⑆ **W9-AWJ-497**

More Praise for Leadership When the Heat's On

"If you're looking for dry theoretical concepts and philosophical musings, don't look here. All you'll find in *Leadership When the Heat's On* are practical examples of how to provide positive management direction and create essential leadership characteristics in today's dynamic corporate workplace. We've purchased copies for all of our managers."

—Ron Craver, Manager Training & Development
Gyrus ENT

"This book has rejuvenated me and my management team. It's been a great aid in helping us focus on what our next goals should be. Danny has helped create a 'bit of Disney magic' for us."

—Donna Sue Davis
Director of Disney Resort Group Sales & Services

"This valuable book contains Danny's unique leadership system that inspires a positive attitude, which is the root of increased productivity—even 'when the heat's on.' We are, without question, a better company with higher operational efficiency because of his incredible system."

—Beecher Hunter, Executive Vice President
Life Care Centers of America

"Danny Cox truly exemplified Leadership Characteristic #2—High Energy. He delivers High Energy throughout this book or in front of an audience equally well. Read the book! Then have him speak to your group. The ROI will be unbelievable."

—Russ Umphenour, President
RTM, Inc.

"A timely message that is very important to anyone in a management position. Danny's energy, humor, and zest for teaching sound leadership techniques are beyond compare.

—Dan Maddux, Executive Director
American Payroll Association

"This book is having an incredible impact on those of us in the public sector, not just the private sector. Required reading for anyone in public service. It helps generate a new level of leadership and customer satisfaction."

—Joe De Ladurantey, Chief of Police
Irwindale, California

"OW! Profound…entertaining…practical. Take your career to the next level and be a better coach for your team. Reading this book is a must. Danny Cox is very insightful and offers real-life, tested techniques for improving your leadership capabilities. Excellent reading for the new college graduate to the seasoned CEO...a resource that you will come back to again and again."

–Steve Garris, Associate Director
Moore School of Business, University of South Carolina

"We have people from around the world attend our customer service course at Stew Leonard's University. We have used Danny Cox to train our 2000 Team members and seen his management system in action. We recommend this book to all our attendees."

–Jill Tavello, Dean of Stew U
Stew Leonard's Dairy Store

"A winner. It's the best, a perfect guide to turn you and your team into record breakers.

–D. Linn Wiley, President/CEO
Citizens Business Bank

"This book is an inspiration with lessons and methods for the growing leader. As we say in the Army—HOO-AH—for a job well done!"

–John Bourgault, Office of the Auditor General
Department of the Army

"A book that hits you between the eyes if you have been managing and not leading. It should be studied time and again because it contains the fundamental recipe for success as a leader. If you need to lead, then this book is for you."

–Jerry Acuff, President & CEO
Delta Leadership Group

I have used the principles, lessons, and examples in this book everyday while guiding my department to a better, stronger tomorrow! This book has set me on both a personal and professional flight plan to unbelievable success!! Thanks Danny."

–Legrand "Chip" Guerry, Chief of Police
Clover, South Carolina

"A very beneficial message and delivered flawlessly. It's a valuable book filled with effective 'down to earth' leadership techniques."

–Dennis W. Larson, Executive Vice President
Central Illinois Builders

"This is a highly readable, content-packed book. Danny Cox's plan for record-breaking leadership comes through with both sincerity and enthusiasm."

–Hansel B. Hart, Senior Vice President
South Carolina Credit Union League

LEADERSHIP WHEN THE HEAT'S ON

BY **DANNY COX**

WITH **JOHN HOOVER**

SECOND EDITION

McGRAW-HILL

NEW YORK   CHICAGO   SAN FRANCISCO   LISBON   LONDON
MADRID   MEXICO CITY   MILAN   NEW DELHI   SAN JUAN   SEOUL
SINGAPORE   SYDNEY   TORONTO

To Captain Maurice "Mo" Abney, USAF

I only thought I knew how to fly jets until he assigned himself as my instructor. He undoubtedly saw something in me that I didn't see in myself at the time. That's the way great leaders operate. Through his insight and coaching I moved to higher levels. The world needs more "Mo" Abneys.

Danny Cox, Author

Library of Congress Cataloging-in-Publication Data

Cox, Danny, 1934-
    Leadership when the heat's on / Danny Cox with John Hoover.— 2nd ed.
       p. cm.
    Includes index.
    ISBN 0-07-140083-4
    1. Leadership. I. Hoover, John, 1952- II. Title.
HD57.7 .C69 2002
658.4'092—dc21   2002006988

McGraw-Hill

A Division of The McGraw·Hill Companies

2 3 4 5 6 7 8 9 0   DOC/DOC 9 8 7 6 5 4

ISBN 0-07-140083-4

This book is printed on recycled, acid-free paper containing a minimum of 50% recycled de-inked paper.

McGraw-Hill books are available at special quantity discounts to use as premiums and sales promotions, or for use in corporate training programs. For more information, please write to the Director of Special Sales, Professional Publishing, McGraw-Hill, Two Penn Plaza, New York, NY 10121-2298. Or contact your local bookstore.

ACKNOWLEDGMENTS

There is an old proverb that says, "When you're drinking the water, don't forget who helped you dig the well." To the many leaders who served as mentors after my boss told me he was looking for my replacement, I say a heartfelt thank you. They helped pull me out of the fire then and continue to be an inspiration to me now.

Thanks to the authors of the business books and articles that have helped shape my growth. No other country in the world has so many "behind the scenes" secrets available through the printed word for increasing productivity.

John Hoover, my collaborator on the first edition of this book and now on this second edition as well, has earned my undying appreciation and respect. His organization and "putting to paper" my systems, techniques, and anecdotes was no small job, but he almost made it look easy.

Our sponsoring editor at McGraw-Hill throughout this process has been Mary Glenn. John and I both thank her for her enthusiastic support of *Leadership When the Heat's On.*

Tedi (a.k.a. Theo) has been my best friend for 38 years and my wife for 37. She has served as a sounding board for ideas and has put in countless hours in typing, retyping, and helping me in proofreading all of the material that has made this book possible. I couldn't have done it without her.

Then there's Ellie Newton. Dear Ellie Newton, who wrote the Foreword for this book. She was the traveling companion of Mrs. Thomas Edison the last few years of her life. Ellie wrote a book of poetry called *Echoes from the Heart.* At the age of 103 she is bright, alert, and still writing beautiful poetry. Thanks to Ellie for being a part of this book and for her continuing inspiration as an uncommon friend.

Danny Cox, Author

P. S. I'll bet this is the only book in history with a foreword written by a 103-year-old!

CONTENTS

FOREWORD

Being born in 1899, I have seen every single minute of the twentieth century, plus two years thus far into the twenty-first century. As a young man, my husband, Jim, had the good fortune to have close, personal friendships and, in some cases, business relationships with Thomas Edison, Henry Ford, Harvey Firestone, and Charles Lindbergh. His insights into and memories of those great leaders and shapers of the twentieth century are documented in his book *Uncommon Friends.* I was a travel companion to Mrs. Edison before I married Jim. You could say that they were all *our* uncommon friends.

Just like his circle of uncommon friends, Jim finally graduated. (He never said, "Passed on.") But what he admired in those men, and the women who stood beside them, lives on. The future Fords and Edisons are still in development, discovering what does and does not work. Danny Cox's book *Leadership When the Heat's On* provides an invaluable technology for these emerging leaders and brings Danny's tremendous personal experiences and acquired knowledge to bear on the increasingly vital subject of leadership.

Jim was in his late sixties and I was in my very early seventies when we opened a real estate office. Although it was a humble start, within a few years our company had grown to 130 salespeople and 15 offices. It was then that we brought Danny in to speak to our managers and salespeople. Every day that Danny was with us in Florida, speaking to our people, I sat in the audience, eager to learn. Danny shared my thirst for knowledge, and a day doesn't go by when he isn't seeking to grow and develop as a leader and as a person. That personal and professional growth over the years filled Jim and me with enough energy to match most thirty-year-olds.

The energy and will to press on when others tire and fall by the wayside is not an old-fashioned virtue. Persistence and dedication will be rewarded in the future, just as they have been in the past. It will take as much courage to venture into uncharted waters in the future as it has in the past. Overcoming criticism, fear of failure, and other adversities will still be defining factors for excellence long after anyone reading these words has joined Jim and his uncommon friends in the boardrooms and on the fishing piers of paradise.

I learned from my husband and from the men and women who shaped his life that leadership, true leadership, is *timeless.*

Ellie Newton
103 Years Young

INTRODUCTION: ANDREWS AIR FORCE BASE, JULY 21, 2001

I'm sitting in the cramped rear cockpit of the F-16 Fighting Falcon, listening to myself breathe through the microphone inside my oxygen mask. Then the brigadier general in the front cockpit asks permission to take the active runway, and it's granted. The needle-nose fighter is now aimed straight down the runway. The control tower operator says, *"You're good to go."*

In a split second, the brakes are released; the throttle is moving forward, and the afterburner ignites. The acceleration is tremendous! I'm pushed hard against the ejection seat, and my crash helmet feels as though it's glued to the cradle provided for it at the top of the seat. With a thunder that shakes the ground, a column of orange flame from the afterburner rockets the sleek, fourteen-ton fighter toward the heavens.

We roll into a tight turn. Inertia pulls the blood from my head toward my feet. I instantly feel the rubber bladders in the G-suit that covers the lower half of my body start to inflate. This *squeezing* keeps the required pressure on my legs and abdomen and forces the blood back into my upper extremities, therefore preventing the vision-stealing *blackout*.

Accelerating with each passing second, we turn toward the Chesapeake Bay. It's a perfect day. Blue sky. A few puffy white clouds. As our fighter rips through the air, I glance at the bay below, filled with sailboats out for a lazy Saturday afternoon. What a contrast in speed!

Twenty-five miles off the Atlantic Coast, we make our supersonic run. Mach 1.0 is the speed of sound. The air speed indicator is moving through Mach .7 (70% of the speed of sound). It's moving up through .8, .9, 1.0. We're through the sound barrier! Now up to Mach 1.1, 1.2, 1.3, 1.4, and then one and a half times the speed of sound. Although this fighter is capable of Mach 2, in the interest of fuel consumption we decelerate to back below the speed of sound. The deceleration is so powerful that, with no effort on my part, my arms are sticking straight out in front of me.

The fighter performs perfectly through a series of horizon-tumbling aileron rolls, then a beautiful slow roll. The throttle is pushed forward as the nose comes up into a loop. The G forces start to build … 4, 5, and then 6. (If I had my 165 pounds sitting on a scale right now, it would be reading a mighty 990 pounds.) We're going over the top, inverted, in a perfect loop. I look *up* through the canopy, which really is *down* at the ocean. I see the sailboats again off in the distance. The thought that pops into my mind is: "They only think they're having fun."

The general asks me if I ever went into vertical flight in the supersonic fighters I flew for ten years. "Yes, many times," I answer.

"Not like this," he says. At full power, the nose comes up to vertical flight. I look at the airspeed and it is increasing as we're going straight up! My logbook shows I have over 2400 hours of high-performance supersonic fighter time, but never have I seen anything like this. What a thrill! This orientation ride is the general's way of helping me understand what his pilots, support staff, and recruiters have to deal with on a daily basis as I present my *Leadership When the Heat's On* and *There Are No Limits* programs for them the next day.ow heading back to the base, I'm thinking about the other fighters that I flew for ten years as a pilot in the United States Air Force. There was the F-86 Sabre, which would go supersonic if you started out at over 40,000 feet in a vertical dive using full throttle and maximum afterburner. And there was my F-102 Delta Dagger, which could fly supersonic straight and level. And the F-101 Voodoo, in which I logged 1200 hours, held several world speed records, including the U.S. coast-to-coast record, and could break the sound barrier in a climb (but not vertical).

And to think that this progression of supersonic fighters literally started with the flimsy little Wright Brothers' Flyer. Finding out what works and what doesn't, and then building on that is what makes great progress a reality. A reality such as this multimillion-dollar fighter I'm in right now.

After landing, the general and I debrief our flight. Briefing before and debriefing afterward, the pilot's never-ending cycle. Plan well, execute well, and learn everything you can from the experience. How many times have I stood on the platform in the briefing room and briefed my flight before a mission? Countless times.

Leadership is a mission. It must be planned for and executed. But do we take the time to learn from our experiences? Have we learned enough to pass on the knowledge to those who come after us? What do we leave to those who will face tomorrow's challenges? After all, the children being born in these early years of the twenty-first century could well see the dawning of the twenty-second century!

After returning to our hotel in Alexandria, Virginia, from Andrews Air Force Base in neighboring Maryland, my wife Tedi and I decide to celebrate this supersonic day. We choose a restaurant located in historic *old town* Alexandria, which was founded in 1749.

The ambience of the restaurant is perfect for a night of celebration and reflection. The Early American style of furnishings, the costumes of the staff, and the lighting help transport us into the past. Before dinner arrives, Tedi, who knows I've been studying my lineage. which goes back to the very start of this great country, says, "Wouldn't you love it if we could invite some of your ancestors here to have dinner with us?"

"Wouldn't that be interesting!" I answer. The Cox family arrived here on this continent in 1607, several years before the Pilgrims. I've had grandfathers with varying numbers of greats before that title, and their brothers and children, who fought in the French and Indian Wars, the Revolutionary War, the War of 1812, the Mexican-American War, and the Civil War.

At this point, our dinner conversation crosses the line into a fantasy encounter with some of my ancestors. Join me, dear reader, as Tedi and I embark on a fictional encounter with men who have learned the timeless lessons of leadership and passed them down from generation to generation.

"Excuse me, sir," the innkeeper interrupts. "These pints of ale are compliments of the gentlemen over by the fireplace." Tedi and I glance across the room and see six men gathered at a round table next to a blazing fire. Tedi and I smileand raise our glasses of ale, and the six men do the same to us.

"Can you believe how authentic the innkeeper's costume looks?" I ask before I take a sip from the tall glass. Tedi finishes her first sip.

"And those men by the fire," she whispers. "Who do you think they are? Actors?"

"Let's find out," I say. And we both stand up and walk toward them. Halfway across the room Tedi touches my arm.

"Danny?" she says. "Was there a big fire burning in the fireplace when we came in?"

"I don't remember," I say. At that moment I notice that there is no electricity in sight, only gas lanterns and candles. We both stop. "But, I didn't think the place was this primitive."

We turn back toward the men by the fireplace and notice that the air is thick with smoke from long pipes filled with Virginia tobacco. "Now this is weird," Tedi says. "This is a non-smoking restaurant. It said so on the front door."

"Maybe it was when we came in ..." I say.

One of the men at the table stands up. He is tall with strong features, yet his smile is gentle and genuine. He wears buckskin clothing, including a coonskin cap. The fringe on the sleeve of his jacket swings back and forth slightly as he extends his arm in our direction. "Come join us," he says. I can't help but notice the large Bowie knife hanging from his belt.

Tedi locks her arm in mine, and we take two seats that have been cleared for us with our backs to the fireplace. I think to myself that these must be where the guests of honor sit, with the warmth of the fire on their backs. The firelight illuminates the faces of the six men. Each of them is dressed in a military uniform or in the working or hunting clothes from a bygone era.

"I'm Danny Cox," I say. "And this is my wife, Tedi."

"We know who you are," the tall man in buckskin says with a smile that makes me feel welcome.

"Tedi and I were just starting to talk about leadership lessons handed down from generation to generation," I say. "If I didn't know better…"

"Best be careful of what you think you know," Mr. Buckskin grins. "Ain't necessarily so."

"Is there a leadership legacy?" Tedi asks, curious about this unusual group, but certain that they can provide an answer. "Are there lessons that have withstood the test of time?"

"Never let fear stop you," a short, stocky man sitting on the far side of the table pipes in. "Nearly every other man didn't believe it could be done." Despite his rugged appearance, the man, speaking with a Welsh accent, is one who has been educated. His blue Revolutionary War officer's coat, with a long row of gold braid and brass buttons on either side, is neat and clean. I recognize him from family portraits. He is my ancestor, General Evan Shelby, Jr. He has been a leader in many battles. "No one had ever fought for and won their freedom like this before. It was a risk of the highest order."

"What inspired you to risk so much?" I ask.

"Freedom," he says without hesitation. "We defeated the British not just for ourselves but for the generations to follow, which includes you. We wanted all to live as free people. No risk was too great for that."

"So leadership is about taking risks," I conclude.

"Tenacity," says a man seated beside General Shelby. He points his long-stemmed pipe in my direction as he talks. "A leader must have a fire inside that burns hotter than anything or anyone who tries to stop him." I can see by the fire in his eyes that this man is filled with intense commitment. He is another of my ancestors, General Shelby's son, Colonel Isaac Shelby. He led a company of the famed Minutemen. When he finishes speaking, he leans over, takes a twig from the fire, and relights his pipe.

He wears a gold medal for gallantry presented to him by Congress. Captain Oliver Wiley sits beside him and Moses Shelby beside *him*. They voice their agreement. I know from studying my ancestors that these men fought alongside Colonel Shelby in the Revolutionary War and, although outnumbered, won a decisive battle against British Loyalists at Kings Mountain in North Carolina. It was the turning point in the war.

"A great leader can't hesitate just because the odds aren't in his favor," the colonel continues. I know he lived by his words. It is a matter of historical record. He went on to be elected the first governor of Kentucky, then was reelected, and was even asked by President James Monroe to serve as Secretary of War.

"It sounds to me that a leader must provide the example and inspiration necessary to reach the goals," I say.

"A leader must be willing to go wherever the work needs to be done," a man across the table says. I recognize him as another of my ancestors, Private Abner Durock, who was wounded in the Mexican-American War.

"Even if there is no possible way to win the day," the man in the coonskin cap adds, in his deep and steady tone. "Leaders must be willing to sacrifice. In the sacrifice we made we left a legacy for those who continue to follow us." By now I have recognized him as my third great-grandfather, frontiersman Davy Crockett. He made his supreme sacrifice in the hopeless defense of the Alamo. But the legacy left by Davy and other martyrs that day inspire freedom-loving men and women to this day.

"Hold to your beliefs," a broad-shouldered man with piercing blue eyes says as he rises to his feet. "Leaders must demonstrate by their own stubborn determination that victory will ultimately come to those who are patient and persevere, no matter the hardships. It is what keeps a valuable idea alive." My great-grandfather, Richard S. Cox, went back to the farm after his release from the infamous Andersonville Prison following the Civil War. How many times had he struggled against the desire to give up?

The moment is overwhelming. I turn and look at Tedi. I can see that she feels the same way. We exchange a smile and turn back to the others at the table. But they are gone. "Would you like another round of ale?" the innkeeper asks.

I'm speechless as I look around the room. The other diners are dressed like Tedi and me. There is attractive, but *electric,* lighting. The innkeeper's costume now looks like exactly that, a costume. There is no more smoke in the air. "Danny," Tedi says, "Look."

I turn to see that there are attractive flower arrangements in wooden and clay containers filling the massive fireplace from which the blaze had lit the room moments before. I follow Tedi's eyes to one of the planters. There, resting against the side of the wooden bucket, is a long-stemmed pipe. Tedi and I exchange glances again.

"They're gone," she says, sadly. "What a shame."

I raise my glass of ale for a toast and Tedi raises hers to meet mine. "No," I say. "They're not gone. Our ancestors live within us, every last one of them."

The answers to leadership challenges of the future are, in many ways, similar to the answers my ancestors left behind. They are the intangible human qualities, rooted in the soul. The souls of all leaders, past, present, and future, are connected by an unshakable sense of purpose, unquenchable spirit of adventure, and unending personal growth. When these qualities become infused into the fabric of your organization, through your efforts, you'll have courageous leadership at all levels. The result is a memorable, long-lasting organization.

Elbert Hubbard, philosopher of the late nineteenth and early twentieth centuries once wrote, "When you begin to thirst for knowledge, you drink it in. You need not go out for it, nor away. The ocean of it surrounds us as the atmosphere."

From over one hundred years ago, that is timeless advice for us as leaders here in the twenty-first century. Find the leadership techniques that work and pass them along. That has been my goal in writing this book. Don't be sidetracked by management *quick fixes* that are nothing more than fads.

This book will start your journey toward a leadership style that will have a very positive, life-enhancing effect on your team members and their families. And, in the foreseeable future, when a team member says to you, "Thank you. You've made a difference in the lives of my family and me," you are a leader in the strictest sense of the word. So fasten your seat belt. Your quest is going to be quite a ride.

May the rest of your life be the best of your life.

Danny Cox
17381 Bonner Drive
Tustin, California 92780
(714) 838-3030
www.DannyCox.com

CHAPTER ONE

THE LEADER FEELS THE HEAT

"The cream of all jobs is to perch on the fence and tell the other feller how to saw wood."

George Ade, Humorist

TICKY AND PETER

According to Peter F. Drucker, a crisis should never be experienced a second time. As leaders, our various stakeholders expect us to be smart enough to learn from a near disaster the first time and to avoid a sequel. You don't have to be a Rhodes scholar to figure out when you're having an experience that's not worth repeating. I learned that lesson long before I ever heard of Peter F. Drucker.

In the small town in Southern Illinois where I grew up, there was a peculiar fellow named Ticky. We all liked him even though his grits weren't in the center of the plate, as we used to say in that part of the country.

One day, Ticky wandered into Orie Hifle's blacksmith shop moments after Orie had pulled a horseshoe out of the fire and laid it on the anvil. It was all but red hot. Orie turned his back just long enough for Ticky to reach down and pick up the horseshoe with his bare hand. When Ticky screamed, Orie turned around just in time to see ol' Tick throw the horseshoe into the big wooden tub of water next to the anvil, where it sizzled and let off a plume of steam.

"Did that burn you, Ticky?" Orie asked.

The rhetorical question didn't throw Ticky off one bit. "No," he shot back, holding his wrist and waving his injured hand back and forth in the air. "It just don't take me long to look at a horseshoe!"

Ticky never picked up another horseshoe, hot or cold, as far as anyone can recall. It's hard to say which man was more eloquent, but when Peter F. Drucker and Ticky agree on a principle as profound as not repeating mistakes, it's probably a good idea to pay heed. As hard as I tried to remember and learn from Ticky's experience throughout my life, I still managed to pick up a hot horseshoe now and again. I'll bet that you have too.

As leaders, it's not unusual to find ourselves breaking a sweat when the temperature is rising all around us. At such times, whatever caused our internal thermometer to climb is not always clear. There's no shame in wiping perspiration off your brow as long as you haven't occupied that particular hot seat before. As I speak at business meetings all over the country, I hear the same confessions again and again about how individuals found themselves in the same predicament more than once..

Getting burned by the same horseshoe more than once is proof that you have not resolved whatever situation or behavior caused the problem the first time. As a supersonic fighter pilot in the United States Air Force, I was trained to anticipate problems before they arose so I'd be prepared to deal with them quickly and effectively. You could say that I was trained to keep my internal early warning system calibrated and operational. A leader in any organization does well to anticipate difficulty, remember lessons learned from experience, and keep his or her mind open to new input and new lessons that might change the way the game is played.

The skilled and effective leader must learn, learn, and learn some more. Effective leadership requires a constant balance between action and caution. And that takes practice. Most people are naturally inclined toward impetuous action *or* excessive caution. But too much of one without the other will take a lot away from what you're trying to accomplish, and might cause failure altogether.

The "ready, fire, aim" executive is exciting to watch and read about in newspapers and magazines, but can bankrupt his or her organization in a hurry and in any number of ways. The "fire, aim, never ready" folks just take their companies down that much faster. On the other side of the coin are those people who wait for every traffic light across town to turn green before pulling out of their driveways. Not only do they never get anywhere, they never even get started. The effective leader will constantly strive to find the optimal balance between contemplation and action.

TEMPERATURE RISING

Smoke in the cockpit is never a good sign. Smoke in the cockpit is always bad. The only question is, How bad?" Smoke in the cockpit when tearing through the sky means you have to fly and land the aircraft while attempting to locate the fire and dealing with it. If a pilot, like a leader, is adequately prepared for crisis management, there is a chance that everyone involved will get out of the situation unharmed. When a crisis arises for the unprepared pilot or executive, he or she had better hope that it's their lucky day, because luck is about all that will get them out of the dilemma. Without proper preparation, even a lucky pilot or executive won't emerge unscathed from a crisis. Part of being prepared for adversity is the ability to locate the source of the problem quickly. Several forces acting on the executive cause the kind of heat that gives this book its title. These forces all apply pressure. When more than one force is at work, friction occurs—the kind of friction you can demonstrate by rubbing your hands together quickly. You can cause your palms to heat up in only a moment. If you're like most people, you'll instinctively rub your arms or legs when you feel a chill.

The dictionary defines friction as "conflicts of opinion or differences in temperament." And the subject of leadership certainly calls forth images of heated situations. Such situations were more than likely caused by unmet expectations. There are more expectations in our lives today than ever before. Expectations of our own, and expectations that others want us to live up to. Our families have expectations of us, as do our employers. Often, the expectations of family and employer are different. Friction occurs when work demands more of our time and attention, which can only come at the expense of our families.

At work, despite recent enlightened approaches to personal life vs. career, career is consuming many people as it never has before. That's where the issue of pressure begins to resemble three-dimensional chess. Even if you achieve some balance between family vs. work, once you get to the office, there are strictly professional conflicts to contend with. If you're in a position of leadership, pressure is your middle name. The "up pressure" from employees' demands slams against the "down pressure" of upper management and/or major stakeholders' demands to improve the numbers. The result is heat. Heat on you.

What happens when the *external pressure* exerted by customers' expectations comes up against *internal pressures* exerted by cost controls, supplier delivery, and other productivity issues? Heat, heat, and more heat. Everyone, from individual entrepreneurs to the heads of multibillion-dollar corporations, feels the innate pressures of the business world, whether the market is up or down, whether the dollar is weak or strong, in sunshine or in rain.

Other than outright consumer demands, external pressure can come from banking and regulatory requirements, regulations, taxes, competition, and a growing list of other issues. Don't forget about the pressure you exert on yourself.

Other than meeting outright employee needs, pressure from within can also come from the need to stay abreast of new technology, to capture and integrate knowledge and intellectual capital, from organizational growth pains, and from a growing list of other issues. *Heat is created at the point at which the manager finds himself or herself squeezed in the vise.*

As a student of leadership, the sooner you accept the fact that you'll be dealing with heat, the better off you'll be. The heat might be caused by top-down pressure rubbing against bottom-up pressure, or internal pressure rubbing against external pressure. For almost anyone in a position of leadership, it's probably both. If you want to figure out who's really in charge of an organization, just find the spot where all opposing forces meet. That's where he or she will be.

If the friction analogy doesn't work for you, it might be because you feel as if you're constantly on the spot. That can get hot. If you've ever taken a magnifying glass and formed a pin dot of sunlight on wood or dry leaves, you know that before long you've got smoke, and not long after that, fire. Even if you've never tested the solar-powered magnifying glass before, you have probably felt as if the collective energy of the whole world is focused on you, with the same result: The intense scrutiny is like a laser beam that can burn a hole right through you.

Whether the greatest pressure comes from the inside or the outside, from right or left, top or bottom, when you're the one in the vise or on the spot, you feel more heat than anyone else. I have yet to meet anyone in a position of leadership who doesn't know it when the heat's on. Unfortunately, those in positions of leadership (I call them managers) who are not prepared or willing to deal effectively with the pressures causing the heat will often simply pass the heat on to those least able to say no.

An effective leader will find ways to control the temperature by managing the causes of pressure. There will always be pressure—more on some days than on others. If a manager's way of dealing with it is to push back hard against whatever force is pressing in, it will likely turn a heated situation into a four-alarm fire. Too often that's when my telephone rings. "Danny," the voice at the other end says, "I've got a four-alarm fire going on here and I need your help to put it out."

That's all well and good. But if you study the principles of effective leadership, it's less likely that you'll ever need to make an emergency call. Instead, you'll find that when problems arise, you will have anticipated them and prepared to address the new demands with appropriate and effective solutions. You'll respond instead of reacting. Heat is a part of daily life for a leader. Properly attended to, *warmth* doesn't need to get *hot*.

WHAT IS LEADERSHIP?

It's important to understand exactly what I mean when I talk about *leadership*. The term can mean different things to different people. You might have noticed that I don't consider words like *executive* or *manager* to be synonymous with *leader.* Some of the many active definitions of leadership include:

To guide
To direct
To begin
To be chief
To influence
To command
To be the first
To go ahead of
To create a path
To show the way
To control actions
To cause progress

LEADERSHIP: THE HONORARY TITLE

All of these descriptive terms can be a metaphor for the act of leading. Any genuine leader will tell you that leading consists of many things. You can probably come up with a dozen or so additional descriptors that apply to your own particular leadership challenge. No matter what your precise definition is, however, the title of *leader* is honorary. Those who are being led bestow it. And when is that? When you've helped them grow and develop as human beings; when they're more ready for life's challenges because of your good coaching.

It happens when you *earn* their respect. Top management can't appoint leaders any more than individuals can appoint themselves as leaders. When I refer to a leader, I'm talking about someone who has earned the title through a successful relationship with his or her team members. Those you have been assigned to lead make your leadership official.

Managers are those who have been given the assignment to lead others, but perhaps lack the skills or motivation to do so. The fact that you're reading this book perhaps indicates that you regard leadership as the art and science that it is. Just studying leadership moves you one step further away from the ranks of those who merely carry out managerial tasks as part of a daily routine, and it brings you one step closer to true leadership. It is possible to manage people and processes effectively without truly leading.

Getting people to do things requires a skill set, and it's one that can be learned, as you'll see. Some managers are better at it than others. But motivating people and providing them with the guidance and means to reach their potential requires a much more elaborate and well-developed set of skills, plus a personal commitment, as you'll also see.

RESPONSIBILITY

The individual quality of effective leadership that looms above all others is *responsibility*. Above all else, a leader is responsible for getting a job done. Regardless of how many people are involved in accomplishing the task, the leader bears the ultimate responsibility. It doesn't matter if you're a new leader, responsible for relatively little, or someone higher up in the organization with other leaders reporting to you. Your leadership will be defined largely by the amount of responsibility you have accepted.

Leadership itself is a challenge, and none of us are truly leaders until we have fully accepted that challenge. Accepting the role of leadership is a personal choice for which the leader assumes full and final responsibility. Leaders are personally responsible. Anyone who sheds responsibility and/or slides it onto someone else's plate whenever possible is not a genuine leader. The good news is that accepting full responsibility can be a liberating experience: There's no confusion about where the buck stops.

Figure 1-1 depicts self-talk that will help you etch the notion of responsibility indelibly onto the inside of your forehead. I call it my "Declaration of Personal Responsibility."

Once you realize and accept that you are personally responsible for your actions, you're ready to become a more effective leader. Your effectiveness as a leader is directly proportionate to your effectiveness as a human being. Sure, there are exceptions to everything. Some people win the lottery. But I'm talking about the long haul, about how life really *is* for people like you and me. To be an effective leader with staying power, you must make a full-blown commitment to the challenge of being an effective person—a person who subscribes to your own Declaration of Personal Responsibility. In fact, why don't you write your own? That will bring you face-to-face with your own sense of responsibility.

THE ARTISTIC SIDE OF LEADERSHIP

Science requires hard evidence. True scientists don't consider something a fact unless it can be replicated forever without exception: gravity, human mortality, taxes, and so on. You could argue that the results of effective leadership can be measured and thereby proved, but exactly what *caused* the results is the unanswerable question. In any organization there always seems to be much less argument about who produced poor results rather than who produced favorable results.

With few exceptions, you'll find every time that *someone else* is responsible for the poor results. But everyone claims responsibility for the good results. Such debates tend to flow up or down the organizational ladder, depending on the quality of leadership. An effective leader will accept responsibility for bad

"I currently possess everything I've truly wanted and deserved. This is based on what I have handed out to date. My possessions, my savings, and my lifestyle are an exact mirror of me, my efforts, and my contribution to society. What I give, I get. If I am unhappy with what I have received, it is because as yet, I have not paid the required price. I have lingered too long in the *quibbling stage.*

"I fully understand that time becomes a burden to me only when it's empty. The past is mine and at this moment I am purchasing another twenty-four hours of it. The future quickly becomes the past as a control point called the present moment. I not only truly live at that point, but I have full responsibility for the highest and best use of the irreplaceable *now.*

"I accept full responsibility for both the successes and failures in my life. If I am not what I desire to be at this point, what I am is my *compromise.* I no longer choose to compromise with my undeveloped potential.

"I am the sum total of the choices I have made and continue to choose daily. What I now put under close scrutiny is the value of each upcoming choice. Therein lies the quality of my future lifestyle.

"Will my future belong to the *old me* or the *new me?* The answer depends upon my attitude toward personal growth at this very moment. What time is left is all that counts and that remaining time is my responsibility. With newfound maturity I accept full responsibility for how good I can become at what is most important to me.

"With personal growth comes the fear of the unknown and new problems. Those problems are nothing more than the expanding shadow of my personal growth. I now turn my very real fear, with God's help, into a very real adventure.

"My life now expands to meet my newfound destiny. *Old me,* meet the *new me!*"

Figure 1-1. Declaration of Personal Responsibility.

news. The same leader will hand over responsibility to his or her team when the news is good. In other words, if you are the leader, take the responsibility when things go badly. When things go well, give the *credit* to your team members. Very few leadership behaviors will win over the hearts and minds of your team members faster than your willingness to take the heat on their behalf.

Leadership is considered to be first and foremost an *art* because it can't be considered a science. Leadership is about human beings, and human beings are inconsistent and unpredictable. Almost everything that human beings do is open to interpretation. Human beings are emotional creatures, and our individual emotional compositions can only be fully known and understood by God. One of the most exciting things about people, as well as one of the most optimistic truths about leadership, is that no matter what bolt of cloth we're cut from, it's never too late to weave new and colorful threads into the fabric of our lives.

As much as some accomplishment-minded folks would like to see human functions in the workplace mechanized, I believe that the complexity of the human being exceeds any possible synthesizing. We must keep our options and our minds open. Knowing how to tap-dance out of tight spots is a terrific and sometimes lifesaving, nonscientific talent. The great leaders throughout time have been truly great *artists,* not scientists. William Shakespeare could have been writing about the challenge of leadership when he said, "All the world is a stage and we are but players." Effective leaders look like vaudevillians more often than they look like Einstein.

The issue becomes how well you play your role. Does your performance truly come from the heart? The kind of picture you paint with your unique palette of colors and selection of brushes is what individualizes you—as a person and as a leader. Your effectiveness is a reflection of or, better yet, a measure of who you are.

NATURAL-BORN LEADER OR NOT?

I will share portions of my personal history with you in the hope that you will be able to visualize how these leadership concepts were integrated into both my personal and professional philosophies. I wasn't born with the knowledge and awareness of what makes a good leader. Nobody was. Leaders are not born, despite the popular moniker: the "natural-born leader." A doctor in the delivery room doesn't hold up a newborn infant and say, "Well lookie here. We've got ourselves a natural-born leader." The local newspaper never reported the birth of a seven-pound, six-ounce natural-born leader yesterday afternoon at Saint Mary's Hospital. The skills of leadership can only be learned through experience and refined by study. As the son of a coal miner, I can tell you that sometimes the greatest lessons are learned through mistakes and by getting your hands dirty.

High Stakes Mistakes

My first sales experience was in selling *sonic booms.* It was during the "golden era of supersonic flight," when we were pushing our fighters up to almost twice the speed of sound and sonic booms were prevalent. The squadron phones were ringing off their hooks with complaint calls from the local populace blaming us for everything from hens that had quit laying eggs, to cats that had left homes, and even hair falling out.

I've broken the sound barrier over 2000 times in everything from the F-86 Sabre, to the F-102 Delta Dagger, to the F-101 Voodoo, to the F-16 Falcon. I have knocked off more than my share of plaster and broken way more than my share of windows, causing many of the complaint calls, I'm sure.

To help solve the public relations problem, I volunteered to become the sonic boom salesman. My extra duty job was to speak to these upset, hostile communities in order to convince them that what they were hearing was "the sound of freedom." It was a *tough* sale. But, it was a learning experience that I used later to build an industry-leading sales team in the civilian world, and no, the civilian team was not selling sonic booms. You'll see how all that happened in a later chapter.

Being involved in so much high-performance flying on a daily basis, and gaining some notoriety as the sonic boom salesman, my next stop was to apply for the crack Air Force aerobatic team, the Thunderbirds. Shortly afterward, they called me to set up an interview.

The Thunderbirds were impressed with my credentials, and their call was the opportunity of my lifetime. After the grueling, six-hour interview, the team leader walked over to me and extended his hand. "Congratulations," he said. "You've made the team." I knew that I'd arrived. My dream had come true. Nothing was going to stop me from being part of the most elite acrobatic team on the planet. Nothing, that is, except the United States Air Force.

I belonged to the "all-weather" fighter command, and the Thunderbirds were part of the "day-fighter" group. The bureaucratic snag came when my request for transfer was denied. All-weather pilots had extra training, and the Air Force didn't feel they could spare me at that time. You can imagine where I thought they could put their "special training." I was not a happy fighter pilot.

Showing the enthusiasm and confidence of a man who had just been chosen to fly with the elite of the elite, I launched into Plan B: I sent in my resignation, figuring that would bring the Air Force to its knees. If they couldn't spare me to the day-fighter command, they couldn't possibly let me walk out the door.

Not only did they let me walk out the door, they opened it for me. They signed my resignation, and overnight I was a civilian, wondering what I was going to do with the rest of my life. What a blow! But upon reflection, it was one of the best things that ever happened to me.

I had no money saved up and no eligibility for retirement pay. What I did have was a wife and three little girls with the very expensive habit of *eating*. So I did what many people were doing in those days: I packed them all in the car and headed for California. My plan was to fly with the airlines. After all, I had some impressive credentials, but the credentials were not going to be my next life-changing obstacle.

That was the second assumption that blew up in my face. There was nothing wrong with my credentials as far as the airlines were concerned. I had 2400 hours of high-performance fighter experience without an accident. But their height requirement was five feet eight inches. "What a coincidence," I told them. "Five-eight is my goal." It wasn't that I couldn't fly the plane. They just didn't want the passengers to say, "You mean to tell me that little guy is going to fly this great big airplane?" Another blow! But once again, as it turned out, a life-changing experience for the better.

Selling It Like It Is

I took a quick inventory of my life's accomplishments and discovered that I didn't have much in the way of employable skills. But if I could convince a hostile crowd of unnerved citizens that sonic booms were worth putting up with in the name of national security, I could sell almost anything. This time I guessed right. In my first year as a salesperson I earned more money than I'd ever made in one year in the Air Force. More important, I didn't have to risk death every day on the job. (Well, there were a couple of customers I wasn't sure about. I wasn't into customer service then like I am now.)

Things started looking up. In fact, I did so well that the company asked me to manage one of their sales offices after only one year of selling. My thought at the time was that the company recognized talent when they saw it. I felt like I was born to lead. After all, I never studied leadership, and I was being dragged up the corporate ladder. My promotion took effect immediately. The only request they made was for me to stay away from my new office until they had a chance to drive over there and fire my predecessor. No problem.

I was instructed not to mess up that office more than it already was. That was the extent of my management training. Not a word about leadership. True to form, I managed that office for a year without messing it up any more than it was the day I walked in. On top of that, we had increased production a significant amount. As I would have said in the Air Force, "There's no sweat to this leadership stuff." I didn't know it, but very dark clouds were building on the horizon.

Much as I expected, the same executives who had put me in that little office the year before showed up again and told me I was being promoted to manager of the top office in the 36-office chain. I could hardly wait to get back to that office. It was where I had started as a brand new salesperson two years earlier. The storm clouds that had been on the horizon, which I still hadn't noticed, were now almost overhead.

Imagine how happy the salespeople were to welcome me back as their new boss. They hated me with a passion I've never seen before or since. I urged them not to think of me as their boss, but as a friend who was always right. Well, I didn't say those exact words, but that's how they interpreted my style. My goal was to turn everyone in that office into a copy of *me*. It made perfect sense at the time. I was red hot. Or so I thought.

Transforming the entire office into Danny Cox clones seemed to be what *my* bosses wanted me to do. If they hadn't been so impressed with my performance, I reasoned, they wouldn't have promoted me. I reasoned further that if

I could get my salespeople to do their jobs exactly the way I had done mine when I was in their shoes, they wouldn't bring me any problems that I hadn't already successfully handled. Therefore, I would never be embarrassed with an unsolvable problem.

Thanks to my "natural" leadership abilities, the number one office was soon number 36 out of 36. One fateful day I was scratching my head trying to figure out the problem when my boss showed up in my office, unannounced. His usual smile and pleasant demeanor were gone. "Cox," he said through clenched teeth. "I can now see that it was a mistake making you the manager of this office, and I feel it's only fair to tell you that I'm already looking for your replacement."

Cloning Canceled

That was not only the shortest but also the most *effective* motivational seminar I ever attended. I searched the room with my eyes as if I were going to spot an appropriate reply to my boss scribbled on the wall or the side of a filing cabinet. All I could think to say was, "I've got to learn how to do this."

"You don't have much time," he shot back tersely as he headed out the door.

"You don't know how motivated I am," I called out as he disappeared.

The scene that followed was classic. There I was, standing in the doorway of my office, watching my boss leave the building, when I noticed that everyone in the office was staring at me. The shoe was on the other foot, and every one of them knew it. They had succeeded in getting the plug pulled on the clonemaker. I felt so small in that moment that I could have walked directly *under* my desk. At least, that's what I wanted to do.

How could I have distanced myself from the very people I depended on for my success as a manager? Why didn't they just fall in line and become the cookie-cutter soldiers I wanted them to be? The more I pondered my dilemma, the more I realized that before I could get the right answers, I would have to start asking the right *questions.*

Before long it came to me. There was no thunderclap. The heavens didn't part and drop a stone tablet at my feet. But when the thought hit, I knew it was profound. I needed to work on *me,* not *them.* My focus had been completely wrong. My eyes had been fixed on the bottom line to the exclusion of everything else. I'd been obsessed with whipping them into shape without any regard for the kind of shape I was in.

Instantly, the truth energized me. Even with my boss out looking for my replacement, I felt a sense of liberation. I realized that *employees can only get better after the manager does.* Students get better right after the teacher does. Children get better right after their parents do. It is unreasonable to expect children to know more than their teachers or behave as maturely as their parents do.

My most important revelation was that I could no longer expect any other individual to become like me.

I had established a track record of expecting people to adopt my agenda, while I had little, if any, regard for theirs. I was getting back what I was giving out. If I didn't give it out, I didn't get it back. Examples: empathy, tolerance, understanding. I was cloning myself all right. I just didn't want to admit that I wanted people to do as I said, not as I did. I didn't express much consideration for my team, and they expressed even less for me. I was about to become a casualty, much like several of my top salespeople did during my reign of as a whip-cracker.

If you think I'm making a case against management by threats and intimidation, you're right. I am a walking, talking case study in how to uninspire and demotivate. Impatience, intolerance, and rigidity have never inspired people; it's scared them, maybe, but never inspired them to reach for higher goals. My friend Ken Blanchard calls intimidation "sea gull management." He describes how the sea gull manager flies into the office, flaps his or her wings, squawks, makes a mess on everybody's head, and flies out again. Twenty-first century employees will work as hard and as ethically as their managers. The heat is not on the employee; it's on the manager.

Work on Number One

As it turned out, I didn't lose my job. I doubt if they could have found a sane person to take over that office after what I'd done to it. After being told that my boss was out looking for my replacement, I rolled up my sleeves and jumped in with both feet. I resolved to become the best manager I could possibly be, whatever it took. My relationships with the men and women in my office became more genuine by the day. And to my amazement, my team members started to respond, and respond quickly. We started to look like and act like a real team. I stopped demanding that they be more like me and started helping them be more like themselves. The system that I devised and put into practice will be revealed in Chapter 3.

Four short months later we were the number one office again. Together, we climbed right back through that field of 36 offices to the top spot. All my people wanted was to be recognized, supported, encouraged, and respected for their individual and unique strengths and abilities. Once I started giving them what they *needed* instead of what I wanted them to have, their production went through the roof. I have conducted seminars for all types of companies year in and year out for more years than I care to mention. And I have yet to see an organization that doesn't see *positive* and *immediate* results when the focus is placed on the growth and development of staff members.

The skills, methods, and techniques—the things I had to learn the hard way—are described throughout this book and are intended to sharpen you as a leader who values your number one asset: your people. They will get better right after you do. By reading *Leadership When the Heat's On,* you have already begun to work on *you.* Congratulations. As your people start getting better, they'll help take the heat off you by easing off on the "up" or internal pressure. Likewise, when productivity goes up, the "down" or external pressure will ease off as well. Your situation will get better, right after you do.

MANIPULATION IS NOT LEADERSHIP

Genuine regard for everyone you deal with is not something that can be faked. People cannot only sense your true sincerity, they will only be fooled by insincere words and deeds for a while before they see you for what you're really doing. That's why confidence artists have to stay on the move, while old, slow-talking, straight-shooters can stay in business on the same street corner for decades.

Manipulation means causing others to act against their will, their better judgment, and possibly to their detriment while providing a perceived, though temporary, benefit to the manipulator. The ultimate cost of manipulative tactics is an eventual decline in morale and productivity. Good leadership is made up of carefully and strategically thought-out, growth-producing techniques that motivate team members to achieve new heights in current tasks, in addition to encouraging new and innovative actions.

Good leadership results in the development of personal and professional potential and in the achievement of team goals. There is no question that morale soars and turnover plummets in an environment of good leadership. Only when the leader's vision includes the goals and ambitions of his or her people will the experience of success be sweet for everyone. And success that is enjoyed by all is likely to be repeated.

LIFTING PERSONAL LIMITATIONS

Effective leadership produces results that relieve "down" or external pressure from superiors, stockholders, and/or customers. It also relieves "up" or internal pressure through improved employee relations. And meanwhile, it expands your personal horizons. Once my office got back to the number one spot in the organization, I learned a new and eye-opening lesson about personal limitations. I would have used the example of breaking through personal limitations as a metaphor for sonic booms during my Air Force public relations experience, but I hadn't learned the lesson at that point.

After reaching the number one position again, our office's production amazingly leveled off at exactly where it had been when I first took over. Once we returned to our previous level of performance, we unknowingly reached our *self-imposed* barrier and went no further. Notice that I emphasized the word *self.* The barriers I refer to are not company-imposed or customer-imposed. They are self-imposed. There is a world of difference, and leaders who understand that can make a difference in the world.

Pilots talk about the "safety envelope" between minimum acceptable performance and maximum performance. There are minimum safe air speeds for various aircraft and weather conditions as well as maximum air speeds, sometimes referred to as "never exceed" speeds. Structural stress tolerances and other safety factors all fall within their respective envelopes. The range between the minimum and maximum is considered the safety envelope. Remember that once leadership improves, organizations and individuals within organizations improve. Once leaders learn to push the limits of their own envelope, others will follow.

I have flown supersonic fighters outside of the envelope and lived to tell about it. That's what being a test pilot is all about. An airline pilot would and should lose his or her job for operating outside of safety specifications. As leaders, we are equally responsible for the safe conduct of our operations. However, to be effective and progressive leaders, we all need to have a little test pilot in us. Otherwise, our self-imposed barriers will constantly stop us. If there were no test pilots or leaders to push the envelope, there would be little innovation and progress.

Self-imposed barriers are not walls around our lives. They are the margins of our lives where nothing has been written yet. A self-imposed barrier is nothing more than the dividing line between our developed and undeveloped potential. Yet we look at that line as though it's a wall. Imagine what the world would be like if explorers throughout history believed that they couldn't go anywhere for the first time. That's what we were up against after my office was back at number one. Our production curve leveled off once we were back at the top of the office's previous performance curve. There was no tangible barrier.

But pushing production higher than it had ever been before meant venturing into uncharted territory. We had reached the collective personal barriers of the team. My people were not by any means slouches. They were the best in the company. We were already receiving monthly awards for being the top office. Success became a barrier for us. Walt Disney is remembered to this day throughout the Disney organization for warning his staff against "resting on our laurels." Ralph Waldo Emerson put it even more profoundly when he said, "He who sits on the cushion of advantage soon goes to sleep."

Good Isn't Good Enough

A great executive once said to me, "Good is the enemy of best and best is the enemy of better." When most people get to be good, they start to think, What's the point of struggling to be best? Isn't good, good enough? Often, when people get to be best, they become comfortable and productivity plateaus, the way it did in my number one sales office.

I wanted to challenge my team to break through their existing personal production records. To launch this plan, I met with each one of them privately and said, "I don't want you to worry about breaking anyone else's personal record. I just want you to worry about breaking your own record on a daily, weekly, monthly, quarterly, and yearly basis." Once they focused on their own record instead of someone else's, they did in fact see instant progress on a daily, weekly, monthly, quarterly, and yearly basis. Energy and morale went even higher and production sharply increased. We broke office, company, and industry records.

Straw vs. Chain

In the Old West, cowboys rode up to the saloon, got off their horses, loosely wrapped the reigns around the hitching post one time, and went in to have a sarsaparilla. I used to watch the old westerns and wonder, Why doesn't that horse just pull the reigns off the post and take off? Someone who owned horses eventually explained to me that as long as the horse *thought* it was tied up, it didn't bother to try to get loose. The same can happen to us. We're tied with straw and think it's chain.

The people in my record-setting sales office proved that they were top performers over and over and over again. As our performance received increasing acclamation and overall attention, I was frequently asked where I got all of those great people. Did I steal top producers from our competition? Did I recruit at the top business schools? Were they all cut to pattern out of the same piece of cloth? The one-word answer to all of those questions is "No." They came from every walk of life—just ordinary people who discovered they could do the most extraordinary things with their newly discovered potential.

One woman in my number one office got tired of earning $25,000 per year as a secretary and took up sales to expand her horizons. She'd been selling full-time for four years when I met her. Her annual commissions totaled $25,000, almost to the penny. She couldn't visualize making more money than what someone else *thought* she was worth. She was tied with straw and thought it was chain!

Through the team-building secret revealed in a later chapter, she broke through her self-imposed barrier almost instantly and never looked back. At last report she had a net worth of $3 million as a result of her sales career. There is no higher honor or more rewarding feeling for a leader than applauding the success of someone who has been positively influenced by his or her leadership.

Reframing

Leaders find out where their people are comfortable. Sometimes it comes down to painting a picture for your people to illustrate what success looks like so they can know what they're striving for. Sometimes you need to put the process in language they understand. Because my top sales office was out in the San Fernando Valley, a couple of my salespersons were seasoned character actors in the motion picture business. Like me coming out of the Air Force, they had no sales training at all.

They didn't make much money as character actors and they didn't make much money selling. One day I handed them our sales training manual and said, "Gentlemen, here is your script. Study it hard because the customers have already read this and know what to say." A glow of familiarity came over their faces. After that they didn't go on sales presentations, they went on sales *auditions,* and did very well. I let them know how proud I was of their accomplishments in blending the old with the new.

Dear Old Dad

There was another salesperson in the office that darn near drove me crazy. He was without a doubt the most frustrating person I've ever had working for me. (I'll bet someone's face just popped into your own mind.) Why was I frustrated with him? I saw potential in him that he, himself, refused to see because of his self-imposed barrier.

His hang-up was that he made $3000 on straight commission, almost to the penny, *every* month. I still wonder, to this day, how he and his family got by on that. He had to pick his sales carefully, otherwise he would exceed his self-imposed limit. If he made his $3000 three or four days before the end of the month, he turned into a basket case. If someone had walked in and said, "I'm buying from you, today!" he would have fainted, I'm sure.

One month I decided, this is *his* month. He's going to go through that barrier or I'm going to die in the effort, I thought. I did everything but move in with him. He couldn't move without me breathing down his neck. I "big-brothered" him to death. He couldn't go to the men's room without me standing guard at the door.

I'm proud to say that in that one month he nearly doubled his productivity. He made almost $6000! He then put square wheels on my wagon. The following month he made *zero dollars*. The next month? You guessed it: $3000. I had forgotten that his breakthrough had to be on *his* terms, not mine.

I brought him into my office and confronted him. I couldn't believe his response. He told me that I just didn't understand. He said he had never had any more money in the bank than his father did when he was growing up. I realized that he had a self-imposed barrier that stopped him just short of ever earning more than his father. That was another eye-opener for me about choosing the right role models.

Using my new knowledge, I took a stab at a solution and said, "Is that the role model you're currently setting for your own children? So they can sit in an office someday at your age and tell their manager that they've never had any more money in the bank than their father had and it's always been that way in your family?"

He shot out of his chair and I sank back into mine, thinking that he was about to come flying across my desk. Fortunately, he was just energized by the revelation. "My God," he exclaimed. "That's exactly what I've been doing. I've been setting an example for my kids to never achieve more than I achieve. My own kids think that this is as good as I'll ever be at what I've chosen to do with my life. Why should they feel any different? I've never given them any reason to." He went out, blew the lid off his self-imposed barrier, and at last report was still pushing his envelope.

WORKING HARD AT NOTHING

Much of the heat that managers feel is caused by *unnecessary* friction. Getting in the habit of doing things that don't work is a good example. We can fill eight or more hours doing things that don't work, then go home and tell our families about how *hard* we worked all day.

If I were to ask you to write a description of an average day for yourself, it would include how you go about your job, what you say to people, what you say back to them after they answer you, and so on. After pages and pages of writing, I would ask you to go back through each item and check off what does and doesn't work. Then stop doing those things that don't work. Sounds simple? Maybe it is. Author Tom Peters called it "a blinding flash of the obvious." By the way, if it were simple to stop doing things that don't work, everybody would instantly get more efficient and productive. Nobody can make an honest inventory of his or her behavior and say that no energy is being wasted on old, familiar, and comfortable habits that crowd out more productive activities.

How can we identify what isn't working? The fact that the behavior has been with us for a long time is the first clue. We probably do it without thinking. It *feels* natural. If anyone asks you why you do something and your answer is, "I've always done it that way," you ought to take a serious look at what you're doing. More than likely, the behavior is unnecessary and counterproductive. If a behavior has a rational and operational explanation, you're probably in the clear.

Every day, sometimes moment to moment, each one of us stands at a fork in the road (see Figure 1-2). One road leads to personal and professional growth, which is an absolute necessity for effective leadership. The other road leads us back to repetitive and nonproductive activities.

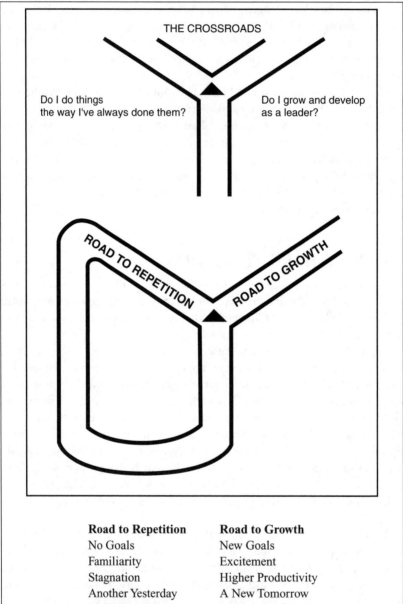

Road to Repetition	Road to Growth
No Goals	New Goals
Familiarity	Excitement
Stagnation	Higher Productivity
Another Yesterday	A New Tomorrow
Making a Living	Making a Life
Something to Live On	Something to Live For
Burn Out	Quality
Amusement	Enjoyment
Problems	Problems

Figure 1-2. The fork in the road.

We tend to choose the road to repetition because it always brings us safely back to a familiar place. Familiar territory makes us feel more comfortable, even if it's nonproductive. Many organizations claim to be steeped in tradition when they're really just stuck in the mud. The future is upon us whether we like it or not. These "traditionalists" are driving into the future with their eyes fixed on the rearview mirror. They are tradition-centered and unhampered by progress.

THE PROBLEM WITH PROBLEMS

The difference between an effective leader and an ineffective manager is not who has problems and who doesn't. Everyone has problems. The difference is whether a person *reacts* or *responds* to problems. The ineffective manager reacts to problems. The effective leader responds creatively to problems and *learns.*

Many people stand at the fork in the road and think, I'll follow the road toward growth just as soon as I resolve the problems currently facing me. It will never happen. Some people wait their entire life for the precise moment when all of their problems clear up. The terms *old* and *bitter* are usually used to describe such people. We learned in childhood that there is no Santa Claus. It's too bad that our parents didn't teach us that there is no magical moment when all of our problems disappear. Why do we wait before striking out on the road to opportunity and success? Take the road that demands the most of you.

Do you need a written guarantee of smooth sailing? Do you need to have every traffic light across town turn green before hitting the accelerator? Forget all of the lights turning green and staying green. It's never going to happen. The only light to worry about is the one right in front of you. Worry about the next light when you come to it.

Lemons to Lemonade

Thank goodness some people are willing to push the envelope from time to time. Many people seem to have the cards stacked against them. If anybody has an excuse not to succeed, the individuals mentioned below would be high on the list.

1. He was labeled unsociable and mentally slow. He didn't start talking until he was four years old. His own father said that he was not normal and would never amount to anything. He was even expelled from school.

2. This man entered the conflict a captain and was busted down to private. He left the military and became a farm laborer. His progression in rank and career were stuck in reverse.

3. This person's childhood voice teacher said that he had no vocal talent at all.

4. This man's employers told him that he didn't have enough sense to wait on customers. He was relegated to stocking shelves at the dry goods store where he worked until the age of tweenty one.

5. The editor at the newspaper where he worked accused him of being "void of creativity" and fired him, citing "lack of good ideas."

6. Consistently at the bottom of the class, this man's teachers said he was too stupid to learn anything, and he was finally educated at the knee of his patient mother.

7. Her parents received a letter from the acting school where she was a student, explaining that her teachers felt she had no talent and recommending that they waste no more money on her theatrical training. She failed at audition after audition, and struggled to overcome a crippling disease. She didn't walk for two years. Finally, at age 40, she landed her first noteworthy acting role.

8. She was born to a 12-year-old as a result of a rape. When she was five years old, she was running errands for prostitutes and pimps.

Have you guessed who any of these people are? (1) Mentally slow and kicked out of school: Albert Einstein. (2) Military failure: Abraham Lincoln. (3) No voice: Enrico Caruso. (4) Lacked the sense to wait on customers at the dry goods store: F.W. Woolworth. (5) Void of creativity and good ideas: Walt Disney. (6) Teachers said he was too stupid to learn anything: Thomas A. Edison. (7) No theatrical talent and didn't get a decent role until she was 40: Lucille Ball. (8) Illegitimate child of the streets: the great gospel singer and Oscar nominee Ethel Waters.

I never get tired of hearing how people swimming upstream, against incredible odds, triumph over problems and setbacks. Dr. Norman Vincent Peale once said, "You're only as big as the the problem that stops you." I, for one, am thankful to these and so many other men and women who were bigger than the problems that would have, and often did, stop so many others. The *world* got better right after *they* got better.

Lunch When the Heat's On

None of those great people were available to me during the dark hours when my boss was out looking for my replacement. However, I started looking for articles about successful people in the business sections of newspapers and magazines. When I came across someone local, I called them up and said, "You don't know me, but my name is Danny Cox and I've just destroyed the number one office in my company by taking it from first place to 36th in three months time. My boss is out looking for my replacement right now. Can I have lunch with you?"

These successful people not only took my calls, they agreed to have lunch with me. Some sensed the urgency in my voice, and others just wanted to meet the person who could single-handedly wreak so much havoc on an organization. The one quality that every one of the successful individuals I called on shared was an entrepreneurial spirit. They all saw me as a challenge, or at least a curiosity. I listened to what they had to tell me, and immediately started to apply what I learned. I have never stopped seeking out the advice and counsel of effective leaders. Take someone to lunch before someone else eats yours. They don't even have to be in your industry for you to learn something. People principles are basically the same, regardless of industry. Learn them and apply them.

DON'T IMPRESS ... *INSPIRE*

Experience a crisis once and learn from it. Don't make Ticky or Peter Drucker say "I told you so." If you're a quick study and an observant person, you won't have to experience your own disasters to learn. Pay attention to what's happening around you in your organization, your industry, and your local business community. Keep up the radar sweep and don't go to sleep at the switch. Thomas Edison said, "The answers are out there. Find them."

There is no way to lead when the heat's on without wrinkling your clothes a little. Wrinkled clothes and dirt under the fingernails never killed anyone. Just remember, when you roll up your sleeves you go to work on yourself first. Your continuous personal pursuit of excellence will set the agenda for everyone in your organization.

Ask yourself tonight, just before you drift off to sleep, "Who am I inspiring by the way I do my work?" Notice I didn't say who are you *impressing*...? When you impress someone with the way you do your work, they say, "You do good work." When you *inspire* them they respond with, "I wish I did my work as well as you do yours." Right now we need inspirations more than ever.

The methods, techniques, and principles of effective leadership must be woven into *your* fabric before anyone will follow and seek the same excellence. Any improvement you make as a leader will be reflected in your organization. Think of it this way: Somebody, somewhere, is going to get better because you took the time to read this book.

CHAPTER TWO

THE EMERGING LEADER PROCESS

"Take a mentor to lunch before someone else eats yours."

Danny Cox

When my boss's search for my replacement launched me into a learning frenzy, the heat was on, and I was not about to go down in flames! I sought out successful people as often as I could and studied everything about them. I was starving for knowledge. Not just head stuff, but meaningful ideas I could transform into meaningful action. To this day I continue to seek those from whom I can learn.

To paraphrase the great twentieth-century philosopher, Yogi Berra, "We're bound to see something if we watch long enough." I keep watching and I keep seeing new and exciting things. Watching is a good habit that has served me well through the years. I discovered the hard way, I didn't know it all—and still don't. Age is irrelevant when it comes to acquiring and refining leadership skills. It doesn't matter if you're new at the game or if you've been working hard at it for most of your life.

The quality of leadership is not determined by the urgency or size of the task to be accomplished. Some of the greatest leaders I've ever observed or read about spent most of their time dealing with common details in order to achieve their vision. What made these people great was the uncommon way they dealt with everything in their lives, whether it was an ordinary detail or a major challenge.

After studying many great leaders over the years, I've narrowed their most powerful qualities into my top ten characteristics of an effective leader:

LEADERSHIP CHARACTERISTICS
Characteristic One: Uncompromising Integrity

Uncompromising integrity is the most important quality. All of the other characteristics stand upon this steel-reinforced concrete foundation. Although the other nine characteristics are in no particular order, integrity *must* be number one. Don't be misled by anyone who tells you that your personal integrity can be different from your professional integrity. Unless you're comfortable living a double standard, your professional integrity must match your private integrity.

Honest Abe Lincoln, who walked miles to return a customer's change, is a classic example of how integrity is reflected in professional conduct. At the core of integrity is a declaration of personal responsibility like the example in Chapter 1. A person who refuses to accept responsibility lacks the moral armor to stand against temptation.

STAYING POWER

It's common in the business world to see people take off like a rocket. We're all initially impressed with their spectacular accomplishments. The press and publishing communities nearly always chronicle the glory of the rising stars, and we spend the big bucks to listen to them address major conferences and seminars. Unfortunately, it is all too common for great success stories to fade into oblivion within a couple of years, if they don't crash and burn sooner. I'm sure everyone can recall a few recent riches-to-rags stories where folks didn't have the integrity to effectively fight the fire when it flamed up. What brought these people down? They had chosen not to make integrity part of their plan.

How many people could have been saved tremendous damage and/or pain if only they could have known which people in trusted positions were charlatans or would turn their backs on the accomplishments that elevated them into positions of power in the first place? In a small town, strangers have to prove themselves, and if someone proves himself or herself untrustworthy, it's a long and difficult road back into the public trust.

Where I came from, we used to describe an untrustworthy person by saying that we couldn't trust him or her any further than we could throw a soggy mattress up a spiral staircase, or that the person was as slippery as a pocketful of custard. If your neighbor told you that about somebody, would you buy from that person? *The Wall Street Journal* should publish a soggy mattress list every month just to snip off the fringes of the business world that haven't bought into the importance of integrity.

Integrity can be an entire book in itself. In fact, there are many great books on the topic of integrity and personal and professional ethics. More than anything else, these books are studies in right and wrong. Before you write me off as an evangelist waving a moral flag in your face, consider that integrity in business is the cornerstone of success. Without a commitment to right conduct, any enterprise is ultimately doomed. I'm talking dollars and cents.

GETTING OUTSIDE OF YOURSELF

One of the strongest indicators of integrity is the willingness to help someone else, even when there's nothing tangible to expect in return. My wife Tedi and I traveled to Holland a few years ago to begin a journey that would take us on a Rhine River cruise to Switzerland. We arrived in Amsterdam and caught a taxi down to the dock our boat was supposed to depart from that evening. When we arrived, there was no boat.

The cab driver drove us around in search of our missing ship. He eventually decided we had paid enough fare and turned off his meter. I told him it was okay to keep charging us, but he waved me off and finally took us to a nice restaurant near the dock where the boat was supposed to have been.

It was Sunday evening and the local cruise office was closed. Once inside the restaurant, the bartender sympathized with our plight and handed us off to a very friendly and helpful waiter who sat us down for dinner and promptly got the restaurant owner, Jaap Mous, involved. Jaap told us to relax while he went out and drove around the harbor, a drive that took him over thirty minutes.

Before long, the bartender summoned me for a phone call. It was the folks at the cruise line. Word of our dilemma had reached them through a sympathetic fellow diner who had heard our story. They were sending a limousine to pick us up. The departure city had been changed at the last minute from Amsterdam to Rotterdam, and we had already begun our trip before they could get word to us in the United States. As we waited for the limo, Jaap and his staff served us a great meal and provided good company with warm conversation. We actually started to feel as if we had known those wonderful people for years, and hated to leave when the time came.

The limo driver got us to Rotterdam in record time. Even though we could see the boat in the distance, he couldn't find the right streets to get us there. Our driver flagged down a local cab driver to ask directions. The cab driver told us to follow him and then escorted us through a maze of narrow streets until we finally reached the right dock with the right cruise ship.

As I trotted from the limo toward the lead cab driver, peeling off bills to compensate him for rescuing us, I was again waved off, just like the limo driver did, and he drove away without accepting anything for his efforts. Integrity permeated each person we encountered in Holland. What a great memory. How many people do you think have heard our Dutch hospitality story? Anyone who would *listen*, that's how many.

It is impossible *not* to share such a positive experience. Think about that the next time you have a choice between giving a customer a positive or a negative experience. If any story is told more often than a positive experience story, it's a negative experience story.

Each one of us is responsible for our own conduct, and as leaders we have additional responsibility for the conduct of our people as it relates to our professional relationships. No organization can force us to compromise our integrity. Heroes and heroines from the beginning of time have been identified by how much they were willing to sacrifice to uphold it. We're never too old to make it a part of our structure. More than any other quality, our customers and employees recognize the amount of integrity we possess.

Characteristic Two: High Energy

High energy also became evident in my study of great leaders. Great leaders do not get involved in petty issues. They know that pettiness is the biggest drain of energy you can have in an organization. These people not only know right from wrong, but also know the difference between *interesting* and *important*. There is a world of difference between the two. An effective leader must develop a sense of discretion and be able to draw clear distinctions between what is truly important to the organization and what is merely interesting, and that can include petty issues.

Much of this discriminatory ability is the result of experience. Take it from Ticky. There is no better teacher than experience, especially *hands-on* experience. However, even the emerging leader, who might lack experience, has a valuable tool at his or her disposal: *common sense*. Regardless of how much your common sense might have been maligned by a critical parent, everyone has some. Our biggest problem with common sense is not whether we have enough to come in out of the rain, but rather whether we trust our own common sense enough to allow it to help guide our judgment.

People often refer to great leaders as people who can "see the big picture" or "stay cool under pressure." In either case, what these leaders are really getting credit for is the level of trust they have in their own judgment. While others are running around like headless chickens, the energetic, effective leader is calling upon his or her sense of judgment to remedy the situation. There are times when even the experienced leader is facing a new and unique crisis, in which case the playing field becomes level. At such times, the experienced leader and the inexperienced leader must both call upon their individual common sense for guidance.

THE SMALL STUFF

Companies are all but destroyed by pettiness. I'm sure you experience pettiness in one form or another almost every day. I've seen entire offices get bent out of shape over what brand of office supplies to buy. Should an effective leader sweat over whether to supply the office with Eagle Brand #2 lead pencils? Believe it or not, such questions can be the subjects of many e-mails. What's even more amazing is that employees sometimes spend enormous amounts of time *discussing* e-mails concerning pencils. They even band together to have lunch and discuss the pencil crisis. Perhaps even start a petition.

How about the office that ceased providing postage to commissioned salespeople? The place nearly came apart at the seams. You would think that lives and careers had been shattered. At the obligatory lunch conference following the announcement, one of the ringleaders in the pending revolt was reported to have said, "If this company thinks I'm going to put out the price of a stamp in order to earn a $1000 commission, they'd better think again!"

Effective leaders have to be bigger than that. Remember that your people won't get better until you do. For the same reason, they won't get *bigger* until you show them *how*. Go with what's important and trash what's not. Any company, from an individual proprietorship to a multinational, can get bogged down and practically grind to a halt under the burden of petty issues that have been turned into mountains.

Petty issues are small and can easily go undetected, but they accumulate like dirt in your air filter, eventually choking off your supply of oxygen. Policies, rules, and regulations are often painstakingly drafted and enforced to smooth out the smallest wrinkles. Tremendous energies are frequently applied to handle minuscule problems. Sledgehammers were not designed to kill fleas.

The larger an organization grows, the greater the tendency to *over*regulate. Of all the companies I've observed, I have yet to see one operate perfectly. Never once has the factor of human error been eliminated. To the contrary, in organizations where the human factor is acknowledged and accepted, there seems to be much higher productivity and morale than in highly regulated organizations.

When relieved of the burdens that petty concerns and endless regulations impose, people have a natural tendency to focus more enthusiastically on the task at hand. Customers get better service, and jobs, in general, are handled more efficiently. You would think that some companies must have a sign in the training center that reads, HOW DIFFICULT CAN WE MAKE IT FOR CUSTOMERS TO BUY FROM US? Surely, nobody *intends* to promote such a dreadful thought. Yet, it is unwittingly true of many organizations with an inward focus on petty issues instead of an outward focus on people and what they need. In the fighter squadrons we used to put it like this:

Some die by shrapnel.
Some go down in flames.
Most die inch by inch, playing at little games.

The big question you and I need to ask ourselves each night is: "Did I play at big games or little games today, and at what will I play tomorrow?"

Characteristic Three: Good at Working Priorities

Effective leaders are also good at working priorities. Setting priorities is important. However, the distance between setting and *working* priorities is often enormous. Most lists of priorities end up in the landfill of life, having never been realized. The difference between merely setting priorities and *working* priorities is similar to the difference between a dreamer and a doer. It's important to dream and to plan, but all the dreaming and planning in the world doesn't accomplish a thing. The *doer* makes things happen. When the heat's on, I will trade you 1000 people who ponder the possibilities for one person who will make things happen. As we used to say back home, it's okay to have a tiger by the tail if you know what to do *next!*

Working priorities are essential for stability under pressure. Why? Because stability under pressure is the foundation of sound problem solving. Many people can solve problems when given enough time and a friendly atmosphere in which to work.

However, when financial demands from above are coupled with production and personnel pressures from below, the friction produces heat. The heat, in turn, frightens off the less confident and leaves those with true mettle to face the problems. Leaders almost always have the ultimate responsibility for problem solving, and their mettle is proven time and again by their stability under pressure.

FIRST THINGS FIRST

The great leaders I've studied work their priority lists from the top down. Even when you and I make our priority lists correctly, we tend to jump in at item number five because one through four are *hard*. Five is where the easy ones start. The great ones don't do it that way. They go after that number *one* priority with all they have. That number one priority gets *number one attention*.

Ignoring the big item at the top of the list won't make it go away. Jumping in at item number five on the list instead of starting at the top is kind of like tearing off a Band-Aid *slowly*. You didn't pause to savor every drop of that awful cough syrup your mom used to feed you with a spoon when you were a kid. You gulped it quickly. The shorter the painful experience, the better. Back home in Southern Illinois, we used to put it like this:

If you've got a frog to swallow, don't look at it too long.
If you've got more than one to swallow, swallow the biggest one first!

If you've been swallowing your frogs in the proper order all day long, then you shouldn't be taking any of them home with you for dinner. Frogs that aren't swallowed grow bigger and *multiply*. The best way to be an effective leader and avoid becoming a frog farmer is to take care of those guys, biggest to smallest, *in order, every day*.

The effective leader will finish with the number one priority and then go on to the *new* number one priority. That's right. When the number one priority on the list is dispatched, the next item on the list is not treated like number two. It becomes the new number one priority. The former number two priority becomes the *most important*. We approach priorities with different intensity, depending upon where they fall on our lists. When number two becomes the new number one, we bring the intensity it deserves as number one.

If we work on our number three, four, and five priorities as if they are third, fourth, and fifth in importance, there is a corresponding drop-off in quality throughout the day. Everything seems exciting and energized in the morning when energy is being invested in the number one priority, but by the end of the day there is a feeling of disappointment and letdown.

The secret to energy at the end of the day is to be working on a new number one priority then. You've witnessed it many times when there was a deadline to meet and the whole office struggled frantically to beat the overnight courier. Energy was high. Do the same with everything. It's a matter of working priorities as if each consecutive priority is number one. Indeed, each one is number one, in its turn.

The effective leader works the list of priorities and doesn't back off or compromise just because of where an activity was originally placed. The great ones get to the point where everything has been crossed off for the day except "pick up the laundry on the way home." Guess what? They pick up their laundry better than anyone else. It's simply a matter of finesse and style. Great leaders pump gas at the self-serve station at the end of the day better than anybody else pumps gas, because it is the number one item on his or her priority list.

Characteristic Four: Courageous

The cowardly lion in *The Wizard of Oz* realized that being a safe plodder was not the way to succeed in life. All of the great leaders I have studied were and are courageous people. I'm not recommending that anyone act irresponsibly. It's simply a difference in the way the courageous person and the timid person approach life. The courageous one is willing to walk near the edge and do things slightly off balance when necessary—not for the sake of living dangerously, but for the sake of getting the job done. The willingness to take risks and accept responsibility for their outcomes is a consistent quality among effective leaders.

The safe and timid plodder is cautiously tiptoeing through life, hoping to make it safely to death. That is substance abuse. It is like eating the banana peel and throwing away the banana. It seems like some people are in a hurry to get to the end so that nothing bad will happen to them.

The safe and timid plodder is the one you will find waiting in that parking lot at one end of town for all the traffic lights to turn green before starting out. Not only is the guy I described in Chapter 1 still waiting in the lot, he probably will be for the rest of his life. Who wants to spend their time in life's parking lot? If that someone is you, I can offer you some assurance: If you're cautious enough, nothing really bad *or good* will ever happen to you.

The safe and timid plodder turns pale or balks entirely when you say, "Let's give it a go!" To put it another way, you have to do what you fear, or fear will be in charge. There is no middle ground. Either you or your fears are in charge of your productivity. Pass that important thought on to your team members. It applies to them and their jobs as well as you and yours.

Characteristic Five: A Committed and Dedicated Hard Worker

Are you a committed and dedicated hard worker? What do you think other people are saving all of their energy for? Where is that reservoir full of energy that they've saved by not pushing themselves too hard? When we observe a dedicated and hard worker, we compliment that person on how hard he or she seems to work. Yet, when we point out how hard they appear to be working, they invariably reply, "I don't work hard. I love what I do. I'd do it for free, but don't let that get around."

They might not say that last sentence, but nobody ever worked himself to death in a job he loves. People work themselves to death in jobs they hate. Working in a job you hate will produce ulcers, a form of cannibalism that begins to eat up the person you're not happy with. I'll bet any doctor will agree that very few happy people come in complaining of ulcers.

The people who love their jobs constantly think about how they can do their jobs better. It's common for them to get a great idea at four in the morning and scramble to write it down so they can get to the office early and try it. Remember, the risk takers are always ready to roll.

You'll also notice that committed and dedicated hard workers don't tend to be depressed people. They don't have the time to waste being depressed. They are in charge of their moods, not vice versa. When their fellow employees get their hands on them, they might slow down, but only momentarily. In fact, that is the exact advice they get from their peers: "You better slow down or you'll ruin your health. One of these days you're going to drop dead from a heart attack."

WORKING IS FOR WINNERS

I don't think anybody believes the solemn advice giver is truly concerned for the high performer's health. When I talk about committed and dedicated hard workers, I'm not talking about workaholics who use their jobs to shield them from personal or family problems. I'm referring to people who have the support and encouragement of their friends and family. I'm talking about achievers whose priorities are in the right place and who have supportive families that are proud of their professional accomplishments. They get the most out of not only their professional life, but their family life too.

When the heat is on and you need to be highly effective and efficient, you want to surround yourself with committed and dedicated hard workers. There is no limit to what you can accomplish with a team of people who love what they do. It's a terrible thing when someone manages people who love what they do and doesn't share their enthusiasm. It's equally bad when an enthusiastic leader doesn't have a committed and dedicated staff. Dedicated and committed hard working leaders eventually develop dedicated and hard working organizations, regardless of whom they start with.

In the best of all possible worlds, each of us would be employed in activities we'd enjoy doing even if we weren't being paid. Most of the successful leaders I've encountered don't give much conscious consideration to what they're paid. They do what they love, and the money comes with it. The big question that stops most people I present it to is: "What would you be doing if money was not a primary consideration?"

The great leaders will always say, "I would do exactly what I'm doing." If you don't give that same answer, perhaps you should consider a change. If a change seems too frightening or uncertain, reread Leadership Characteristic Four.

Characteristic Six: Unorthodox and Creative

Effective leaders in any field are a bit unconventional, with an urge to create. If the truth were known, they are also a bit mischievous. These people bore easily. They're not likely to stick very long with something that's not working. If you need something monitored for a long period of time that's not likely to produce much in the way of results, it's better to give that assignment to someone who is worried about saving his or her energy. Those careful plodders make good kettle watchers. The effective, enthusiastic ones won't have the patience to wait for a phone to ring before acting.

The effective leader is an innovator. You might have heard them described as people who would rather ask forgiveness than permission. I'm not talking about irresponsible loose cannons. Recall important characteristics such as sound judgment, common sense, and personal responsibility, and you'll begin to see how these great qualities of leadership complement one another.

I had a few of these folks working for me, and they came into my office from time to time and said, "Danny, I just tried this or that unorthodox thing." I would turn pale before asking, "You did *what*? What happened?" not really wanting to hear the answer.

"They gave us a big order," came the reply. After I started breathing again, I said, "Congratulations!" with all the confidence in the world. "Good work."

PERFECT FAILURES

Experience can't be beat, and if you learn something from a failure, then it becomes a "perfect failure." I think that's a terrific way to put the educational value of a failed attempt into perspective. Every organization should have its share of perfect failures. Ticky had one when he picked up that horseshoe. It's okay to have new perfect failures, but they shouldn't be reruns. Learning eliminates reruns.

In my Air Force days, I flew a supersonic fighter in air shows, in front of 75,000 people, at 25 feet off the ground. Not many people have done that. When you see a tree shoot past your wing tip at 700 miles per hour, just under the speed of sound, you know you're living in the fast lane. It was always important to remember when flying at 25 feet off the ground that you should gain a little altitude before rolling into a turn. The penalty for forgetting one measly time would have been a 700 mile-per-hour cartwheel. The sky is *not* the limit. The ground *is*. You can only *tie* the record for flying low.

After my big teardrop-shaped turn, I would make another pass over that runway, 100 miles per hour slower, at 600 miles per hour ... upside down. Hanging in the cockpit by my shoulder straps, I had to also remember that, while flying upside down, the control system is *reversed*. Thank God I never had a lapse of memory. The one word I never wanted to hear myself use during an air show was "Oops."

My point is that the gray hair I sport these days didn't come from flying upside down at 600 miles per hour. My gray hair came from the unorthodox people who worked for me and constantly invented new and unique ways to do business. I'm proud of my gray hair, and I'm proud of those people who taught me so much about innovation.

Characteristic Seven: Goal Orientation

Great leaders I have studied also possessed the goal orientation needed to face tough decisions. Tough decisions don't have to be big ones either. How about making a few simple changes in your life, like turning off the tube at night and having someone who can teach you something over for dinner? How about reading or taking some quiet time to be creative? These might seem like insignificant things, but they can represent some of the subtle differences between the life of an immensely successful person and someone who can't figure out why they can't seem to get ahead.

At other times, tough decisions might involve cutting some people out of your life. If friendships do not include mutual regard and reciprocal support and encouragement, the chances are that the relationship will become the battery charger for someone else's inoperative alternator. I'm not saying to turn your back on people in need. I'm saying that you need to associate with people who are taking the same career and lifestyle bus that you are. Like likes like. As the Good Book says, iron sharpens iron. Choosing your associations intelligently is more than being fussy about friends. It's a matter of *shaping your community*.

All of these issues require a sense of where you intend to go, or goal orientation, if you prefer. Selecting appropriate people to spend your time with is an example of knowing the difference between those who take responsibility for what they can become and those who cry because they haven't arrived there yet. When someone takes responsibility, breakthroughs begin to happen.

When people on your staff become a contradiction to the goals you have established in the best interests of the organization and its people, it's time to part company. I'll talk more specifically about the art of firing nonproductive people in my chapter on team building. Keeping a nonproducer in a job where she or he is not contributing is not doing your organization or that individual any favors. We are not placed in jobs to keep them the same; we're placed in jobs to make things better.

A goal-oriented fellow (whom I'll tell you more about in Chapter 4) once told me he never works hard to pay bills; he works hard to have *fun* with the money. Otherwise, you won't have enough to do either one. I hasten to add once again that you ought to love what you do, even if you aren't paid to do it.

PAIN? NO PROBLEM

I did a program once with former heavyweight champion George Foreman. Even though he is the *former* champion, I still called him Champ. If I'm not tall enough to fly with the airlines, I'm certainly not big enough to survive annoying George Foreman to his face. As we had lunch together that day, I observed his nose from across the table. Let me tell you, a heavyweight boxer's nose is a work of art.

George Foreman's nose is a monument to goal orientation. It has been sculpted by some of the strongest, meanest punchers ever to step into a ring. I can personally attest to the pain you feel when you take one right on the nose. It gets your attention right quick.

I was on the varsity wrestling team at Southern Illinois University. Moving around the mat one day, I was looking for an opportunity to take down my opponent, the Missouri state champion. I was feeling confident. For some reason, I felt like that day was going to be special. I was right. Not for the reasons I thought, but it was special. That day was going to be an experience like no other.

I looked at his feet and decided to surprise him with the old flying-tackle type takedown. I launched and dove for his feet. For future reference, if you ever do that, you will want to make sure your opponent is not about to do the same thing to you at the *same time*.

My coach had taught me to keep my face up so I could see were I was going. "Watch for your opponent's mistakes," he always said. He was right. I kept my head up and noticed that my opponent had made a mistake. In midair, I saw that he wasn't as well-coached as I was. He had lowered his head and was completely unaware that my nose was about to do great damage to the top of his approaching skull.

POW! The only way I can describe the pain is to have you imagine an atom bomb going off inside your nostrils. Skyrockets went off inside my head. White-hot flames shot up behind my eyeballs. The lower half of my nose was now covering my mouth. Everything was bleeding but my hair. I shiver to even think about it.

My wrestling experience made me admire George Foreman's nose all the more. I looked at that thing and wondered how he could have endured the incredible pain of so many powerful heavyweight boxers popping him on the nose. So I asked him exactly that. "If I see what I want real good in my mind," he replied calmly, "I don't notice any pain in gettin' it." Perhaps that philosophy brought him back for a chance at the heavyweight championship at age 43.

That's sound thinking for a professional boxer or anyone else. Our kids could do with a dose of sacrifice to attain something worth having. But remember that people need to be led by example. Some people come to me and say, "Danny, you don't understand how sensitive to pain I am." When that happens, I ask them if they've ever been working around the house or garden, cut themselves, and not noticed it right away. I know I have.

I've gazed more than once at an awful-looking wound and wondered how and when I sustained the injury. The point is, our minds can only concentrate fully on one thing at a time, and the mind will shut out even a painful cut when we're fully committed to a task. If you picked up a knife and said, "I think I'll cut my finger now," the pain would be instant, wouldn't it? Goal orientation produces a drive and energy that shields us from the pain and weariness of accomplishment. So if you're experiencing pain in getting what you want, it's because you aren't seeing what you want clearly enough.

Characteristic Eight: Inspired and Contagious Enthusiasm

The great leaders I've studied have inspired enthusiasm. They're like a pilot light on the burner. I'm sure you have friends like that, or work with people who can light up a room just by walking in. Their genuine enthusiasm is contagious. As a leader, your people look to you for enthusiasm. Not that they need to borrow yours, it's just that it seems inappropriate to have more enthusiasm than the boss. They need permission from you to let it loose. Enthusiasm comes from witnessing the accomplishment of your daily *goals*, not just your *tasks*, which are part of a larger plan.

Actually, some people simply have too much enthusiasm to be held back. Chris, a woman who worked for me several years ago had everything going against her. She came from a very poor background. Her family worked in the tomato fields of California and she worked right alongside them as she grew up. Because of the demands of life in an agricultural labor family, she never made it past the eighth grade and speaks with a heavy Hispanic accent.

Nevertheless, she worked her way to the top of her field and broke every record our company's top salesperson ever set. This woman outsold an entire office of 20 people. When I asked Chris how she did it, she twinkled and said, "God didn't make me with an off switch." Life would be so much simpler for many of us if we didn't have an off switch that keeps getting bumped.

I was the one in the leadership position, but she was the one who inspired the rest of us in that organization. My most responsible leadership maneuver was to pave the way for her to keep doing what she was so excited about doing. I was not about to allow anything or anyone to pour cold water on her pilot light.

YOU ARE CONTAGIOUS

I hope this next thought will pop your eyes open like a good whiff of ammonia. I mentioned earlier that inspired enthusiasm is also contagious. If you don't have inspired enthusiasm that's contagious, whatever you do have is *also* contagious. That's a scary thought, but it's true. If you're hoping that the people who work with you won't get what you've got, rest assured that they probably already have.

Growth and improvement as a leader, especially a leader under pressure, requires genuinely inspired enthusiasm. If you're confused about how people can have such enthusiasm about what they do, skim the previous seven leadership characteristics, remembering that there is a distinct, interactive relationship between these qualities.

If someone is showing phony enthusiasm as a compensation for some other inadequacy, anyone working with them will detect it quickly. People with phony enthusiasm change jobs and locations frequently. They hop from job to job, always, impressing everyone with their enthusiasm when they first arrive. However, if it's not genuine, it will quickly fade.

As leaders, each of us needs to examine our own enthusiasm to determine if it truly emanates from our love of what we do. At the same time, we need to be sensitive to what drives the enthusiasm of our people. If there is any doubt in either regard, then we once again find ourselves standing at that fork in the road. Which road you follow should be determined by whether your enthusiasm and the enthusiasm of your people are driven by the accomplishment of or progress toward goals. Accomplishment is the appetizer of enthusiasm, followed closely by sound relationships that build character.

Characteristic Nine: Staying Levelheaded

Effective leaders are levelheaded people. They grasp facts in a hurry. They have the ability to organize chaotic situations. They see things as they really are, as opposed to how they wish they were. Effective leaders don't *react* to problems, they *respond* to them. Reacting is like a reflex knee-jerk that will invariably produce the same type of behavior that helped generate the heat in the first place.

Responding means using the type of common sense judgments that take the organization down a new and better road. When internal pressures combine with external pressures to produce a storm of uncertainty and disruption, the realistic leader can bring order and set corrective measures in motion. This is a leadership quality for tough, heated moments.

These people prefer to fix problems rather than talk about them. I'm sure you know the different types. Some people come to you constantly with worried expressions, reporting problems that seem unsolvable. These same people will discuss the problems at length with anyone who will listen. Interestingly, long after the problems are solved or no longer relevant, these people are *still* talking about them.

Not those who approach life realistically. They act without being told to because they understand that in the real world problems aren't stopping places, they are *decision points*. Problems are not to be feared. Problems are to be expected. The levelheaded leader doesn't go into a state of shock when he or she is on the hot seat. Instead, they confidently deal with the situation. When others are panicking, the effective leader must stay realistic and see the situation as it really is.

REALISTIC WITH A CAPITAL R

I learned about being realistic on a test flight. I know what it's like to be flying a supersonic jet fighter, alone, with 79,000 horsepower, at 60,000 feet, 1200 miles per hour, 20 miles per minute, upside down … on fire. There I was, with every red light on the control panel flashing in my face. At least I *think* they were flashing in my face. There was too much smoke in the cockpit to really see them.

Not having read Peter Drucker at that point in my life, and forgetting what I should have learned from Ticky back in the Ozark hill country where I grew up, I wound up in such a precarious position more than once. At any rate, I did my best to *be realistic* in the face of disaster. It started with self-talk.

Be realistic, Danny, I would tell myself. You are a test pilot with the right stuff. You're used to living on the edge. This is America up here. The nation is depending on you. The whole world is listening in on the emergency frequency. Remember that before you touch the microphone button.

Once I felt under control, I reached over to shut down whatever I thought was causing the fire with one gloved hand and simultaneously pressed the microphone button on the control stick with the other. I hit the button and called control center. "Mayday, Mayday, Mayday," I said in the most macho voice I could muster. "I'm at 60,000 feet, upside down, on fire. Clear the traffic pattern, I'm bringin' her in."

As I remembered it, each word of my transmission was clear, calm, and distinct. A Hollywood actor in a simulator couldn't have been more composed. As far as I could tell, I couldn't have been calmer ordering ham and eggs at the Officers Club. Of course, after I managed to get down safely (don't tell me God doesn't answer prayers), the controllers invited me in to hear a playback of my emergency transmission. For some reason, that calm, composed, macho voice ended up sounding like a panic-stricken, crazed chipmunk.

My sense of realism in the heat of the moment gave way to the adrenaline pumping though my body at such intensity I didn't even recognize my own voice later. It never failed to give the controllers a chuckle. My high-pitched babbling was so fast that sometimes they even had the prayer recorded. I didn't get my thumb off the button quickly enough and I usually broadcast my negotiations with God. The Test Pilots' Prayer is, by necessity, *brief:* "God, get this thing back on the ground and I'll taxi it in for you." There has been a time or two in my civilian life when I've used that same prayer. A good example was the time my boss came in and told me he was looking for my replacement.

The people with the information we need to develop the leadership qualities I'm listing are all around us. Remember, leaders are not born. They simply drink from Elbert Hubbard's "ocean of knowledge." Nothing promotes a levelheaded sense of realism as much as knowledge. Lack of knowledge results in ignorance, prejudice, and narrow thinking.

Characteristic Ten: A Desire to Help Others Grow and Succeed

Every great leader I studied had a desire to help others grow. That desire is at the core of Dale Carnegie's success. He made millions by helping and encouraging others to make millions. True leaders not only want their people to succeed, but also to grow and develop. When an organization functions in a nurturing environment where pettiness is eliminated and ideas are openly exchanged, the result is synergy.

With synergy, the organization and the individuals within the organization will become more than the sum of their parts. Every once in a while a sports team will rise above its potential, as the sports analysts say, and win the big game or championship or even the gold medal against all odds and predictions, defeating higher-rated teams in the process. Whenever this happens, we are witnessing individuals and their organization achieving synergy. However, as my sales staff once proved, you don't have to be rated as a preseason champion to succeed.

We should *never* pour cold water on anyone's dreams. Being unenthusiastic, down-in-the-mouth, and generally nonsupportive is the fastest and most effective way to choke any hope of synergy and growth out of your team members. Believe me, if you're like soggy cereal at the company breakfast, then its time to have a personal "moment of truth."

Don't shy away from the people you need the most. One way to pump energy and enthusiasm into your office or company is to fill it with the most talented and skilled people available. Unfortunately, hiring somebody better than you is the exception, not the rule. When it comes to hiring and promoting, it's common for bosses to protect their territory and/or image by making sure they surround themselves with people who won't push or challenge them too much. That usually leaves the most talented and skilled people on the outside looking in. No manager would ever admit to such a thing, but it is so common that it might be done unconsciously.

There are many reasons not to hire someone better than you. None of them are good. But they're powerful reasons just the same. For example, if you hire someone less skilled and talented than you, that person probably won't bring you any challenge that you can't handle. That person probably won't push you to learn anything that you don't already know or bring you any problem that you haven't solved before. On the other hand, that person won't bring creativity, new and different ideas, or the kind of innovative thinking that can help you and your company reach new heights. Opting for comfort can mean opting out of getting better.

GET YOURSELF IN PERSPECTIVE

By working hard on tasks that reflect your true priorities and values, people around you will take notice. One of the things they will observe is that you're not admiring yourself as you go. You're not doing things with one eye on the mirror. People get inspired when they see someone doing courageous and daring things. Hiring someone who is possibly more talented than you shows that you care more about your team's overall success than your own image. That inspires others to go beyond their own self-interests for the good of the team. It takes a big person to admit that there is always room for growth and improvement.

Developing good people depends upon your willingness to support and encourage them, no matter how farfetched their ambitions seem to be. When I was flying fighters out of Tucson, Arizona, I met Hal Needham. In those days, Hal was a stunt man in the movies, falling off horses or crashing cars for $500 per stunt. We became friends. We both lived life a little differently than the average person.

If Hal would have told me back then that he intended to become Hollywood's top stunt man, I might have said, "Hal, there's no way you're going to do that. You're not going to live that long. You've already had 43 major bone breaks, not including fingers and toes."

If he would have said, "Danny, I intend to write a movie someday that will rank in the top 10 movies of all time, sharing box office honors with *Gone With the Wind*, *The Sound of Music*, and *Star Wars*," I would have said, "Hal, you're an ex–tree trimmer with a ninth grade education. Are you planning to write that script with a crayon clutched in your fist?"

If he would have told me he also intended to team up with another friend of his, who is a butcher by trade with a *hobby* of engineering, and build a rocket-powered supersonic car, I probably would have said, "Stop right there, Hal. You're talking to one of the world's foremost authorities on supersonic machinery ultra close to the ground, and I'm telling you there is no way an automobile will ever go supersonic. The rubber won't even stay on the wheels at those speeds." Then I would have patted him on the shoulder sympathetically and said, "Hal, old buddy, I think you've fallen off one horse too many. Let me drive you back to the hotel. You need your rest."

Fortunately, Hal didn't describe his many dreams to me until after I had learned not to pour cold water on other people's ambitions. Sure enough, years later he called me and said it had been some time since we had seen each other and we should get together for dinner. As we sat there in Malibu, watching the waves roll in, he told me how he had become the top stunt man in Hollywood. He told me how he had written and directed *Smokey and the Bandit*, which was tied with *The Sound of Music* for fourth place in all-time box office sales. I never imagined I would ever hear the names *The Sound of Music* and *Smokey and the Bandit* in the same sentence, but at the time, they shared that distinction in motion picture history.

He went on to say, "Danny, next week I'm doing something I want you to be a part of."

"What's that, Hal?"

"I've got this friend who is a butcher by trade and his hobby is engineering. We've built a rocket-powered car and I want you to be there when we punch it through the sound barrier."

"That must be quite a car!" I said.

"It's 18 inches wide and 40 feet long," he went on. "It even has metal wheels."

"Of course," I said confidently. "Rubber would probably come right off at those speeds."

This former tree trimmer with a ninth grade education was blowing me away. He went on to say that they were going to run the car on the dry lake bed at Edwards Air Force Base. So, there I stood, one week later, on the same lake bed where the space shuttles land, my wife on one side of me and Chuck Yeager on the other. Chuck had been the first man to *fly* through the sound barrier, and he was now watching Stan Barrett, the man Hal had selected to drive the car, squeeze himself into that tiny cockpit.

It took Stan 20 minutes to maneuver his body into the 18-inch-wide car. As he twisted and turned, inch by inch, it occurred to me that he *wanted* to get in. I couldn't imagine how long it would have taken to get *me* into that car, not because I'm wider than Stan Barrett, but because my kicking and screaming might have slowed down the process. Once Stan was inside, they *bolted down the canopy!* That means you're encapsulated in there until somebody comes and unbolts you. What a thought! I don't think I have enough of the "right stuff" for that.

The speed of sound varies with temperature and other atmospheric factors, but that day the sound barrier was at 730 miles per hour. That's about 500 miles an hour faster than the drivers come down the straightaway at the Indianapolis 500. Imagine *tripling* the speed of the Indy cars racing past the grandstand. The countdown commenced and the rocket engine ignited. Even with our ear protectors, the noise was deafening. A rocket engine delivers total thrust instantly. As Stan later described it, "It's a whole lotta gone in a hurry."

They told Stan it would take three runs, one run per weekend, to punch through the sound barrier. He said, "I'll risk my life three times for that." My wife and I were about to watch run number 16. The rocket car roared down that long dry lake bed out of sight over the horizon, although we could still see the 50-foot rooster tail of dust and smoke. When they unbolted Stan, he still hadn't reached the sound barrier but he had driven 637 mph, faster than any human being had ever traveled across the face of the earth.

He said that he felt he just couldn't drive any faster, but weekend after weekend he'd squeezed inside to give it another go. The following week, Stan tried again. Seventeen seconds after ignition, he was traveling nine miles an hour faster than the speed of sound! That put him into the *Guinness Book of World Records* as the *first* to break the sound barrier on the ground. Stan later gave me a picture of the event and pointed out that his rear wheels were a foot off the ground while he was supersonic.

"Did you know that you were only on your nose wheel?" I asked.

"It's hard to know anything when you've got your eyes closed and your fingers in your ears," he replied.

I should include *a confident sense of humor* as my 11th characteristic of great leadership. The great ones all seem to have it, from presidents who have just been shot to test pilots who are out of control.

After the successful run, Chuck Yeager and Hal walked over to the car. Chuck pointed up to the American flag on the tail fin and said, "Where else but in a *free country* could a tree trimmer from St. Louis with a ninth grade education finance a $2 million car and run it 17 times at an average cost of $75,000 per run, built by a butcher who only had a hobby of engineering, and driven by a man whose schoolteacher had lifted him out of his seat by his cheek as a youngster saying that he would never amount to anything?"

Don't ever pour cold water on somebody's dream. And, for heaven's sake, never pour cold water on your own.

YOUR VALUES EQUAL THEIR VALUES

An organization will never rise above the quality of its leadership. With the 10 leadership characteristics as your guiding pillar of fire, you can lead some pretty wild folks successfully across a challenging desert and produce great results. When building a new team, the selection process is guided to some degree by what jobs you need handled.

That's the easy part. Deciding who can best handle the job and/or is going to contribute the most to the team's effort is more difficult. To determine someone's potential as a team member, regardless of job description, I suggest you use the 10 leadership characteristics:

1. Uncompromising integrity
2. High energy
3. Good at working priorities
4. Courageous
5. Dedication and commitment to hard work
6. Unorthodox and creative
7. Goal orientation
8. Inspired and contagious enthusiasm
9. Levelheaded
10. A desire to help others grow and succeed

Use this list as a 10-step report card for your evaluation of each potential leader using a 1 to 10 scale for each of the 10 characteristics. You might want to rewrite your own version of what constitutes a great leader, adding or substituting characteristics that are relevant to you and your organization. Remember that your criteria need to be consistent for *everyone*. Whether you're assembling a new team or adapting an existing group to a new leader or a new assignment, consistency in your values is critical.

In short, I'm suggesting that you look for the same qualities in new people you expect from yourself as their leader. Make sure you're not trying to clone yourself. You're simply setting forth what you believe constitutes the highest ideals in business conduct and using those ideals as a *standard* measure.

You can learn a lot from how someone tells you they intend to behave. Someone who never intends to make another mistake is naïve, unrealistic, or both. I might immediately suspect him or her to be a safe plodder and not the creative and unorthodox type I'm looking for. Suppose an interviewee told me, "Danny, when I get going, I'm likely to make a mistake now and then. But I would rather keep pushing hard than just sort of crawl along. I always try to learn from mistakes, and rarely repeat them." I would probably hire that person and put them in the office next to mine so some of that enthusiasm might rub off on me.

LEADERSHIP DEVELOPMENT

Top performers in your organization might look to management positions as a way to move up in the organization. There's no doubt that they deserve to be rewarded, but moving them into management positions might not be the best thing for them or the organization. It's a mistaken notion that managers don't do much and are paid a lot. That's why team members often refer to such a promotion as "retiring into management."

Your job as a leader includes doing what's best for your team members and the company as a whole. That means you'll need to do some educating. Start with Henry Ford, who said, "Asking who ought to be the boss is like asking who ought to be the tenor in the quartet." The job of boss should go to the person best qualified to handle the complex responsibilities of leadership. That might *not* be the highest performer in the office. Leadership is a different animal than selling or engineering. This doesn't mean that a salesperson or engineer won't make a fine leader. I started in sales. Some high-visibility CEOs were engineers by training and education.

Leadership Evaluation: Phase One

Sit down with anyone who is a potential leader and go over a management checklist. Ask for the the candidate to rate himself or herself on:

- Numerical skills
- Communication
- Product knowledge
- Independent thinking
- Leading change
- Ability to cooperate with peers, team members, and upper management
- Sensitivity to people's wants and needs
- Getting along well with people in general
- Team orientation
- Tactfulness
- Self-confidence
- Respect for authority
- Treating opposition fairly
- Accepting criticism
- Resolving conflict
- Attention to details

You'll need to design your own list so the items are appropriate for your business. From this example you should be able to see that a candidate who thought that managing was a cakewalk might start forming another opinion. That's education. Managing is not easy. If anything, it's much harder and more challenging than anything the candidate has done in the past. If you teach the lesson well, many candidates for management positions will excuse themselves and take another look at the position in which they found success.

Leadership Evaluation: Phase Two

If the candidate still thinks that he or she is leadership material, you can move on to the assignment phase. Just talking about the many challenges of leadership will never have as much impact as rolling up the old sleeves and doing it. Make temporary assignments for the candidate that will place him in a typical management situation. The way he handles the assignment will demonstrate to both of you the candidate's management capabilities.

For example, you might have the candidate write an assessment of each of the team members' strengths and weaknesses, and how the strengths can be maximized in each individual.

If the number one task before effective managers is the growth and development of each of their team members, you need to have a good idea of how mentally prepared the candidate is. The candidate needs to know that growth and development of the team members will be his or her number one priority. The assessment exercise will bring all of that out. Here are some other assignments you might give the candidate:

♦ Give a specific recruiting assignment in which the candidate is required to find somebody for you to interview. Put a deadline on it. This will tell you if he or she understands what to look for in a potential team member, and why.

♦ Have the candidate sit in on an interview; preferably not his or her recruit— in case you have to turn the person down. It could ruin a friendship, if that's how the potential manager knows the person. Recruiting talent is a major portion of the manager's job. Candidates have to observe what they would be facing, in order to decide if management is the right move for them.

♦ Give administrative planning and organizational assignments. Help the prospective manager see how the responsibility rests on the manager's shoulders to keep quality records and information management systems straight.

♦ Have the prospective manager lead a meeting. Getting up and speaking in front of the group might be the blow that knocks them out of the running. Many people have a hard time making presentations, but a manager must be good at it.

♦ Have the candidate train a new person. Make sure that the aspiring manager has the patience and temperament to bring the new employee along and to see that the newcomer's needs are met.

♦ Appraise a disguised or fictionalized termination. In your role-play scenario, tell the candidate what you've tried with the problem team member, and see if the candidate has other suggestions for turning the team member around. Then place the candidate in your chair, walk around the desk, and pretend to be the employee facing termination. "Okay," you say. "Terminate me." If the candidate doesn't have the stomach for firing people, they're not management material. I'm not saying that a hatchet man makes a good manager. But a good manager has to be able to set someone free if the situation isn't working out.

The candidate should see by now that a manager's job is truly complex and multifaceted. If they previously believed that managers just sit in the office and read reports, they won't think so anymore.

Leadership Evaluation: Phase Three

If your company has a management development program, your candidate is likely to be enrolled by now. However, he or she might have remained under your watchful eye long enough to get a feel for whether management is the right choice. As your candidate makes her way through the management development program, you should schedule regular review sessions to evaluate her progress. Have the potential manager complete a manager's evaluation checklist, such as the one in Phase One. More than anything else at this stage, you're checking to see if the candidate is still interested in making the move to management.

FINDING THE RIGHT PERSON

You might not have a managerial candidate chomping at the bit. In that case, you need to go out looking. To determine who has the most potential based upon peer respect, go directly to team members and ask, "Whom do you go to with a problem if the manager isn't around?" Often you'll discover that you have a highly respected and well-qualified individual right under your nose—someone who is already demonstrating good coaching and people-building abilities.

A FINAL QUESTION FOR YOU

On a leadership scale of 1 to 10, how do you stack up on each of the characteristics and what is your total score? Would your employees give you the same score? If not, take a moment to analyze why you think theirs might be lower. Subscribing to the 10 qualities of effective leadership will not only make you a better leader when the heat's on, but you'll also become a calming agent for your staff by never picking up a hot horseshoe for the second time.

CHAPTER THREE

THE FIRST STEP: TEAM BUILDING WHEN THE HEAT'S ON

"Gettin' good players is easy. Gettin' 'em to play together is the hard part."
Casey Stengel

Often, after doing a keynote talk at a convention or a corporate leadership seminar, some manager will call me aside and say, "Danny, how do you get rid of the mavericks in your organization, those people that are hard to handle?"

"You don't," I respond quickly. "As a matter of fact, you go get more of them."

"But if I did that, I'd have to learn how to ... "

I finish his or her sentence with, " ... handle all that incredible new horsepower."

If your goal is to develop a workforce or sales force that does exactly as they're told to do, you'll soon find out that they do only what they're told. Initiative and creativity will be stifled. In today's competitive world, that is not what you're after.

The greatest leaders go out of their way to recruit premier talent. It's logical. The organization won't get better any faster than the leader does, and one sign of good leadership health is the willingness to applaud the accomplishments of others. If others are never allowed to soar any higher than the manager does, then there will always be a lid screwed tightly over the organization's potential and the potential of every individual in the organization.

PUT PETTINESS BEHIND YOU

In any organization where the manager refuses to hire anyone better than he or she is, or to allow anyone to receive higher acclaim, there will surely be pettiness. Effective leaders are big enough to permit others to be bigger than the leader. Leaders who have the 10 qualities you read about in the previous chapter will be eager to hire the best and to get the best out of everyone they hire.

Many people assumed I must have recruited top talent by raiding or hiring people who were already successful at other companies, in order to achieve the record-breaking production we achieved. That was not the case. I began with what was left of the team when we hit bottom. As we climbed back, I added new team members from many different backgrounds. One of them was an ex-rodeo steer wrestler. The people working for you have just as much potential. Perhaps even more.

Imagine taking your entire team into a very special room and turning out the lights. Then, magically, only the undeveloped potential in each person would glow. It would not only be an unforgettable sight, it would be blinding. As you look at each team member, see in your mind his or her bright potential. It's there.

This chapter on team building is one of the most important in the book because building the best team possible is the very foundation of effective leadership. Many exciting aspects of team building will be covered. In addition to building a good team, there are the tasks of establishing effective communications, focusing the organization, and laying the foundation for motivation. Getting a quality team firing on all cylinders can relieve much of the down pressure you feel from above. Likewise, the up pressure from below can be reduced or practically eliminated by a well-functioning staff, free of disruption and friction.

VIEW FROM THE SHOULDER

The victories belong to everyone in the organization. How often have you seen a football team charge over to their bench after winning the big game, hoist their coach onto their shoulders, and parade around the field? It's a ritual after a particularly meaningful victory. But look closer. A bunch of players, sweaty, battered, and bruised after sixty grueling minutes of punishing competition, run over and hoist up a person who hasn't carried the ball one time or made one tackle in the entire game.

What's wrong with this picture? The way many managers think, if they were to allow their team to go out and perform tasks they themselves are not capable of, the team would charge his or her office following a victory and demand to be carried on the boss's shoulders. But that's not how it works. The team still comes to the leader and lifts him up to celebrate the victory.

Damage occurs and hostilities erupt when the manager expects or, worse yet, demands that the team honor him or her for something they have accomplished. You never see the football coach demanding to be lifted onto the players' shoulders. Can you imagine the coach at the postgame interview taking all the credit for the victory? How would that make the players feel? Would they play nearly as hard for that coach again? I doubt it. Nevertheless, organizations frequently heat up because of friction between those who deserve praise and applause and those who attempt to steal the spotlight.

Switching sports, I heard the great UCLA basketball coach John Wooden, the Wizard of Westwood, tell a great story about young Bill Walton. This talented but undisciplined player had a few days off and didn't shave. He wanted to grow a beard. Coach Wooden forbade this. At the next practice, Walton walked up to his coach and said, "Coach, I've decided to grow a beard."

"You know that's not allowed," Wooden replied.

Walton said he was aware of that rule, but he believed strongly in his right to do it anyway.

Wooden looked up at him and said, "Bill, I admire anyone who has strong beliefs and will stand up for them. I'm going to miss you, but I admire you."

Bill Walton turned around, walked into the locker room, and shaved. That kind of great leadership helped make Walton a superstar in college as well as in the National Basketball Association. At this writing John Wooden, in his 90s and living alone, still receives a phone call each week from Bill Walton. Bill expresses his love and appreciation for the impact his old coach had on his life. It would truly be a noble goal for all of us as parents and leaders to have our kids and the people that were our team members calling us in our 90s to say "Thanks" and "I love you."

RESPECT STARTS WITH YOU

It's an up pressure issue as well as a down pressure issue, and one of the most complex tasks facing any leader. People don't care how smart or talented you are. They really don't. What people care most about is your attitude toward them. Only after you have established credibility, based on genuine regard for others, will others extend the same regard for you as a leader. Humility and equal regard are the ingredients for quality leadership. A fire extinguisher to battle the flames of jealousy and suspicion should be filled with the genuine ability to build other people up.

A leader cannot clone himself or herself. The ultimate result of a "make everyone just like me" approach is disaster. Cloning reduces most of your talented and enthusiastic human resources to a small group of paranoid people. It's simply a waste of terrific people. I ought to know. I did it … at first.

HOW TO REDUCE THE UP PRESSURE

There are many ways to create friction in the workplace. You have control over some of the causes and you don't have control over others. Demands from above for increased performance at reduced costs always tend to raise the temperature. These edicts from on high are very much like being told to run the engine hard but not being given the money to buy oil.

It's vital to let your people know that you understand the demands are difficult, if not impossible, but you'll be right there alongside them to confront the challenge and experience the victory, no matter how great or small. It's exciting when individuals and organizations break through self-imposed barriers. Major directives from above are really nothing more than challenges to your team members' self-imposed barriers.

Remember, the leader's mood is contagious. If the leader has a case of panic-scramble-for-survival, then everyone else is going to be infected. The way many managers react to pressure from above often increases pressure from below. Here is a partial list of things to avoid:

- Threats
- Disciplining in public
- Playing one person against another
- Not listening to input from the team
- Not publicly accepting responsibility
- Allowing favorite people to goof off
- Criticizing honest effort that comes up short
- Taking credit away from those who deserve it
- Abandoning ship while the crew fights the fire
- Attempting to force square pegs through round holes
- Doing anything that questions the loyalty of the team

This list could go on and on. Anyone with experience working in an organization, large or small, in either a leadership or a support role, has surely experienced these and other transgressions a thousand times. I know I have.

HOW TO REDUCE THE DOWN PRESSURE

As leaders, things we do can increase or decrease pressure from above as well as from below us. How well we do our job makes a big difference in how comfortable or uncomfortable everyone in the organization is. By the time my boss came to me with smoke coming out of his ears to say that he was looking for my replacement, my staff had been severely burned already. Let's look at how to reduce the heat.

Ten Sleepless-Night Questions

Getting better so your people can get better is an ongoing process. The following list of ten questions will help you focus on how the dynamic between leader and staff is actualized. Try to push back the limitations of self-imposed barriers as you honestly answer these questions.

+ Either I'm in charge of my organization or outside influences are. Which one is it? When you read this you may be in a tough market and answer by saying, "Well, right now the market is ..." Don't ever forget that great leaders always perform better than the current market.

+ If my people were as good at their jobs as I am at being their leader, how good would they be? Do I need to set a better example as a leader?

+ I know my employees will improve as they see me improve as their leader. How much improvement have they seen in me in the past 12 months? The past six months? The past month? (They could do a surprisingly accurate chart on your development as a leader for those periods.)

+ If one of my people were to ask me to describe my own personal plan for growth as a leader, what would I say? Would I have to make up a quick answer?

+ On an individual basis, how does each one of my people feel after a conversation with me? Am I playing favorites with the way I communicate with each one?

+ As a whole, my people get as much out of their time as I do as their leader. How are we doing?

+ The people in my organization have their future with me planned as well as I have mine planned with them. How far into the future is that?

+ My people are committed as much to the success of my organization as I am committed to the success of each individual. How much is that?

+ My people take as much pride in working with me as I take in having them work with me. How proud are we?

♦ When an organization succeeds, the leader stands in the midst of the group and says, "They did it!" If the same group fails, the leader must stand out front and say, "I am responsible." Am I willing to accept that responsibility?

DIFFERENT DEFINITIONS OF LEADERSHIP

Many people talk in terms of management. I prefer to reduce management to its more basic component of leadership. Management, of course, must include some amount of leadership. The pattern seems to be that the less effective one is as a leader, the more one immerses oneself in managing. Remember, you aren't truly leading until the people under your leadership award you that rank. Until then you're merely managing. I formerly subscribed to a very traditional definition of management that went like this:

Management is getting the job done through people.

This definition places a higher value on getting the job done than on the success of the people involved. A fiery, Type A–personality boss might find no fault in that. To such managers, employees are like replaceable batteries. The myth that goes along with that thinking is that a new battery is better than an old one. This is true of batteries perhaps, but not of people. Employees are like tools to be selected for whichever job is appropriate. The job is supreme. The employee exists to serve the job. If the job suffers, the employee suffers more. You've heard the tales of searching out the innocent and punishing those who were not involved.

Not anymore. Times have truly changed in that regard. The new news that really isn't new news at all is: When people aren't led properly, the job suffers. It's always been that way. Management was simply not in the mood to accept responsibility for helping team members grow. The new employee we hear so much about needs to trust the people he or she is going to work with as well as the organization itself. Employees are much too valuable to treat like interchangeable parts. When team members soar, so does productivity. The pivotal point between people soaring and people being shot down is the quality of leadership they receive.

Think for a moment about the concept of trust as it applies to the leader and the individuals in an organization. Successful employment for each individual depends upon the trustworthiness of the leader, which is trustworthiness as a person. Most managers are used to asking if an employee is trustworthy. What a switch it is for the shoe to be on the other foot. Yet that's where the responsibility belonged all along.

I confess that Danny Cox was one of those managers who once used people as tools. I would pull them out of the toolbox to get a job done and then toss them back into the toolbox until I needed them again. It's not hard to see why I was taking my office down the tubes. I systematically deprived my people of their humanity by devaluing their individual and unique identities and talents. Shortly after my boss told me he was looking for my replacement, I coined a word I use to this day: Humanagement.

HUMANAGEMENT

Humanagement is simply the ability to use the job to develop the person while having fun in the process. Instantly, my entire emphasis changed and I stopped managing my people like a bunch of livestock and began leading them as people. It occurred to me I could help each individual unlock the talent he or she had inside, as well as to:

♦ Set more meaningful goals (personal and professional)

♦ Better understand and plan their time

♦ Use more of their creativity

♦ Better handle their stress

♦ Feel safe pushing their envelope

If I had an office full of happy, growing people, I thought, there's no telling what we could accomplish. Sure enough, when they began taking a new and enriched mind home at night, instead of a sore, tired, and aggravated one, our entire universe expanded beyond anything we previously thought possible.

Don't forget the "while having fun in the process" part of my definition of Humanagement. By that, I don't mean you open the office with a joke every morning. My experience has proven time and time again that people who grow and develop to the point where they can handle problems they would not have been big enough to handle in the past are happier people. They're happier because they are more fulfilled and actualized as human beings. And when an office full of people becomes more fulfilled and actualized, morale goes up. Productivity goes up with it. I've never seen it fail.

With high morale comes low staff turnover. With low morale comes high staff turnover. With low staff turnover comes more bonding and team spirit. High turnover results in suspicion and a lack of personal investment in the job. It's difficult to feel a part of an organization if the probability of losing your job is high.

There are the managers who swear their organization has a terrific atmosphere but that people leave because the money is not competitive. On the other hand, there are those bureaucracies where people stay forever even though they're miserable. Perhaps someone could develop a logo for such companies built around the name:

In both cases, nobody is having any fun. People are leaving the first organization because they're not happy, not because they can make more money elsewhere. The value of having fun on the job ranks above money. The ability to enjoy the work and the working environment has a stronger hold on people than higher wages in an unpleasant job and an unpleasant environment.

IS THE MANAGER HAPPY?

You might not enjoy your job as manager. Many people who accept management positions actually long for the good old days when they loved what they were doing. The tragedy is that they had to allow themselves to be promoted away from the rewarding activity they used to enjoy in order to make more money. This practice of promoting people beyond their comfort zone produces a crust of unhappy and somewhat resentful managers setting a new, downbeat tone for those who are still enjoying what they do.

Those managers who recognize that they've been caught in this trap can remedy the situation in a couple of ways. First, they can acknowledge what has happened and attempt a return to what made them happier in earlier positions; or second, they can engage in learning new and effective leadership skills that will bring new vitality to their management position. They should never simply accept the leadership role and then grumble about it. Nor should they attempt to do their old job from the manager's office, thus pulling the rug out from under others in the organization.

ALL EYES ARE ON YOU

All of this ties in with what was discussed earlier about your attitude as a leader being contagious. I believe that nobody in your organization is going to enjoy their job more than you enjoy your job as their leader. They will try. You often see renegade bands of merrymakers attempting to liven the place up. But if the experience of truly enjoying the workplace and all of its relationships doesn't emanate from you, the leader, it will eventually rain on everyone's parade.

As your people watch you for clues and cues, a new level of self-correcting staff supervision begins to develop. The old Golden Rule comes into play just as naturally as falling off a log. People begin to give themselves and each other the same type of attention and support you give them. What does this mean to you? It means that the up pressure is eased off.

Your people can become virtually self-regulating. They will solve problems among themselves they formerly brought to you. Wouldn't it be nice to hear your people talk in terms of solutions instead of problems? They will even go so far as to police one another if the team has reached a high level of cohesion. Those who build each other up and support one another can and will hold each other to higher standards of ethical conduct and productivity, without you having to be the cop.

When you see a bunch of happy folks burning up the track, with the leader at the wheel and the staff hitting on all cylinders, odds are you're looking at a well-balanced and self-regulating organization. A supersuccessful organization is one that has surely blown through self-imposed barriers. It's a cinch the leader isn't sitting on everybody's lids.

THREE CHARACTERISTICS OF AN EFFECTIVE ORGANIZATION

Creativity

These days, many businesspeople hear the word creativity and automatically think of finances in the same way that stretching used to be something you only did during exercise. That's not what I'm talking about. The creativity at the top of the list of organizational characteristics refers to the originality of thought and execution, which are becoming increasingly necessary in today's business arena.

When the heat's on, chances are that the same old way of handling situations just won't cut it anymore. In fact, the same old routines are probably what got you into trouble in the first place. Down pressures are changing in nature and intensity. Up pressures are coming from the rapidly changing dynamics of a workforce with a new identity. If we lack originality in our thinking and behavior as leaders, we're clearly oblivious to the vise slowly closing on us.

Creativity in thought and action is necessary to stay at the head of the game as well as to avoid being overtaken by problems. Creativity is the steam that powers the locomotive of progress. Mark Twain used to tell the story about the train that was so slow they moved the cowcatcher from the front and mounted it on the back of the caboose to keep cows from climbing aboard from the rear. Creativity will keep you and your organization moving along in the right direction.

Energy

Any effective organization has a certain energy you can sense as soon as you enter the office. Even if there's only one person sitting in the office at the time, you'll be able to feel it. The thought might even pop into your head that this could be a fun place to work. Andrew Carnegie, the great industrialist, said, "I've found there is little success where there is little laughter."

When you walk into the other kind of office, the one with low or no energy, you feel that too. It's almost like walking into a big refrigeration unit: the chill makes you shiver. Even if there's only one person sitting there at the time, you still feel the chill. Some offices might as well have a sign on the wall that says:

FUN IS FORBIDDEN. ANYONE CAUGHT ENJOYING WHAT THEY'RE DOING
WILL BE PUNISHED

Where there's no fun, there's no energy. How long does it take to detect energy or the lack of it in the office you've just walked into? Ten seconds? No, five. Within five seconds of being greeted you can tell how much fun it is to work there. The thing to remember is that your customers can tell the same thing within five seconds of being greeted by one of your team members. Five seconds is all it takes to discover how much fun it is to work for you.

Change

Change is what happens when you mix creativity and energy. An effective organization is a changing organization. I don't say that the other way around because it is possible for management to change the look, staff, location, and a thousand other things about an organization in an attempt to artificially produce effectiveness. As Alfred E. Newman, *Mad* magazine cover boy, said: "Just because everything is changed doesn't mean it's different." That's wisdom.

Change that does not emerge from a healthy combination of creativity and energy will look, feel, and taste synthetic. I've never heard of the chef getting a compliment on rubber chicken. Creativity combined with energy produces change from within the organization. Changes imposed from the fringes of the organization feel like impositions. Changes from within are self-regulated and guided by realism. Impositions are irritating.

BUILDING BLOCKS OF AN EFFECTIVE ORGANIZATION

The foundation of any effective organization requires the following four basic components. Two or three won't do. All four need to be present in order for the foundation to be strong enough to support the organization's future growth.

- A sense of urgency
- Commitment to excellence
- Healthy discontent about the way things are
- Appreciation for the awesome responsibilities of leadership

A Sense of Urgency

Right now, I'm extending my arm four to six years into the future and pluck-ing something out to give you. Here it is: the yellow pages from the future. For some people, it's the stock exchange index or the Dun and Bradstreet direc-tory. For many it's the company organization chart. Is your name listed? In what capacity? Are you surprised at what you see?

If you have a sense of urgency about your growth and effectiveness as a leader, you and your organization should be in a prominent position. If you don't, chances are there won't be a trace of you left. Your attitude, shaped by your sense of urgency, will be largely responsible for producing the results you're looking for.

Commitment to Excellence

We live in the age of the consumer. The greatest businesspeople throughout time have been consumer-oriented. However, the consumer's power today is so great that any business that fails to be responsive will surely perish. Thanks in large part to the media, and the fact consumers are increasingly aware of their power, the heat on business has been turned up a few degrees. But the actions of some companies would lead you to believe that the customer service thing is only a fad. If you tell your customers, "We don't have to serve you like we used to, that was a fad," they'll make sure that it's you and your organization that become a passing fad.

Our society assumes the consumer is entitled to fair value for his or her money. As consumers ourselves, we strongly defend this notion. Yet, in a cli-mate where business is guilty until proven innocent, the pressure is on leaders to avoid living a double standard or requiring their people to compromise their ethics. It should not be the threat of exposure that motivates us to service our customers' needs.

A strong desire to do the right thing, beginning with ourselves and per-meating every personal and professional relationship we have, marks our commitment to excellence. Remember the ethical model where the best choice benefited the greatest number of people for the longest period? That makes excellence a goal we never fully achieve and, hopefully, never stop pursuing. I think everybody's grandmother said at one time or another, "If it's worth doing, it's worth doing right." That's good leadership advice, Grandma!

Healthy Discontent About the Way Things Are

A healthy discontent is like a little burr under the saddle making it slightly uncomfortable to sit back. Unhealthy discontent is made up of complaining, moaning, and groaning. When Walt Disney told his people not to rest on their laurels, it was because he was a leader who understood the consequences of complacency. Constantly looking for new directions and ways to improve what we're doing doesn't need to spoil the pride and sense of accomplishment that comes from a job well done. But we must continue to grow in new directions.

Walt Disney illustrated the need to constantly scan the horizon for growth opportunities when he resisted his advisers, who were urging him to produce a sequel to the enormously successful *Three Little Pigs*. They pressured him and he reluctantly agreed. After the sequel turned out to be a box office bust, Disney called his advisers together and announced a new law, one that's heard around the Disney organization to this very day. He simply told them, "You can't top pigs with pigs." Sage advice.

Appreciation for the Awesome Responsibilities of Leadership

Do you have room to grow? Look at it this way: what are your team members saying about you to their spouses and children at home? You're not a topic of conversation; you are *the* topic of conversation. What are they talking about? How well you've been working with them. Before you run back to your office and fire all those "sorry so-and-so's," read on.

When someone comes to work for you, they are essentially laying their life on your desk and saying, "I trust you and I trust this organization to do right by me and my family." That, my friend, is a heavy responsibility. For example, if that person wastes a year or two of his or her life, that time will never be recovered. It's gone. People's lives should be enhanced and opportunities should abound for them and their children because they had the good sense to come to work for you. Working successfully with you can mean a college education for the kids or simply an overall quality of life they might not otherwise enjoy. Your effectiveness as a leader has a long reach into people's lives. Never forget that. All of us have room to grow.

A CHALLENGE FOR YOU

If I were to say, "For the next five years, you will not be allowed to hire any new people," would you rethink how you lead the people you have now? If no new blood was allowed to enter your organization, could you continue to grow and prosper? You bet you could. If you truly faced a moratorium on hiring, I have no doubt you would begin discovering some diamonds in the rough.

The diamonds were there all along. You, the leader, haven't been sufficiently motivated to uncover them. You will be amazed at the untapped potential in your people if you look at them through different eyes and fully own up to the long reach you have into their lives.

THREE STEPS TO GROWING AS A LEADER

Learn How Successful Leaders Think and Act

This is about the reading and studying I've been harping on. Don't wait until your boss comes in and tells you he or she is looking for your replacement. If I had known then what I know now, my boss never would have come in and set my pants on fire. I would have paid $10,000 for a single copy of this book back then. Maybe even twice that.

The way others successfully handle pressure can be an education that ensures you'll never have to experience similar situations. When we observe someone who never seems to be on the hot seat, it might well be that while we were scrambling around with our nose to the grindstone, that person's head was up where they could look around and learn a thing or two from other people's experiences. A head that's up and looking around means:

- Attending seminars, live or on-line
- Reading books, magazines, and newspapers
- Taking to lunch people from whom you can learn
- Monitoring your own people for things you can learn
- Gobbling up audio/video multimedia training programs

When I was having difficulty in my sales office, it came as no big surprise that nobody wanted to come to my sales meetings. However, I heard there was a car dealer down the street who had terrific sales meetings. People came out of his gatherings full of enthusiasm and excited about their jobs and each other. Even though he was in a totally different industry, I had lunch with that car dealer and learned how to put on a great sales meeting.

Do What Successful People Do

It's not enough to merely study. True learning is the application of knowledge. Things get exciting for everybody when successful techniques are put into action. Keeping all of your great new knowledge in your head won't do a thing to increase productivity.

I speak three to five times every week, all over North America plus a few other places, and I don't think I've ever been in front of an audience that didn't have at least a few educated failures. Some of them possess enormous amounts of information about the latest leadership methods, yet they've stagnated or are failing. They sometimes ask me, with a cynical smirk on their faces, "What's the point of all this leadership babble anyway, Cox? I've been coming to these seminars for years. I read all the new books. But nothing ever changes in my organization."

When I ask them how many of the new techniques and strategies they have incorporated into their organization's daily routines consistently, they hesitate to answer. The truth hurts. Isn't that true for most of us? Isn't there a gap between how we do our jobs and the way we know how to do our jobs? I can't tell you the number of times that thought has popped into my head. You know the one: I know I can do this job better than this. My advice is: "Use it or lose it."

There's no use cluttering your mind with information you don't intend to use. It's better to focus on applying the most basic of the concepts you know. If you do, energy and creativity will take care of the rest. The content of your intentions will determine the content of your results. You must do what you know in order to know what you're doing.

Develop Leadership Characteristics

The following list of characteristics is a report card on your effectiveness as a leader. I established this list in the last chapter. It appears here as a tool for grading your effectiveness. Grade yourself 1 through 10, with 10 being highest, in the left fill-in column. When you're finished, I'll tell you what to do in the right fill-in column.

1. Uncompromising integrity   ____ ____
2. A high energy level   ____ ____
3. Good at working priorities   ____ ____
4. Courageous (willingness to take risks) ____ ____
5. Committed and dedicated to hard work ____ ____
6. Unorthodox and creative   ____ ____
7. Goal oriented   ____ ____
8. Inspired and contagious enthusiasm ____ ____
9. Realistic and levelheaded   ____ ____
10. A desire to help others grow and succeed ____ ____
11. *Total Leadership Score*   ____ ____

Now that you have scored yourself, go back and score yourself again, in the right fill-in column, the way your people would probably rate you as a leader. See yourself through their eyes. If you're gutsy, you might want one or more of your people who have read the last chapter to do the rating. Whether the two scores match or not, the score your people give you is the real one. That's right. You're only as effective as your people's perception of you.

Fortunately, I didn't have such a report card to circulate at the time my boss was looking for my replacement. If I had, my personal self-rating would have been far different from the rating my staff would have given me. They might have coined the phrase "less than zero" long before it ever became a movie. In retrospect, I must admit their rating would have been more accurate. The rating the staff gives their leader is always the most accurate measure of effectiveness.

WHOM TO HIRE

Mavericks. Hire as many strong people who make things happen as you can. The people I'm talking about are sometimes referred to as "hard to work with" or "hard to control." I'm not suggesting that you create chaos. You already have a good system to guide your leadership process, and you can lead some wild folks successfully through challenging times. Bishop Arthur Moore said it best: "I would rather restrain a fanatic than try to resurrect a corpse."

When building a new team, the selection process is guided mostly by which jobs need to be handled. That's the easy part. Deciding who can best handle the job and/or who will contribute the most to the team's effort is more difficult. To determine someone's compatibility with you as a leader and the balance of the staff you will select, I suggest you use the 10-step report card you used for your personal evaluation. You might want to rewrite your own version of what constitutes a great leader, but keep your criteria consistent for everyone.

Whether you're assembling a new team or adapting an existing group to a new leader or a new assignment, consistency in your announced values is critical. In short, I'm suggesting that you look for the same qualities in new people you expect from yourself as their leader. Are you cloning yourself? Again, no. You're simply setting forth what you believe constitutes the highest ideals in business conduct and using those ideals as a standard measure.

If you're not afraid to hire people who might be better than you, and you're big enough to encourage all of them to realize their full potential, you're on your way to building the most effective team possible. If you use a different report card for your staff than you do for yourself, you've created a double standard. The closer people come to realizing their full potential, the lower the up pressure on you and the greater the morale among your people.

Hiring, like most things, is largely a judgment call. More often than not, people tend to repeat patterns of behavior. For example, if a person has moved from job to job without much stability, it's likely he or she has yet to learn or put into practice some of the characteristics that would reduce that kind of inconsistency. It's important to check references and get an accurate picture of a person's previous patterns. When interviewing new prospective team members or getting to know existing staff better, it's always wise to discuss specific issues relating to the 10 leadership characteristics.

The ideal team would score itself and each individual member, including their leader, high on the 10 leadership characteristics. There would probably be characteristics for each person that rate higher than the same characteristics for the leader. I would hope that to be the case in any organization I was leading. The synergy would be tremendous.

Recruiting Made Easy

When you have a team that's really functioning well, your people don't want you to dump sugar in the gas tank or toss a wrench in the gears. They want things to run as smoothly and effectively as you do. Hiring is as important to the people already on your team as it is to you as a leader.

Because of their relationship to you, as leader, and to each other on the team, your people become your best recruiters. Good people want to work with good people. Not only will your people encourage you to hire quality talent, they'll go out and find it whenever possible. Your people will actually talk you and the organization up with their own personal testimonials.

Recruiting Questions

My favorite hunting grounds for new talent, especially sales talent, include restaurants and grocery stores. Grocery checkers and waiters/waitresses are good at dealing with people and handling problems. They can think on their feet and they're usually upbeat. They are generally organized and customer-focused. Most of all, they have great memories and learn inventories, sales materials, and procedures quickly. They absorb training well and apply the lessons learned to their assignments. When I come across someone who catches my eye as a potential team member, I ask them a series of questions starting with, "Are you planning to do this for the rest of your life?"

The prospective team member usually answers "No."

At that point I hand the person my business card, saying, "I'd like to talk to you about your next step."

Invariably they look at the business card and ask, "What is my next step?"

"Meet with me next Tuesday or Wednesday," I say, offering them choices. "Which is best for you? Morning or afternoon?" This is how I manage to get many talented people to take a new look at their lives.

Recruiting Visual Aid

I developed a tool that delivers multiple benefits. I called it a "Brag Book." The first and foremost use of the Brag Book is to show possible recruits how proud you are of the people on your staff. The initial message is clear: Come on board and we'll be proud of you too; this is an office where talent and hard work are appreciated. Lay the book out in a logical sequence so the new recruits can follow along and get more and more excited at each step.

A Brag Book can be a big three-ring binder, a photo type album, an internal Web page, or even linked to your public Website. Some firms use film and video production and interactive CDs to present this information. Regardless of the media, the impression you're after is all-important. And new recruits are not the only people you're trying to impress. Here's how to lay out the information:

1. The production record of the firm's top salesperson for one year (for sales recruits). Recruits for other departments can be shown the accomplishments of a top performer in their area. This shows the recruit that at least one team member is currently doing well. You'll want to get permission from the top performer before you advertise his or her accomplishments. Few accomplished people will have a problem with the fact that their peers, and possibly new team members, will also see the presentation. You could keep the top performer anonymous, but it's unlikely that you'll have to do that. The production record is essentially your first page

2. Next, display a graph of office production to show that the whole team—not just one person—is performing well. This is the time to emphasize that you're leading a team effort and the whole team will welcome the recruit and his or her contribution.

3. On the next page, display lifestyle pictures. With permission, show photos of a team member who took his or her family on an exciting vacation to an interesting place, perhaps a trip to Europe. If your team members have interesting and diverse hobbies like deep-sea fishing/diving, building boats, or skydiving, show those people in action. Your recruit will see that your team members do more with their lives than just work. And your current team members can learn a thing or two about one another as well.

4. Include biographical sketches of your team members that demonstrate the diversity of backgrounds in your organization. One person might have come to you after being laid off somewhere else. Another might have switched industries. Somewhere in there the recruit might find a familiar situation. The point is: Anyone from any background can find success on your team.

5. Prepare a picture page of people in training. Emphasize the activity and the nice surroundings for workplace learning. This tells your potential recruits that they won't be dropped into unfamiliar waters and expected to sink or swim. They can expect good coaching and education. This is a good time to show the recruit a training manual.

6. Show collateral materials on your company's goods and/or services. If the recruit is in sales, he or she will want to know that you're greasing

the skids for your people. In general, advertisements and write-ups on the company show that the public is aware of what you do and that it's newsworthy.

7. A "Hall of Fame" section featuring several different outstanding team members is fun to put together. It's best to have several categories so your people have numerous categories to shoot for. These can be: Most Sales in a Day, Week, Month, Quarter, or Year, as well as Largest Order Ever Sold, and Most Number of Products, etc. You'll find that people are proud to be included in the Hall of Fame, so much so that when a new record is set and someone else's picture goes into the record book, don't be surprised to see new energy and productivity from the *former* record holder. It's good, healthy competition.

8. People love a come-from-behind story. If you can locate photos that depict the organization's humble beginnings, put those in next to photos depicting the company's current success.

9. Put in a projected growth map. This will tell the recruit that the organization is continuing to grow and that he or she can come on board and grow into the future with the rest of the team if they so choose.

10. Include your own biography as the team leader. This makes it easier for you to talk about your own background and accomplishments. Help the recruit see that you're a competent manager, skilled at people building, and they'll be in good hands with you at the helm. Most of all, make sure you emphasize your commitment to the growth and development of every team member. This is not bragging as much as it's a statement of pride on your part; pride in your team. This opens the door for the recruit to ask questions about your background without you getting on a soapbox.

The Brag Book is a strong recruiting tool. If nothing else, it shows new people and your existing team members that you care enough to document the organization and its people. Don't use it, in any form (printed, on-line, multimedia), unless you've already decided that you want to hire the recruit. It can get sticky if you sell him or her on you and your team before you're sold on the recruit. If you don't ask yourself anything else in your selection process, make sure you ask these questions:

♦ *Will this job give this person what they're looking for?*

♦ *Is it the best career choice, based on what I've learned about this individual?*

♦ *Is this person someone I will enjoy coaching, mentoring, and generally helping to grow and develop?*

Research the Topic of Recruiting

Take the time to interview your top team members. A lot of potentially valuable information could be right under your nose to sharpen your saw as a recruiter. Start with these three questions:

♦ *How did you find out about this company in the first place?*

♦ *What made you decide to join this organization versus the competition?*

♦ *If you were going to start a recruiting campaign, what would you emphasize?*

In special, creative sessions called "Imaginars," I asked my team members questions like the three I just mentioned. I dug deeper whenever I could and pressed them to list everything about our organization that was truly unique. When we finally distilled our ideas into the most outstanding unique factors, I took down the items and used them in presenting our organization to new recruits. The exercise was also good for team members, since they came away with increased pride in the company they worked for.

The list of unique factors spawned a list of questions that I presented to potential recruits who still wanted to interview with the competition. Without identifying our firm on the sheet of paper, I sent the recruits on their separate ways with a list of questions to ask these competitors. Almost without exception, the recruits came back to us after getting the questions answered. By asking the questions, they had proved to themselves how superior we were.

What are the unique factors in your organization? If you haven't done so already, get your people together, using the creative techniques that appear in later chapters, and find out what separates you from your competition. Find out why your people came to work for you and why they're still there. Gather this vital information about your own organization and put it to work for you.

LEAN ON ME

That might make a good song title, but it's a lousy way to relate to your people. A good leader is not a person to lean on. A good leader makes leaning unnecessary. Oh, sure, they have to lean on you a little at first, but one of your first goals should be to get them to a point where they can stand on their own. The same holds true for good parenting. Some managers only feel important when someone needs them. You know the type. They carry pagers and cell phones everywhere, 24 hours a day, seven days a week. They thrive on solving their team members' problems for them. Does this help the team member grow? No, it only causes resentment.

THE FENCE TECHNIQUE

When my boss came in and announced that the search for my replacement was on, I did what any sane and logical manager would have done. I went to the beach. As we used to say back home, "The creek don't clear up till you get the hogs out of the water." My salespeople needed some breathing space, as well. I needed to be alone with my thoughts, the waves, the sand, and a legal pad of paper. That's where it dawned on me. There was a barrier or fence in my organization. My people were on one side of the fence and I was on the other. And the fence looked different, depending on which side you were on. With this revelation came my first major team-building technique. (See Figure 3-1.)

There was only one uniting factor in all of the people on the other side of the fence. They hated me. It wasn't a healthy bond, but it was a strong one. My challenge was to reunite with my people and put an end to our segregation. I could have invoked the power of my position, such as it was, and *ordered* my people to join me on my side of the fence. However, that option immediately seemed hopelessly impractical. Experience had already taught me that yelling at people simply doesn't produce cooperation.

Another option available to me was to crawl around to their side of the fence and try to recreate the wonderful camaraderie we'd had when I first came on board approximately two years before as the new salesperson and they took me under their collective wing. The most obvious problem with that approach was there wouldn't be a leader anymore. That seemed unacceptable. Being in their clique wasn't the answer. In fact, from a leadership standpoint, it was a bad idea all around.

Then it occurred to me that I was not going to reunite with all of my people at one time. At best, I was only going to earn their trust on an individual-by-individual basis. However, whom to start with seemed like an important deci-

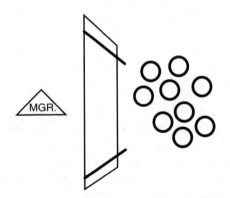

Figure 3-1. The "fence technique"—the team-building secret.

sion with implications down the line. My first thought was to go after the highest producer in the office. But something told me that would foster professional jealousy among the other team members. The situation would become even more divisive. What I needed to do was get someone over on my side of the fence whom the others would really listen to.

It dawned on me then that the most influential member of the team was not necessarily the superstar, but the person whom the others respected the most. The most respected person is the one who has demonstrated dependability and consistency over time. More often than not, this is a salt of the earth type and a midrange producer who cares about his or her fellow team members.

Using these new criteria, I rated my team members, starting with the most respected, then the next most respected, and so on. Already, I was incorporating the values of my people into my thinking. The ratings I used were their ratings, not mine. So I went to work on the number one most respected person on my list. Before long, that person was actually saying some decent things about me. Why? Because of the system covered in the following section ("Team Building: Relying on Strengths").

As I continued to execute my strategy, number two on my list headed for my side of the fence, then numbers three, four, and so on (see Figure 3-2). Once I had won about a third of the people over—the most respected third—others started heading my way from the far side of the fence. I realized then that it was unnecessary to give all of the team members a respect grade, only the top half.

Your people vote every day to decide which side of the fence to be on. This is true even if you've been managing the same group of people for many years. They will get better right after you do. The first ballot is private and the second is public. In other words, each person decides secretly on which side of the fence he or she feels most comfortable. It's a personal decision. Then, when the staff is working together, they poll each other and make a group decision.

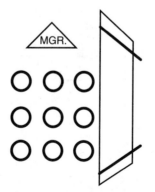

Figure 3-2. The goal: all on the same side.

Initial decisions are not permanent. People who decide to join you can drift away again. To get them back on the team, you use the same system that brought them over in the first place.

TEAM BUILDING: RELYING ON STRENGTHS

While still out on the beach, I laid out a plan, actually a chart as sketched in Figure 3-3. After listing the people in order by respect, I designated the first column after their names as "Weaknesses." This column can become very long, very quickly. Why? Because we notice weaknesses first and then have a tendency to concentrate on them. You might ask, "Why write all those terribly negative things down?" This list will become a *map through the mine field.* Up until that time, I couldn't have cared less about their strengths or weaknesses. No wonder I was in trouble.

The next column was "Strengths." I stared at the blank column and it stared back at me. It was as though I had writer's block. Perhaps I hated to admit that she (the first person on my list) had any. But she was the most respected person in the office. She *had* to have strengths. I forced myself to concentrate on her strengths.

It might have been mathematical ability, loyalty to the company, a good sense of humor, an appreciation for the finer things in life, and so on. Things I wouldn't have necessarily associated with strengths on the job began to add up. I realized that what added strength to a person as a whole were those qualities they could apply to their job. My focus began to shift from the huge pile of weaknesses to the huge stack of strengths. The old dog was learning a new trick.

Once I realized how many strengths a particular employee had that weren't being recognized or put to use in our organization, I was bursting at the seams

Name	Weaknesses	Strengths	Strategy

Figure 3-3. The million-dollar plan of action.

with enthusiasm the next time I considered her strengths. The strengths' column was as long as the weaknesses' columns. Don't think that she didn't notice that I was enthusiastic about her potential.

Then another person ceased to hate me with a passion. Why? Because I reflected back to that person the things that were important and valuable to him. What he thought and felt became my priority, instead of ramming my priorities down his throat. Have you ever heard anyone say they hate someone because they feel understood and respected? As I touched upon earlier, it's a natural human tendency to like someone who shows an interest in you. Your interest in that person might be the only thing the two of you have in common. There is no stronger common bond.

We can transplant hearts and other vital organs from one person to another, but we can't transplant strengths. Nevertheless, managers and parents try it every day and there has never been a successful operation. Our job, therefore, is to be a catalyst between their strengths and the way we'd like to see the job done.

You'll keep adding to both lists over time. A word of caution: The responsible leader does not leave these lists lying around the office. This is an exercise for you and you alone. Keep your lists at home. Each evening take only a few minutes to pick a couple of your team members from your chart to connect with the next day in a coaching session. Select one or two of the strengths from their individual lists that you can show them how to use more of in some part of their jobs.

The following is a partial list of strengths. It can spark your search for more nuggets in case you can't think of enough strengths for some team member on your list. (You'll notice that I didn't include a checklist of weaknesses. You don't need any help with those.)

__ Accountable	__ Bilingual
__ Active	__ Capable
__ Adventurous	__ Character
__ Ambitious	__ Cheerful
__ Analytical	__ Civic-minded
__ Anticipates	__ Committed
__ Appearance	__ Common sense
__ Appreciative	__ Communication
__ Articulate	__ Compassion
__ Aware	__ Conceptual
__ Believable	__ Confident

__ Conscientious

__ Consistent

__ Cooperative

__ Courageous

__ Courteous

__ Creative

__ Customer focused

__ Dependable

__ Detail oriented

__ Determined

__ Dignified

__ Diligent

__ Dynamic

__ Eager

__ Educated

__ Efficient

__ Empathy

__ Energy

__ Enthusiasm

__ Ethical

__ Excellence

__ Experienced

__ Extroverted

__ Flexible

__ Goal oriented

__ Grateful

__ Hard working

__ Health oriented

__ Helpful

__ Honest

__ Imaginative

__ Impressive

__ Independent

__ Industrious

__ Influential

__ Initiative

__ Innovative

__ Inspirational

__ Intelligent

__ Integrity

__ Interested

__ Interesting

__ Judgment

__ Kind

__ Knowledgeable

__ Likable

__ Listener

__ Logical

__ Loving

__ Loyal

__ Mature

__ Memory

__ Motivated

__ Negotiator

__ Open-minded

__ Optimistic

__ Organized

__ Patient

__ People oriented

__ Perceptive

__ Perseverance

__ Planner

__ Poised	__ Service minded
__ Polite	__ Sincere
__ Positive thinker	__ Spirited
__ Precise	__ Stability
__ Prioritizer	__ Strength
__ Problem solver	__ Successful
__ Professional	__ Tactful
__ Punctual	__ Tenacious
__ Qualified	__ Thoughtful
__ Quick thinking	__ Time management
__ Reliable	__ Tolerance
__ Resilient	__ Trustworthy
__ Respectful	__ Understanding
__ Resourceful	__ Upbeat
__ Reputable	__ Uplifting
__ Responsible	__ Versatile
__ Sales oriented	__ Vitality
__ Scrupulous	__ Willing
__ Self-assured	__ Wisdom
__ Self-disciplined	__ Witty
__ Self-starter	__ Writing
__ Sense of humor	__ Youthful
__ Sensitive	

Communicate with Their Strengths

Don't just make these lists. Use them. Learn to do the most important thing you can ever do with people—your children included—communicate with their strengths. Once I understood that, I realized I had been unaware of their strengths as I communicated with their weaknesses. How is that possible? By saying, "If I were you, I would ..." Trust me on this, if you've ever used that phrase, no one heard the end of your sentence. All they hear is you comparing your strengths to their weaknesses. You can understand what an explosive situation that is. You might as well be saying, "If you had my strengths instead of your pathetic pile of weaknesses …"

Quickly, I dropped "If I were you, I would …" from my vocabulary and started saying, "With your strengths, I feel the best way to handle the situation you're involved in would be for you to ..." People will listen to that. Their response, stated or unstated, is essentially: "Coach, you understand my strengths better than anyone I've ever worked for. You always have good ideas about how I can use my strengths, not yours, to handle the situation. Thanks for taking this time with me."

If you apply this system of being aware of your team members' weaknesses but talking to their strengths, you will have paid for your investment in this book many times over.

Breakthrough! Breakthrough!

If you feel that the thrill is long gone out of your leadership position, I guarantee if you will commit yourself to identifying and developing the strengths in your people, you'll experience a resurgence of excitement in your career. It will require you to really observe, analyze, and study each team member's habits, actions, and responses to critical situations. It's a quest that will help you continue to discover new strengths in individuals, including your kids.

Your enthusiasm for the continuing development of your team members will never wane. There's a great old classic movie called *Magnificent Obsession*, in which the mentor tells the star, who is about to make a major life change, "This will obsess you, but it will be a magnificent obsession." Finding strengths will be your magnificent obsession. The only time you get to work on your people's weaknesses is when they ask you to. Any attempt on your part to work on their weaknesses before they're ready is wasted time, both yours and theirs. They may come to you for assistance with their weaknesses after you've done a good job communicating with their strengths. By then, what was remembered as a glaring weakness by both of you could be completely overshadowed by growing strengths that make the weakness no longer a problem.

A Case in Point: Dinner with Bugs Bunny

One of the best illustrations of hidden strengths I've ever encountered was in my dining room. The late maestro of character voices, our friend Mel Blanc, was having dinner at our home a few years before his death. Mel is known for his 400 or so voices, including Bugs Bunny, Tweety Bird, Elmer Fudd, Foghorn Leghorn, and so many others. Over after-dinner coffee, Mel told us about a terrible car wreck he'd been involved in on Sunset Boulevard and what happened afterward.

Following the accident, Mel was brought to the hospital unconscious, and he remained that way for several weeks. Doctors repeatedly attempted to get a response from him by asking if he would lift a finger, squint his eyes, or in some other way acknowledge that he heard them trying to communicate. He never responded. The doctor's hopes were fading when one day a neurosurgeon on his rounds visited Mel's bedside and started reading his chart. Not expecting a response from Mel after all this time, the doctor mumbled, "Let's see how Bugs Bunny is doing today."

To the doctor's amazement, Bugs Bunny answered him. The line couldn't have been more classic: "What's up, Doc?" It was in the rabbit's familiar voice. True story. I got it straight from the rabbit's mouth.

According to Mel's account, the rejoicing doctor said, "Say it again, Mel. You're back." There was no response. After several more attempts to communicate with Mel, the doctor had a hunch. "Bugs," he said, "how's Mel?" Sure enough, the voice of Bugs Bunny came out and said, "He ain't so good, Doc."

Before the evening with Mel Blanc was over, I had shared with him the substance of this team-building concept. He agreed that his experience was relevant in that the doctors kept trying to communicate with Mel Blanc, who was almost killed in the car accident, while Bugs Bunny didn't get a scratch. Mel pointed out there were over 400 strengths inside of him just waiting for somebody to talk to them. When someone did: Bingo! Just like your kids and the people who work for you: Bingo!

Try This Exercise

Everyone in your organization has strengths inside, just waiting for you to talk to them. There's no telling how helpful these strengths can and will be to you once you become aware of them and communicate with them. Peter Drucker pointed out that strong people always have strong weaknesses. That's logical when you think about it. Show me a successful person, and I'll show you someone with a few chinks in his or her armor.

Drucker then went on to stress that focusing on strengths makes demands on performance. Once you identify a strength in a person and talk to that person about it, don't be surprised if they say, "You're exactly right, and watch this." They want to confirm your insight by putting that strength into action. Sarah Bernhardt, the great actress, understood this. She said, "When you tell a woman she has a beautiful profile, she begins to live sideways." I think the same is true of the male gender.

To illustrate what Drucker was talking about, I often set up a situation where you and I are working in a local auto repair shop. We repair automobiles for a livelihood and I'm your working manager. I'm working on a car in the stall next to where you're working on another car. One day you walk into my stall and say, "Danny, I've got a problem. I've got a one-half-inch bolt here and I need to borrow your adjustable wrench." It always seems that the manager has an adjustable wrench.

If I'm a weak manager, I'll go ahead and loan you my adjustable wrench. If I'm a pathetic manager, I'll go ahead and do the job for you. The healthy leader will recognize what is ultimately the best for you and, consequently, what is good for the organization, and help you locate your own half-inch wrench. I will then ask if you have any questions on how to put the wrench on the bolt and which way it should be turned. This is to confirm that you know how to use your newly discovered strength, a wrench in this case. Once that's accomplished, chances are good you will never come back to me, your manager, in search of a half-inch wrench again. You and I now know you have what it takes to do the job properly.

You must also recognize your own strengths. You know that you have many that you yourself haven't discovered. So start your own quest by looking for experiences where you must use more discipline, tact, creativity, speed, etc. You will then be better prepared and qualified to help your people to enjoy a far more productive business and personal life. They will look to you as a true leader, and their respect for you will grow more and more each day.

THREE LEVELS OF MOTIVATION

Motivation is the by-product of desire. Desire and motivation can't be separated. They are always at the same level. True motivation can't be cranked up any higher than the level of desire. To best understand how desire increases, and motivation along with it, you must learn more about the three levels of motivation.

> *Level Three: Commitment*
>
> *Level Two: Goal Identification*
>
> *Level One: Compliance*

The lowest level (Level One) is *compliance,* which is essentially doing something because you were told to do it. There isn't much motivation or personal desire involved. Character is not built at the compliance level. The next higher level (Level Two) is *identification with the goal.* Identification gives the individual a feeling of investment in the goal and produces increased desire and motivation. The highest level of motivation (Level Three) is *commitment.* There is no greater motivation than when someone feels the goal is truly their own. "Because I said so" is all the management ability needed to get somebody to Level One. Simply order the person around as if they can't think or reason for themselves and have no special ability or investment in getting the job done other than to avoid being fired. To help people reach Level Two, you must clearly and simply communicate the benefits of achieving the goal. Include them in why the job needs to be done and how it's in their best interest for all to do it well. When there is something to gain, people invest more. Many a company turnaround has started at this level.

To reach Level Three, a person needs to understand why they're uniquely suited for the task. Show that person how his or her strengths (not yours) can be used to help achieve their part of the goal. Not only will they feel that there's a personal benefit for a job well done, but more important, they'll bring a part of themselves to the job.

Nobody in your organization will be able to sustain a level of motivation higher than you have as the leader. If a person rises above the leader's level of motivation, they have to leave you and go somewhere else. Therefore, it behooves you to internalize the goals of your organization and build everyone else up to your level of commitment. I've heard it described as "organizing energies around a goal." What a responsibility! What a challenge! What a growth opportunity!

MENTAL ACTIVITIES

In order to get someone to any given level of motivation, the leader has to know and understand the mental activities associated with each of the three levels of motivation. The mental activity associated with Level One motivation, or compliance, is desperation. If the highest motivation a person has to do his or her job is the paycheck, he or she is definitely on Level One. The folks who operate at the compliance level of motivation can be called the "Another day, another dollar," crowd.

Goal identification (Level Two) is practically a leader's job description. Can you put your team members into the overall picture of success so they can see themselves there? The mental activity necessary for goal identification is reasoning. When your team members start to ask, "Why not me? Why not now?" they're on their way to true goal identification. Former President John F. Kennedy was trying to get the entire country to Level Two when he asked, "If not me, who? If not now, when?"

The mental activity that corresponds with commitment is intuition. At Level Three, your team members will be highly committed to achieving the organization's goals. At such a high level of commitment, the subconscious kicks in and begins to silently work on anticipated new problems because of new action and their solutions. When a team is functioning at Level Three, you'll find that there is less hand wringing and more action.

Techniques for Enhancing Motivation

There are several things you can do as a leader to help your people internalize the goals of the organization:

♦ Be an outstanding example as a leader. Your team members know how much you have grown as a leader, even since last week. If they charted your growth as a leader over the past year, what would your chart look like? Never forget how visible you are in a leadership position. Different folks look for different things from their leaders, but they all look to their leaders first.

♦ Give each person individual attention. A little positive feedback goes a long way. Prepare by giving some thought to each member of the team and making mental notes. Then it will only take a few moments to give him or her several personalized strokes. This could happen as the person walks past your office or as a "chance" meeting by the coffee machine. The key is to make sure that they hear you and appreciate how sincere you are.

♦ Recognize and highlight individual growth. Recognition is all the more powerful when it's public. Even if it's for someone's minor victory, it should be acknowledged and highlighted. If it's some spectacular achievement, then *hire the band.* Make a point to recognize it in team meetings, in company newsletters, on bulletin boards around the office, and even on your intranet or Internet Website. When someone is publicly recognized, they become a standard bearer for the team.

PLATE SPINNING

In the days when I was struggling to rebuild my team, I realized I didn't even have a good visual concept of what an effective leader looked like. The more I learned in my crash course, the more I began to visualize a leader as the plate spinner on television. You've seen those performers who have about 25 poles, put one plate up at a time, and spin it. When they get up to the sixth or seventh plate, they run back and touch number one through five and so on until they have all 25 or so spinning.

There are a couple of parallels between the plate spinner and the effective leader. The first is the decision to spin plates in the first place. Nobody I've ever heard of ended up on stage in Las Vegas spinning plates by accident. They decided to commit to it, no matter what. I'm also convinced that practice over time makes a person better at plate spinning, just like experience over time helps people become more effective leaders.

Then comes the selection of the plates. A manager might select the best plates possible. The smoothest, best-balanced plates with the lowest friction factor will get the manager's attention. But there are only a couple of plates with superior qualities. What about the empty poles down there? Too often, the manager settles for plates that simply look like the better ones. I call that hiring "warm meat with a pulse beat." It's not a healthy and fair practice for you or the warm meat.

When you put plates that never should have been there in the first place up on the poles, whose fault is it when they don't spin as well as you'd like? You just created more work for yourself as well because you have to spend the lion's share of your time keeping those unbalanced plates going. The time you spend with them is quality time you could be spending to develop plates that were a better choice to begin with. Too often, managers allow pride to keep them working on plates long after both the plate and the spinner should have parted company.

What spins the person's plate is communicating with his or her strengths. When you spend your time away from your strongest plates, you run the risk of losing them or, at least, losing their edge. By the same token, a plate spinner can't get all of the plates spinning and then stand back to admire the spectacle. Before long the plates or your organization, as the case might be, will come crashing down. Absentee management doesn't cut it. The leader/plate spinner must stay involved and stay in motion to be effective. I'll bet you never thought of yourself as a professional plate spinner, did you? But you are if you're an effective leader.

AN EMPLOYEE'S EYE VIEW

As I rebounded from having one foot in the grave at one point in my career to eventually becoming a first vice president with that organization, I became more focused on developing my creativity. I knew there just had to be some in there. Strangely, though, my people were not always excited about my terrific new ideas. To them, my great ideas often were nothing more than additional work and complications. I thought they would love the change of scenery, but I wasn't considering their point of view.

You might have seen the illustration of the tennis ball that's one color on one side and another color on the other. When you hold it up to show someone, you see the color that's facing you and the other person sees the other color. You can't see the other color until you place yourself where that person is or turn the tennis ball around.

Once I realized this, all the brainstorming and creating of new ideas had to include scrutiny from as many perspectives as possible. We would send staff on retreat from time to time to simply examine new ideas from as many angles as possible. We wrote all of the perspectives down and discussed them. Contrary to what many managers believe, they are not smarter than their people. If the manager is smarter than his or her people, then that manager hasn't staffed the organization very effectively.

If you're struggling with up pressure in your organization, a method for instant relief is to put your own point of view on hold for a time and genuinely examine your team's point of view. Even if you don't go along with them, feeling that their point of view has been given real consideration will ease tension.

As you examine all points of view, give your staff the credit they deserve for knowing their jobs and having the intelligence to know what works and what doesn't. All of your wonderful and creative ideas aren't worth any more than the level at which your people buy into them. As I mentioned earlier, nobody enjoys working on the lowest compliance level of motivation.

LETTING OTHERS HAVE YOUR WAY

An effective leader attempts to become as familiar as possible with how the people in the organization think. Here's the formula for getting a handle on how others process information:

1. *Input*
2. *Evaluation*
    A. *"Now" filter*
    B. *Memory movie*
    C. *Imagination*
3. *Response*

Input

The input the leader provides to the organizational thought process will influence the conclusions reached. The better the quality of the input, the more effectively you will influence the conclusions. We are bombarded with input from the time we get up in the morning until the time we go to sleep at night. Radio, television, newspapers, magazines, billboards, the Internet, and conversations with others are only a few examples of the data we're given to process each day. The challenge to the effective leader is how much and what type of input to give people individually to help them understand the merits of the leader's thinking.

Evaluation

Next, you must allow your people to evaluate. The jury must be allowed to go out and deliberate on their own. If you keep their feet to the fire, they will not feel that their conclusions are truly their own and will not invest themselves in the new ideas. Give them good input and then give them time and space to process the information by mixing it up with their own thoughts and feelings. Everyone has a "Now Filter" that will prejudice his or her perspective. A person suffering from jet lag will respond to the same input differently when he or she feels better. So the question often becomes, is now the best time to give my input? Timing is important.

Knowing your people well is valuable in avoiding common mistakes, like giving a morning person a big frog to swallow late in the afternoon. All of us have unique features, and it doesn't require a tremendous amount of scrutiny to figure them out. That's what listing strengths is all about. The "Memory Movie" follows the Now Filter. The input is run through the Now Filter to determine how, in this moment, it should be received and processed. Once it is, our minds automatically submit the input for a memory check to determine if we've ever encountered anything like this before. If the input data has been experienced before, the Memory Movie will play back the experience, complete with the favor or disfavor with which it is recalled.

As a leader, you have the ability to not only turn another person's Memory Movie on, but to direct it as well. Think about Niagara Falls. See? I just switched on your Memory Movie and took you to a precise memory at the same time. Your Now Filter must be really clean. Any input will trigger and potentially direct a person's memory banks. Sometimes this is necessary to help focus your organization.

Response

We use imagination to answer the question, "What am I going to do with the input I've received?" Will we put the input to use, ignore it, or what? If the leader delivers well-considered input, the people in his or her organization are likely to creatively put the input to use in ways that are consistent with the leader's goals for the organization.

The more effective a leader becomes over time at hitting people's buttons, or positively influencing their decisions through good input, the more cohesive and effective the entire organization will become. The ability to deliver quality input is an acquired skill that improves with experience. However, if you understand the process, you're light-years ahead of someone who blindly stumbles across the truth.

MORE ON NOW FILTERS AND MEMORY MOVIES

Influence can be negative as well as positive. I was flying with my regular crew member, Ken Butler, who unfortunately knew how I thought. He flew in the backseat and knew how to hit my buttons. I can now confess that I used to spend quite a bit of time flying my jet fighter inside the Grand Canyon. As it went, I was playing cowboy one day, darting in and out of the maze of canyons.

I leveled off just above the canyon rim and noticed a steel tower ahead and to my left at the edge of the canyon. I kept my eye on it and asked Ken if he had any idea what it was. In his coolly calculated voice, he said he didn't know but there was another one just like it on the opposite side of the canyon.

The wings nearly tore off that jet as I yanked the control stick back to my stomach to change our course from straight and level to straight up. We were pulling about a million g's, or it felt like it, when I heard hysterical laughter coming from the backseat. A quick glance to the right revealed there was no tower on the other side of the canyon as my now hysterical radar observer had reported.

Ken knew all too well how to switch on my Memory Movie and direct it. My memory check immediately recognized his input as high-power lines, and my imagination kicked in to not only create the nonexistent second tower, but to string the nonexistent cables between them and visualize the disaster as I flew straight into them.

What did I do with the input? I took evasive action, much to his delight. He exerted tremendous influence on my behavior through extremely simple, but effective, input. This guy wasn't through with me, though. On final approach to a base in New Mexico sometime later, he got me again. I tell you this story because it's fun and also to illustrate that we're always vulnerable to erroneous input.

I had never flown into this particular base before and wasn't familiar with the area, so naturally I was cockier than usual. That 79,000 horsepower goes to your head quickly. As I turned onto final approach, I noticed some people standing beside the runway. I called the tower to confirm that I was on the correct runway. The controller in the tower that day was as cocky as me. He said the people were a surveying crew, but if I needed a wider runway, he would try to find one for me.

That's all it took to get my attention. Everyone has their weaknesses and their Achilles' heels, and this tower operator had just found mine. You can do many things to a pilot that they will ignore and let roll off their thick skin, because, after all, pilots are bred to coolly handle crises. Just don't cast aspersions on a pilot's ability to land his or her aircraft. That's crossing the line. The controller in the tower knew it. My ego was now on a mission.

I felt I had no choice at that moment but to execute the most perfect landing ever witnessed by that tower operator or the surveying crew next to the runway. However, I sealed my own fate by telling the radar observer my intentions. I told him my landing was going to be so perfect that we would have to ask the tower if our tires had touched down yet.

There we were, on short final, and everything was perfect. My chest was swelling in anticipation as we approached the end of the runway at 220 miles per hour, which is about 10 miles per hour faster than the space shuttle lands. You had to fly this beast down. I used to refer to my 22-plus-ton aircraft as a supersonic manhole cover. We were moving at a good clip as we crossed the end of the runway and a smile crept across my face. The air speed was bleeding off perfectly as we settled closer to the runway. Tears of joy began to form in the corners of my eyes.

We were about 10 feet off the deck, only moments from the sweetest touchdown in history, when my radar observer made his move. "Danny," he said quickly in a voice edged with panic. "Are you sure you put the landing gear down?" Needless to say, I tore my eyes off the runway and quickly refocused them down in the cockpit on the three landing gear lights. It seemed as though those illuminated lights were smirking, as if to say, "Yes, the landing gear are safely down—but you've been had!"

I did not touch down on the end of the runway. I *struck* the end of the runway, and what followed were three separate and distinct landings. Once again, my radar observer nearly wet his pants laughing. But he wasn't through.

As I taxied off the active runway, he said, "Danny, do you want me to log all three of those landings?" He could no doubt tell I wasn't amused because he tried to console me by saying, "If nothing else, you really impressed that surveying crew with how strong the landing gear is on an F-101 Voodoo."

INPUT—EVALUATION—RESPONSE

In the two stories I just told you, I received input, I evaluated, and then I reacted; kind of a knee-jerk reaction, to be more exact. Please note that on both occasions I set myself up to be victimized by my radar observer's devious input. If I had used my Now Filter more judiciously, I would have placed myself in a better position to respond more appropriately.

The more familiar you become with your people, the better you'll understand how they filter the *now*, what's stored in their Memory Movies, and how they're likely to respond to the input you provide. The effective leader is one who is sensitive to each of his or her people on each person's level of evaluating and responding to data. A good leader also recognizes that pressure and heat often stem from inappropriate input. We can take a potentially enormous amount of heat off ourselves as leaders by paying more attention to the input we provide to those we report to and those who report to us.

CHAPTER FOUR

THE SECOND STEP: GOAL SETTING WHEN THE HEAT'S ON

*"Aim for the chopping block. If you aim for the wood,
you will have nothing. Aim past the wood, aim
through the wood; aim for the chopping block."*
Annie Dillard, Author

EYES ON THE PRIZE

A number of years ago, while my grandson Rex was still in kindergarten, the boy caught a serious case of spring fever. It hadn't been that long since he and his mother were free to come and go on their own schedule. So he probably didn't think it would be a problem to talk his mom into playing hooky with him. Southern California offers many things for a boy and his mom to do.

"Mom," he said. "It's too beautiful outside to go to school today. Let's go to the beach."

"No, honey," his mother replied. "You have to go to school today and I have to go to work."

"Then how about Disneyland?" Rex figured that he needed to suggest a more exciting place to go. "Think of how much fun we could have there," the little salesman continued.

"No, Rex," his mother sighed. "You have to go to school today."

"Why?"

"If you don't go to school, they will put me in jail."

Rex looked up at her for a moment, put his hands on his hips, cocked his head to one side, and asked, "For how long?"

That's keeping your eye on the prize! The attraction for you and the people you're leading is the promise of a future that's better than the moment. Whether acting as individuals or in concert with others, we must progress toward something. Our natural tendency in high-pressure situations is to avoid whatever is troubling us. Effective goal setting changes our focus from what we're trying to avoid to what we want to achieve. There is an enormous difference. Thoughts about what we're trying to avoid tend to be negative. Thoughts about what we want to achieve tend to be positive. Negative thoughts weaken us. Positive thoughts energize us.

Rewind the calendar a few years and picture you and I standing beside my fighter that is capable of flying nearly twice the speed of sound. You're about ready to crawl into the rear cockpit for a ride with me as your pilot-in-command.

Before climbing up the side of this sleek, needle-nosed, high-performance fighter, you might have a few questions, the first being, "Which way are we going to take off?"

My answer? "We're parked in this direction, so we might as well take off across the ramp in this direction."

"Which way will we go once we're airborne?" you might ask.

"This direction's as good as the other 359 available to us," I would respond.

"How high are we going to go?"

"Till it quits climbing."

"How far are we going to go?"

"I don't know exactly, but until we run out of fuel."

That's when you'd quit using the word we and ask what are *you* going to do when *you* run out of fuel?

"We'll worry about that when it happens. So it's time for you to crawl in, sit down, shut up, and hang on."

Would you? I don't think so! Yet many managers try to manage that way and can't figure out why they can't get a long-term commitment from their team. To build a strong, committed high- performance team, each individual must be able to describe in detail what the leader's vision is for the organization and how it will be accomplished.

THE REAL REASON YOU WORK HARD

How do we fall into the avoidance trap? Have you ever found yourself not wanting to do some aspect of your job but knowing you had to do it? I recall feeling that way when I left the world of supersonic flight and found myself knocking on doors as a civilian trying to earn a living. Fortunately for me, I had a person who took me under his wing. Everyone in the office warned me about Jim Raco. They said he was meaner than a bear with a sore toe. But he was the one with all of the trophies and the plaques. I started to suspect some professional jealousy, because his clients sure loved him.

One morning he walked by my desk and said, "Danny, let's go out and knock on some doors." I didn't tell him how much I detested knocking on doors. Instead, I did what any reasonable person can be expected to do. I lied. I told him I just had too many things to do in the office. "What things?" he demanded. I wasn't ready for that one and babbled about this and that, but not very convincingly. He cut me off by asking, "What could be more important than finding somebody out there who needs our help and is willing to pay well for it?"

I had to admit I couldn't think of a thing more important than that, at least not without a little more time to think about it. He said, "Come on, then, let's go." I agreed, but he got to the car faster than I did because, while he was walking, I was dragging my feet. I still didn't want to go out prospecting. But off we went. He sat proudly behind the wheel of his gold Cadillac Eldorado in his custom-tailored Italian silk suit, looking every inch a success. By contrast, I was slumped into a kind of a heap in the passenger seat.

As we drove I asked, "Was there ever a time when you didn't want to do this? Be honest with me 'cause I'm about ready to throw in the towel." He told me he knew how I felt. But I didn't believe he could have ever experienced the kind of doubts I had at that point. Then he proceeded to describe the physical symptoms of doubt and anxiety, including the sweat on the upper lip, the queasy stomach, the weak knees, the tongue sticking to the roof of the mouth, and so forth. The shocker came when he told me he had felt that same way only 20 minutes earlier.

I immediately suggested we both go back to the womblike safety of the office, reasoning that we had nothing to offer anyone given our pathetic emotional dispositions. He replied, "Danny, that was 20 minutes ago. I don't feel that way now." Naturally, I asked him how he managed to climb out of his fear. "If I were to give you $1000 right now," he asked, "what would you do with it?" I told him that I would pay bills with the money. "Wrong!" he thundered. I knew right away my answer wasn't what he was looking for. Being the quick study I am, I took another quick stab in the opposite direction. "I would have fun with it," I offered. Now we were connecting.

"What would you do?" he asked.

"Oh, I don't know," I stuttered.

"What would you do?" he demanded. Clearly, I was losing the train of his thinking again. It occurred to me he wanted me to be specific about what I would do with the $1000 to have fun. "I'd like to take Tedi to the National Air Races in Reno in September" I said.

As we drove, he prodded me to explain in detail how much I wanted to attend. The more vividly I pictured my anticipated experience, the more excited and interested I became. I described the different classes of airplanes and what they sounded like as they roared by. I described the hotel I wanted to stay in because of the balconies from which you can watch the sunsets over those rugged Nevada mountains and the lights of the city at night.

He pressed me to describe in detail my favorite restaurant and the terrific steak dinner I remembered getting there, right down to the freshly baked loaves of bread. He said, "Wow! What an incredible trip that would be!"

Then he asked me to figure out what my commission would be if I could get a listing that day and sell a house. In those days my share of the commission would have been just about $1000. At that moment, the difference between this man, who was the picture of success, and I became clear. I had a blinding flash of the obvious. I just didn't know what to call it at the time. My mentor knew what he was working for, while I was just wandering out that day to see if I would be lucky.

NOW SPREAD THE WORD

Then he asked why I was so anxious to stay at the office that day and forfeit the $1000 and my trip to Reno. He told me to think of what I would say to Tedi that night if I were to go home and say I'd stayed in the office rather than earning a trip to Reno for the two of us. I said, "Could you drive faster?"

When we finally stopped, I hit the ground running. I knew where Tedi and I were going to be in September! An hour and a half later we were back at his car. I had a big smile on my face. As a result of the prospecting we'd just done, within the next two months we made three large sales. But I'm getting ahead of the story.

As I closed my door I looked over at him as he slid under the steering wheel of that luxurious car. I expected to see a smile on his face as well, but he had a very stern expression. He said, "I'm going to tell you something that I don't ever want you to forget."

I was a willing pupil by that time, and I said, "Whatever you say, I'm going to write it down."

After a very long pause, he said, "Don't ever work hard to pay bills. Work hard to have fun with the money—otherwise you won't have enough to do either. Pay bills *or* have fun."

It was a life-changing moment. "My gosh, Jim," I said. "I've been working hard to pay bills!"

"Then change your focus," he said as we pulled away from the curb.

A few months later, in September, after an exciting day of watching airplanes race 40 feet off the ground, Tedi and I stood on the balcony of our hotel room. We toasted our friend Jim Raco and made a commitment to *never* again work hard just to pay bills. And we haven't. That thought of never working hard to pay bills but to have fun with the money was worth a few sleepless nights for me. Jim Raco had opened my eyes. As leaders, it's important to understand the value of helping our people open their eyes. What they can't envision (just as I wasn't envisioning having fun with my money) can't help further the company's goals ... or their own.

Since my enlightenment, I've taught many, many people to have fun with their money, if they wanted to have enough money to comfortably pay their bills. That lesson made their lives better and made them more enthusiastic contributors to the company's vision. Once they have seen a personalized vision through their own eyes, they won't lose sight of it as easily, even when their eyes are closed. When people get in the habit of working on personal goals, they will automatically work on company goals.

The vision we invite our people to share with us is the *future* as it best suits the organization and the people who make up the organization. Helping your people experience the future through their own eyes is critical to effective leadership. Do you know what you're working for? Can you see it in great detail? If you can't, how can you help your people to see what they're working for? Helping your people truly see what they're working for is one of the greatest, lifelong gifts you can ever give them.

Mad magazine's Alfred E. Newman, said, "Most folks don't know what they want, but they're pretty sure they don't have it." Leading your team blindly without clear goals renders all of your sophisticated navigation equipment useless. Being driven by a sense of dissatisfaction with the present is not enough if there is no clear course established. This is to say that a clearly charted course is the second best thing to a distinct goal. At least with a clearly charted course, you and your organization know in which direction you want to go. You are intending toward something, even if the something is not well defined.

GO BOLDLY WHERE YOU'VE NEVER GONE BEFORE

There have been a few times when I've thought, "I don't know where I'm going, but I'm making good time." When I realized I could cover a lot of ground and make good time while going in circles, my appreciation for goal setting increased. The tragedy in repeating yesterdays is that we never make any progress. We might crack the whip and increase the speed with which the organization moves around in circles.

We can attack the innocent by replacing the entire staff, only to set the new staff out on the same old track. We can try this and try that, stopping every once in a while to scratch our heads and wonder why nothing's working. Unfortunately, if we don't understand the obligation to be merchants of hope, we will scratch our heads bald before we figure out why, every time we set out for tomorrow, we end up at yesterday.

Every time we reach the crossroads, we can develop a bad habit of repeatedly making the same wrong turn. As I touched on earlier, we know yesterday is safer and less threatening than even today. So, without admitting it consciously, we can fall victim to avoiding mistakes rather than breaking new ground. This is why it's a natural tendency for people to repeat unproductive and uncomfortable behaviors. Rather than trailblazing toward something unknown but promising, we feel safer repeating the familiar. The familiar might not be pleasant, but we know we can deal with it because we've developed the habit of dealing with it every day. When you see someone going boldly where they've never gone before, you're watching someone courageous.

Don't let your personal goals and/or your team's goals live in someday. Before defining specific methods and techniques for effective goal setting, it's important to establish that goals must be achievable. Does that mean pick only easy goals? By no means. It simply means that a major goal can be intimidating until it's broken down on an individual-by-individual and day-by-day basis. The entire organization must see the goals the leader helps to establish as attainable, especially when broken down by an individual daily commitment. Talking about goals without achieving anything reduces a leader's credibility and the organization's enthusiasm.

A QUICK QUESTION-AND-ANSWER SESSION

I have a friend who graduated from not one but two reform schools as a youth. You could say he was twice as reformed as the next guy. His life is straightened out now. He made two multi-million-dollar fortunes in two separate fields. He says he had a personal challenge to succeed in a second field because he didn't want people to say the first one was just luck. When I asked him how he did it, he replied that he (1) asked himself some questions and (2) listened to the answers. We can ask ourselves questions all day long, but do we really listen to our answers? Listening is the key. He asked himself these questions:

1.   What do I really want?
2.   What will it cost me in time, money, and energy?
3.   Am I willing to pay that price?
4.   When should I start paying the price?

Question four is where the rubber meets the road. Answering the others is easy. If the time to start paying the price is someday, then the first three questions have little meaning. Someday never comes, and dues to be paid someday never get paid. Scheduling your start date on someday ensures you'll never get started. The time to start is every time you stand at the crossroads. The way to start is to take the road to tomorrow and not the one to yesterday. Take the road that demands the most of you. The only acceptable answer to question number four is now.

OKAY, SO LET'S DEAL WITH *WHY NOT?*

Many people say to me, "I'd like to achieve great things, Danny. But, I've got problems." I'll buy that. So, let's look at these problems and see how they fit into the goal-setting picture. Goals should not be just new things somewhere in the future, but also a commitment to solve past problems that are still experienced daily. Many people tell me they have goals, but they aren't closing the gap. I suggest that perhaps it's because they have one foot nailed to the floor, and that makes them spend each day walking around in a circle. It sounds like repeating yesterday, doesn't it? When I ask what has their foot nailed to the floor, they point to the problems they experience daily.

Pull the Nail Out of Your Foot

That experience tells me our first set of goals should be the solution of present problems that continue to hold us back. Otherwise, the future is nothing more than your, often repeated, past. It's time to extract the nail that has become the pivot point of your everyday life.

Planning in order to simply avoid disappointment causes goals to be set too low. If a plan doesn't fail from time to time, you're probably playing it too safe and need to aim higher. A buddy I used to fly with once banged up an airplane pretty good. He was okay, so we kidded him about the incident. His response has stuck with me ever since. He said, "If you don't bang one up every now and then, you're not flying fast enough."

Often, when I'm asked to do a series of speaking programs across the country for a particular company, the first meeting is at the corporate headquarters. It's generally held in a plush boardroom with only the upper executives in attendance. If I had to put a title on this meeting, which I don't, it would be, "How to Identify the Nail(s) in Your Corporate Foot." In other words, what's keeping your company from beating the competition?

The first thing I ask is if they have weekly problem-solving meetings at the corporate level. The answer is always something such as, "By all means! Once a week. They generally last all day." When I ask if notes were taken and a copy printed for all attendees, the answer is always affirmative. It's time for the setup. "Since I'm going to be working in depth with your company," I explain. "Would it be possible for me to see last week's problem-solving meeting notes?" In chorus the answer is yes. Someone is designated to retrieve last week's notes. Before that person gets out of the room, I say, "While you're at it, bring some meeting notes from six months ago, a year ago, and 18 months ago. Then we can spread them out across this conference table and see how your problems have evolved over the last year and a half."

This request is generally greeted by a firm voice saying, "You don't need to see the others, but we will bring you last week's meeting notes." They don't want me to see the notes from the past meetings because they're all the same!

Now, for a moment of truth: How long have you been working on the same set of problems? The answer I too often receive is, "A long time." My quick response is, "Then you must have found a cozy, comfortable set of problems." Perhaps this person has become comfortable with that nail in his or her foot.

A Problem by Any Other Name

We must all continually ask ourselves if we've been working on your set of problems too long. Since this isn't a question we're used to asking or answering, it will be helpful to first examine what the term *problem* really means. The dictionary states that a problem is a perplexing question or situation, especially when a solution is not clear. That definition is very broad and will apply to most problems as we understand them. So let's move on to a self-inventory that will help each of us identify what we individually consider to be problems.

1.   What is my biggest unresolved problem? In business? In my personal life?
2.   What am I doing about it?
3.   If I'm not doing anything about it, why am I not doing anything about it?

Who's Working on Problem Number One?

I often do programs for companies that don't have an answer for the third question. If I ask what the company's biggest unresolved problem is, I'm often told that massive turnover in the sales force is considered the most threatening. I quickly ask who has been assigned to work on that problem, and I'm told just as often that nobody has been assigned to work on the company's number one problem. The company can identify what its primary problem is, yet it has taken no action to specifically address it.

This scenario is extremely common. Sometimes the company will throw someone at the problem until that person is reassigned or quits. But as a rule, the problem is *not* being addressed, even though it has been identified. Upon closer examination, I usually discover the company's efforts are being used to address problem number 13 or so. Problems number one through 12, it seems, are considered just too difficult to approach. In most cases, the problems the company spends most of its time addressing are the least threatening.

I'd swear some people get their Ph.D.'s in worrying and stewing: They're really good at it. When I say, "What would you do if I could snap my fingers and resolve those problems?" the worriers get a panicked expression on their faces. Without unresolved problems, what would they do? The company wouldn't need them anymore if there weren't any problems to worry about and stew over. Many people truly believe that unresolved problems represent job security.

A friend of mine asked me those questions while I was still flying fighters. He was at my house, eating my food, and still had the audacity to challenge me by asking what I thought our squadron's biggest unresolved problem was. Question one wasn't all that threatening, so I told him that sonic booms and all the uproar they caused in the community were at the top of our list. There seemed to be no limit to the volume (in either sense of the word) of complaints caused by sonic booms.

Then my friend nailed me. "What are you doing about it?" he asked.

I couldn't come up with a good answer because, at the time, the Air Force wasn't coming up with a good answer. I finally said what I hear so many executives saying today: "We're just trying to figure out how to live with the problem." After a blinding flash of the obvious, I took it upon myself to become the sonic boom salesman I told you about in Chapter 1. I created that job and then filled the vacancy. There wasn't a line of people waiting to apply for a job selling a concept with as high an objection factor as sonic booms. I was the only applicant.

Intending to play on the locals' sense of patriotism and national defense, I entitled my 30-minute presentation "Better Boomed Than Bombed." I spoke to Rotary Clubs, Lions' Clubs, Elks' Clubs, churches, schools, and anyone who would have me. The first half of my presentation was always pretty well received. Before long it occurred to me why my audiences began getting restless at about the halfway point. It was about then that they figured out I was not only the salesman for sonic booms, but also a major distributor. They got that unmistakable look that said, "He's the one." It took every ounce of convincing I could muster to wave the flag, play the Star Spangled Banner, and close with the Battle Hymn of the Republic before they could tar and feather me. Well, almost every ounce.

Believe it or not, I felt tremendous gratification experiencing the effort of doing something about a problem I had a hand in creating. It's safe to say that most of us know the emptiness of leaving things unresolved. However, anyone who has had the experience of swallowing the biggest, ugliest frogs knows how liberating it feels to be part of the solution.

Learn to Distrust Effortless Solutions

There are none. Solving problems requires effort and investment. I think of effort as simply gritting your teeth and going for it. Working hard at something you love doesn't mean forgetting to work intelligently. I'm not suggesting you attack problems like a bull in a china shop. You should always bring the best of your experience and abilities to bear on resolving troubling issues. However, the most important component to your solution is *when* to make the effort. The answer to that is *now.* Another self-inventory helps to bring us to now:

1. Is your year planned out? Have you specified your professional and personal growth goals? Are your vacation times blocked out?

2. If not, why not?

3. When are you going to start?

I don't know about you, but without asking myself tough questions and insisting on honest answers, I'm likely to find that the prime of my life has passed me by. That's what answering question number three with someday will do for you. Today is when we need to make the investment that will get us where we want to go. Now is not a moment too soon to start. Learn to ask yourself, "What am I going to do about this tomorrow morning?"

As leaders in hot situations, a little historical research will usually confirm that we're in hot water due to neglected problems and unresolved issues. A look back through our daily planners will reveal how much time we scheduled to attend to tasks directly related to goal setting and fulfillment. While we wait for problems to go away on their own or for an easy solution to miraculously appear out of nowhere, a river of opportunities is flowing past us. There will be no special day when fireworks go off and sirens sound to announce it's time to safely set out toward your desired goals in life. Trust me, that day never comes. You might as well get down to business now or grow old waiting on life's sidelines. It's time to bite the bullet.

GOALS: THERE'S NO ESCAPE FROM NEGLECT

Deciding not to have a specific goal *is* a specific goal. In the random selection of the universe, the odds are extremely remote that you'll stumble across the opportunities and conditions under which your dreams will be fulfilled. As George Bernard Shaw said, "People are always blaming their circumstances for what they are. I don't believe in circumstances. The people who get on in this world are the people who get up and look for the circumstances they want, and, if they can't find them, make them."

There are no magic mornings when it all comes together, and no fairy god-mothers to wave their wands and make it all come true. Failing to set goals is equal to believing in the mythical phenomena I just described. This all might sound to you like motivational hype, but I know of no line of reasoning that has more practical value. If you don't like to be accused of believing in fairy tales, then give me a logical argument for why your goals have been neglected.

CONCENTRATE ON EFFECTIVE GOAL SETTING

Dr. Alexis Carrel, Nobel Prize winner, once said, "Life leaps like a geyser for those who drill through the rock of inertia." Goals are the drill bits that cut through the rock of inertia. The more exciting the goals, the faster they pene-trate. If goals are the drill bits, then self-discipline is the drive shaft. Dr. Carrel went on to say that "self-discipline is always rewarded by a strength that brings an inexpressible joy. Therefore, goals that motivate us have gifts for us in the form of accomplishment." Your goals should be big enough to turn you on.

If a look back through your daily planner doesn't reveal much conscious effort toward setting and achieving goals, then how about a look ahead? Do the future entries in your daily planner reflect a more concerted effort to devise and execute an effective plan for the balance of the year? Anyone who answers no to those questions is practicing what I call an "on the ropes" style of management. The manager's daily plan is to go into the office and see what happens.

These managers allow all sorts of fires to break out and then expend all of their energy chasing them and putting them out. Because they feel so over-whelmed with continual crisis, they're likely to tell you they simply don't have the time to spend on planning and goal setting. Instead of being on the attack, they're on the ropes. Instead of being on their toes, they're on their heels. Instead of operating from a position of balance, they're continually off balance.

Remember your modeling relationship with the people in your organization. If the leader is operating off balance, on his or her heels and on the ropes, how can the rest of the organization be expected to operate any differently? The goal: Adopt behaviors to infect your entire organization. I stated earlier that your organization is going to get whatever you have, good or bad, and that idea is certainly no less true for goal setting.

ACCEPT THE RISK AND FACE UP TO IT

There's an undeniable risk in goal setting. However, the risks are far, far greater if you *don't* set goals. By not setting goals, you're truly leaving the future of your personal and professional affairs completely to chance. Going into the office each day to "see what happens" is a greater risk than going in and attempting to carry out a well-thought-out plan, no matter how ambitious.

It's impossible to grow and realize new potentials if nobody pushes the envelope. Pushing the envelope is what risk taking is all about. Behind every major breakthrough is a series of perfect failures. It wouldn't hurt any planning session to routinely ask the question, "Are we pushing the envelope on this?" It's even better still to ask, "Am I pushing my envelope?" I recommend that you put that question on your wall. If you find that you're never answering yes to it, you shouldn't be surprised if your organization doesn't seem to be growing or going anywhere.

THREE STEPS TO A NEW REALITY

A new reality is an achieved goal. We are headed into the future at the same rate the second hand sweeps around the clock, whether we like it or not. We can't hold back time. So, given that the future is coming, how are we endeavoring to shape it? What are we doing *now* that will leave our mark on our future? Here are my three steps to shaping a new reality:

Step One: Visualize Your Goal Vividly

You must clearly see what you are intending toward. Generalizations about your intended goals do you no good. The greater the clarity of your vision, the more focused and efficient your efforts toward it will be. The more diffused your vision, the less efficient your efforts will be. I don't know of anyone who wants to waste effort.

Step Two: Break Your Goal Down into Daily Tasks

When goals loom enormous on the horizon, it's natural to feel intimidated and to become reluctant to even approach them. Be realistic about what a human being can accomplish in a day, and don't expect any more of yourself or others. Realizing goals is far less dramatic that way, but you will eventually get there.

Step Three: Act on Your Goals Every Day

I'm not suggesting that you work seven days per week, but don't let a workday go by without even a small step that moves you closer to your goal. Progress is progress, no matter how small, and the feeling of accomplishment is just as sweet in many small doses as it is in one large one. However, breaking the task down into smaller disappointments will not minimize the feeling of disappointment at never achieving the big goal. If you don't know what to do on a daily basis to achieve your goal, then it's not a goal—it's a fantasy.

GUIDELINES FOR GOAL SETTING

Goals should be:

1. Measurable
2. Realistic
3. Challenging

Time allotments for goal planning should be as follows:

1. Short-term goals range from the immediate to one year
2. Mid-term goals range from one to five years
3. Long-term goals are more than five years

The goal-planning process can be described like so:

1. Make a written list of your goals and divide them into the appropriate short-, mid-, or long-term categories.

2. Establish a timetable for each item. If the steps seem unreasonably large, break them down further. Don't fall prey to the myth that a goal that's not achieved by an exact deadline is no longer worth achieving.

3. Concentrate on results.

4. Begin and don't stop.

5. Celebrate when a goal is achieved, and simultaneously replace it with a new goal. If you don't select a new goal, you and your people are likely to experience a letdown. Something must always be out there to be anticipated if we're to keep the spring in our step.

6. Evaluate your progress. When? For personal goals, evaluate each year on your birthday. It takes courage to write yourself a letter outlining all of your goals for the next year and to seal it up to be read one year later.

State of the Office

The state of the office meeting is a special, annual session during which you describe the growth over the past year. Then you present your team with a challenge to do better in the year ahead. This meeting needs to make a positive impression, just like the Brag Book I described in Chapter 3. You might want to serve refreshments above and beyond what you serve at a regular weekly meetings. You might want to have music playing as people are gathering. Set the meetings in a more unique location than your regular sessions.

Break It Down

The goal you set out for the year ahead might seem overwhelming to your team members if they think of it as a prohibitively large figure. So be prepared to break down the goal into smaller, less threatening segments. Daily bite-sized portions of the overall goal always seem more doable. Break it all the way down to the incremental improvement each team member will have to accomplish on a daily, weekly, and monthly basis.

Cap off the meeting by putting your credibility on the line. Acknowledge that you are fully aware of what you're asking of them, and then promise that they can expect to see as much or more improvement on your part, as their leader. Lay out the tasks that you feel most support your team's efforts, and commit to presenting a monthly progress report on how well you're accomplishing the promised improvements. This leaves the door open for you to speak to any one of them about their progress.

Sell Them Their Own Chair

Commissioned salespeople have clear and measurable goals. Even if your team members perform less easily measured tasks, you need to establish the clearest goals possible in order to coach improvement. In the case of salespersons who wanted to earn $80,000 per year, I began the goal achievement sessions by asking each person present what $20,000 would buy in the present market. My only requirement, besides giving a realistic answer, was that the purchase be a fun thing, like a car or boat. Not paying bills. I wrote down the answers they gave me on the board.

Then I asked, "What if I told you that some of you may already be paying that for your chairs?" At that point I rolled out an office chair with a sign on it that read, chair for sale by owner $20,880. I explained that an $80,000 annual income breaks down to $6,660 per month. That's $290 per day and $29 per hour. Wasting three hours per day costs $87. That's the daily payment on the chair. The weekly payment would be $435, the monthly payment $1740, and the annual payment $20,880.

Next, I discussed how easy it is to waste three hours. Coming in late gets you off to a bad start. Spending too much time on the telephone with a person or persons who want to be chatty takes more time. It's easy to spend too much time on the Internet. Taking a two-hour lunch and not using good time-management practices throughout the day also adds to the time leak. Overall, it's not hard to waste three hours per day. By the time I finished explaining about wasted time, I had their attention.

Figure 4-1. The other side of the *For Sale* sign.

I turned the for sale sign on the chair over and revealed the other side (see Figure 4-1). This illustration never failed to get the point across that time is valuable and wasting it could have personal consequences as well as consequences for the team as a whole. My salespeople had some fun with this. If someone came in and asked, "Where's Bob?" somebody was always quick to say, "He's sitting over here making a payment on his chair."

SOME COMMON ROADBLOCKS TO GOAL ACHIEVEMENT

The following roadblocks might be impeding your progress without you being fully aware of their presence. An effective leader is vigilant and monitors the organization for signs of frustration and loss of interest among the staff. When roadblocks are detected, there are several remedies available.

Goals are not understood or seem unattainable. If this is the case, look to your own presentation of the goals to the team members. Did you take the time to think through, from their point of view, their possible reaction to these new goals? Did you break the goals down into doable segments for each person? How clear was your communication in the presentation itself?

The effort doesn't appear to have adequate rewards. When rewards don't seem forthcoming or consistent with the level of effort required, it's time for the leader to start selling. Actually, the time for selling is when the goals are being established. If the team members feel the prize doesn't match the effort required, the leader must evaluate the equity of the situation and then either correct the imbalance or, if the effort and reward are in balance, frame the goals in such a way that the reward becomes clearer, thus increasing motivational influence.

Procedures for goal achievement are too rigid. Flexibility is one sign of a confident and creative leader. Too many people impose rigid structure on their organizations because they lack basic confidence in their own abilities and the abilities of their team. Focusing on results instead of methods will open the door for your people to contribute more of their own originality. Have the courage to let them run with the project, and apply gentle guidance at most. Good people will develop good methods.

Success is feared. Many people are much more familiar with mediocrity than they are with success, and therefore lack the drive to pursue goals. Fear of success is natural if you have little experience with it. Remember my salesperson who was afraid to earn more money than his father? To contradict the frightening aspects of actually doing what your organization sets out to do, you can broaden the sense of accomplishment to include the whole team, and thereby reduce the uncomfortable spotlight on those who have a problem with attention.

YOU NEVER GO WRONG WITH PERSONAL GROWTH

You can continually encourage your people through promoting personal growth. Helping people to push their personal envelopes will prepare them to not only enjoy success, but to expect it more often. Good coaching of the team will prepare them to enjoy winning. When some of the members of your team grow and expand their horizons, the others will notice and, hopefully, internalize that desire. A team that internalizes the expectation and enjoyment of success will become synergistically greater than the sum of its parts.

I know of a company that adopted these principles for goal setting and put them into practice. The result was an unprecedented increase in productivity. More important, the increases were not short-lived. The application of these principles established lasting improvements. These principles also have broad implications and applications far beyond the world of business. Parenting and teaching are two of the obvious applications that come to mind.

The leaders in this organization made a commitment to become involved with the personal growth of their people, as we've already discussed. The leaders engaged in personal and consistent counseling. Without consistency or personal interest, the counseling efforts would have been meaningless. Many managers, parents, and teachers tend to get uncomfortable at the thought of personal counseling. They prefer to keep an arm's-length relationship and focus on bigger goals and accomplishments, or perhaps problems and other issues that shift the focus away from personal growth.

One reason these people—and you might be one of them—experience such discomfort is that taking a personal interest in the personal growth of another requires an investment in one's own personal growth. Remember that the other person isn't going to get any better until you do. Facing one's own personal roadblocks can be downright terrifying. I know. I used to avoid personal growth issues at all costs, both my own and for others. But you can't become an effective leader without an investment in the welfare of your people. It simply can't be done. That's why courage is on the list of leadership characteristics in Chapter 2.

You should now have a clear image of a leader who is secure enough in their own personal growth to extend himself or herself to others in order to help develop theirs. I'm not suggesting that you remove the boundaries that separate a leader from others in the organization. Your roles are different. However, the principles that guide your conduct are not. There is no room for double standards in effective leadership. Likewise, becoming inappropriately close to your people on a personal level, to the point where you have a dual relationship, is not fair to you, not fair to the individual involved, and not fair to others in the organization.

We dispelled the notion early on that people work primarily for money. This is where that knowledge is extremely helpful. If a leader doesn't demonstrate care and concern for the personal growth of his or her people, it's unreasonable to expect the individual to truly care about the best interests of the organization. You would be amazed at how many managers I encounter believe that people work only to collect a paycheck. Nobody who thinks that way is getting as much out of their staff as they can. That kind of thinking leaves unrealized potential buried deep.

The sample company I'm referring to began with a very simple goal: They wanted to make each month more productive than the month before. They approached the goal on an individual basis. The individual goals were measurable, realistic, and challenging. Here are some of the specific techniques they used to build up their people:

- Individual counseling sessions were held monthly between the manager and each member of the team.

- Each individual's production was never compared to anyone else's production. The only issue was how much that individual had improved since the previous month.

- When individuals had their best month of the year, they received a letter from the vice president. If every month was better than the previous one, those people accumulated a pile of letters.

- When an individual had the best month of his or her career with the company, he or she received a letter from the president.

I can already hear some executives saying, "I have more important things to do than write letters to my people just because they earned more money for the company this month than last." To these executives, I say there isn't any more important or productive use of your time than to help your people grow and develop. There is no more effective way to ensure the growth and prosperity of your company. That's what leadership's all about.

Refusing to get involved with people on that level makes me suspect an executive isn't in touch with his or her personal growth issues. The organization will get better as soon as the leader does. People love to break their own records, and that applies to leaders as well. When a significant number of your people start to break their own individual records, you'll feel team energy starting to build.

TAKE THE TIME FOR A PERSONAL MOMENT OF TRUTH

If you want to test yourself and determine how strongly you're committed to personal growth and goal achievement, answer these questions as truthfully as you can:

1. What were my major goals in the past 12 months, both personally and professionally?

2. What were my major personal and professional achievements in the past 12 months?

3. Did my achievements match my short-term objectives and/or move me closer to my mid- and long-term objectives?

4. In what ways do I need to improve in each of those areas?

5. What do I need to do to improve?

6. What changes would I like to see in my personal and/or professional life?

7. What can I do to make these changes occur?

8. Which personal and professional strengths do I feel I'm not using?

9. What is my plan for growing as a leader over the short-, mid-, and long-term?

10. What's my next step up, and whom will I choose as my replacement?

11. How do my peers feel about my reaching my goals? Are they correct in feeling that way?

12. What do I need to do tomorrow morning to start making great things happen?

If these questions are answered truthfully—and you truly listen to your own answers—you can't help but be propelled toward improved goal setting and increased efficiency in fulfilling them. With that much truthful information about your personal and professional affairs, it would require a conscious effort to ignore the obvious and stay on your treadmill. The greater your ability to get in touch with your honest needs and desires, the more effectively you will be able to set and achieve meaningful and worthwhile goals.

GOALS AND VISION

By definition, a goal is an objective. A football player's objective is to carry the funny-shaped ball across the goal line. A basketball player's main objective is to put the round ball through the hoop. A hockey or soccer player's objective is to put the puck or ball into the net. In other words, put it in the goal. A sales professional's objective is to make the sale. Objectives can be very simple and specific. Some goals are harder to achieve than others, but they are still easy to understand.

A vision is a way of seeing something in the future. If an athlete wants to win the big trophy at the end of the season, then he or she must score many goals along the way. Many people can score goals, but only one scores enough to win the top prize. If you want your department or company to be number one, you must develop a vision. The vision is what it will look like and feel like to be number one. Making your vision a reality will require the successful attainment of many goals.

As you can see in Figure 4-2, you and your organization are standing at a place called the now. Your vision is somewhere off in the future. If you set goals for yourself and your team members without aligning them to your overall vision, the goals might radiate outward like spokes on a wheel. Your goals need to be aligned in such a way that each one moves you closer to the vision you have chosen.

In order to make the vision real and attainable, you need to put a time frame to it. Not many successful leaders say, "We're going to be number one someday. I can't say when, but someday." That someday might as well be never. As the leader, it is up to you to focus your team members' time and energies toward the ultimate vision. You start by breaking down the vision into the series and/or sequence of goals necessary for attainment.

To create your own vision chart, as in Figure 4-3, you need to determine:

1. Which goals will move you closer to your vision?

2. Who will be responsible for executing those goals?

3. When are the completion dates for each goal and reaching the vision?

4. What resources will your team members need?

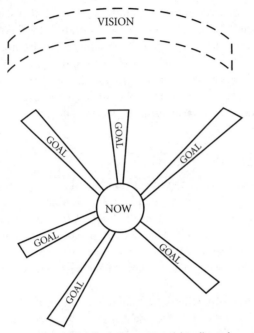

Figure 4-2. Goals that are not vision-directed.

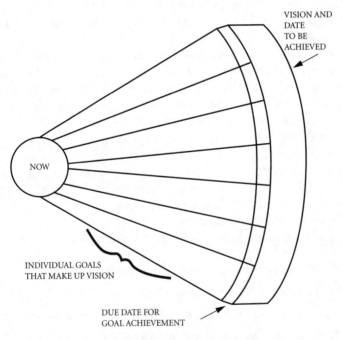

Figure 4-3. Goals and vision alignment.

INVOLVED AND ENTHUSIASTIC

As always, the more you involve your team members in forming the vision, the more passionate they will be in seeing it through. The greater the pride, the greater the passion. In order to know when the goals have been reached, you must set up completion criteria when you launch the project. When team members are involved in setting up milestones, they won't feel as if the benchmarks have been imposed on them. And don't forget to plan a celebration for when the vision is realized. People enjoy the anticipation as they work.

My final thought for you on goal setting:

If you don't have a goal, make finding one your first goal.

CHAPTER FIVE

THE THIRD STEP: TIME PLANNING FOR HIGHER PRODUCTIVITY

"You can transform something important into something urgent, if you wait long enough."
Danny Cox

PUTTING TIME INTO PERSPECTIVE: WORDS FROM THE FUNNY, THE FICTIONAL, AND THE PHILOSOPHICAL

Robert Benchley was more than a great humorist. He was also bullish on human determination when he said, "Anyone can do any amount of work … provided it isn't what he's supposed to be doing at the time." There is an important piece of truth in that for each of us, as individuals seeking personal and professional excellence, and as managers of others.

Want more wisdom? Henry David Thoreau said, "It's not enough to be industrious, so are the ants. What are you industrious about?"

I think Andy Capp, the great British couch-based philosopher and cartoon character, said it best: "The trouble with time is that it disappears while you're trying to figure out what to do with it."

105

Today Is Here

Today is here; I will start with a smile and resolve to be agreeable. I will not criticize. I REFUSE TO WASTE MY VALUABLE TIME.

My time is equal to all others'. Everyone draws the same salary in seconds, minutes, and hours.

Today I will not waste time because the minutes I wasted yesterday are as lost as a forgotten thought.

Today I refuse to spend my time worrying about what might happen. My time will be spent making things happen.

Today I am determined to improve myself so that tomorrow's opportunity will not find me lacking.

Today I begin by doing and not wasting time. One week from now I will be more than the person I am today.

Today I will not imagine what I would do if things were different. Things are what they are. I will succeed with what I have.

Today I will not say, *"If I could only find the time."* There is no hidden time. I must take what's available.

Today I will treat others as if this were my last day on earth. I won't wait to be what I have dreamt about being tomorrow, for tomorrow never comes.

Author Unknown

Figure 5-1.

Want some prose to frame on your wall and help you live and work more effectively? Figure 5-1 is one of my favorites.

Another helpful insight from an anonymous source helps me to keep time in perspective: If you had a bank that credited your account each morning with $86,400 and carried over no balance from day to day, allowing you to keep no cash in your account, canceling all unused funds at the end of each day, what would you do?

You have such a bank. It is called time. Every morning, each person's account is credited with 86,400 seconds. Every night, each second not put toward a good purpose is canceled. Time carries no balance forward. Nor does time allow us to borrow against future allocations. We can only live on today's deposit and invest our time toward the utmost health, happiness, and success.

How many sports teams that were defeated by a shot at the buzzer or a field goal with no time remaining wish there was one more period to play? "If wishes were horses, beggars would ride." The good news is we can all essentially gain that extra period by starting to play more effectively from the beginning. Time management is more about good starts than miracle finishes. Figure 5-2 lists some of my own thoughts on the birthplace of a brighter future.

Birthplace of a Brighter Future

As I concentrate on each word of this thought, *now* slips by me into the past. My past is nothing more than a history of how well I dealt with each irretrievable *now*. So if yesterday is history and tomorrow is prediction, only the present exists.

The future is nothing more than an approaching series of *nows*. During each of those *nows* I will make a decision whether or not future *nows* will be different. A brighter future grows out of a brighter *now*. Therefore, my future improves only as I make better use of the current moment.

It's the time remaining that counts. My willingness to accept responsibility for improving my time will determine the quality of the rest of my life.

The speed at which *now* becomes the past is staggering. Yet, if I commit my God-given strengths to improving each of these approaching *nows*, the faith in my bright new future will be exhilarating! For I realize the same velocity that carries this *now* into the past can carry me at the same rate toward exciting moments of the future whenever increasing goals become reality.

A year yet to be is unborn, untarnished, and full of promise. One of those brand-new years, bright with potential, accomplishment, and joy will be delivered to me tomorrow at dawn. My choice is to accept it as it is given or, through habit, mold it into the shape of years past.

The challenge is clear. The choice is mine

Danny Cox

Figure 5-2.

The following thought was found in the pages of *Boardroom Reports*:

All you can do with time is spend it or waste it. Find the best ways to spend available time and the appropriate amount of time for each task. Concentrate on the best ways to spend time, instead of worrying about saving it.

The skilled time manager I'm describing accomplishes 95 percent of his or her work in less than the allotted time. She or he accomplishes a great deal and knows it. She feels comfortable with an efficient, steady pace. These people have quality time for family and friends, as well as themselves, while finishing more quality work than others, who work longer hours at a more frantic pace.

Time and productivity are inseparable issues. We have all memorized the maxim, "There is never enough time to do it right the first time, but there always seems to be enough time to do it over again." The truth in that statement hits me in the wheelhouse. How about you? Speed might not always kill (as the popular saying goes), but it usually will cost you plenty in the long run.

Doing it right the first time requires time planning, or darn good luck. If you're like me, good luck is a rare commodity—certainly not common enough to stake a career on. It has also been said that making your own luck is simply a matter of doing the necessary things in order to be ready and available when opportunity appears.

WHY PEOPLE DON'T PLAN THEIR TIME

I'm going to list some of the most commonly given excuses for not planning time, so we'll all feel at home. More important, the meaning behind the excuses helps us understand how we often get ourselves all tangled up.

- The excuse, "It takes too long," really means, "I would rather focus on a day-by-day or short-term basis and just see what happens."

- The excuse, "I don't have enough information to plan well," really means, "I don't have enough faith in the information I've gathered so far, so I'd better wait."

- The excuse, "It's impossible to predict the future," really means, "I would have to give up acting on impulse and develop new disciplines."

FOUR OF THE BIGGEST TIME WASTERS YOU'LL ENCOUNTER

In a recent survey of business managers, people named their own lack of time management for 92 percent of the failures among those under their supervision. This raises the ominous question, "How do managers waste so much time?" Several primary reasons top the list:

- The most common contributor to wasted management time is doing an employee's job for him or her. This occurs much more frequently than we might think and can easily cost managers one-third or more of their efficiency.

- Another cause of lost productivity in management is doing tasks that can be handled by someone with less responsibility. As one great entrepreneur said, "I may be able to do it better, but I can't do it all."

- It's common to find a manager spending a disproportionate amount of time on a favorite or pet project at the expense of items that are more valuable to the organization as a whole. Keep in mind the difference between interesting and important.

- Repeating instructions is another time killer. The lesson employees learn from this misguided practice is that they don't have to take action until the boss instructs them for the third time. Unfortunately, senior employees pass on this rule to anyone just coming on board.

Let's never forget to turn lemons into lemonade whenever the opportunity presents itself. For example, the practice of favoring pet projects could be turned into a motivational maneuver by scheduling favorite activities at the end of the day or upon completion of another project or task. The headline in all of this is:

MOST PEOPLE WASTE TIME THE SAME WAY EVERY DAY

MINOR CORRECTIONS FOR MAJOR IMPROVEMENTS

Minor corrections can mean major improvements. For example, if a manager figures out a way to save only 10 minutes every workday, that savings will total 42 extra hours gained at the end of a year. That would be like having a 53-week year, and would result in one heck of an increase in productivity—all from just 10 minutes per day. What are some of the most valuable expenditures of a manager's time? Training new people, for one. Equal, if not more important, is the continued nurturing and development of veterans within the organization. We must never forget our obligation, both to our people and the organization as a whole, to keep the furnaces stoked in our human fleet.

Then there is planning for the future. Whether it's next week, next month, three years or more down the road, a ship under a full head of steam isn't very useful to anyone if it has no destination. Seeking out new opportunities, challenges, and markets are productive uses of management time. How about establishing new personal and business goals? Organizing a better system for your business and your home? Creative and innovative thinking are time investments for a better tomorrow.

LIBERATED TIME

Peter F. Drucker, the great management expert, has many suggestions for ways in which we can all profit from liberated time. Here are three of his most important:

Record your time   Don't count on your memory for an accurate assessment of how you spend your time. Would you trust your memory more than the register in your checkbook? I promise you that documenting your time usage for three days will convince you beyond any doubt how much you need time planning.

Manage your time   Peter Drucker was so convinced of the importance of time management that he said, "Until we can manage time, we can manage nothing else." Managing means being aware of and proactively appropriating time to tasks rather than letting time "get away from us." Plan your time, but also time your plan. Give yourself some time pressures as motivation.

Consolidate your time   To increase efficiency, group chores together.

STOP DOING WHAT YOU KNOW DOESN'T WORK

Doing away with the unnecessary and inefficient is the first step toward higher achievement. However, most people continue to repeat ineffective patterns, even after they've become aware that their efforts are not working. In fact, the Muddling Manager's Law specifically states, "If you are unsure of what you're doing, then do more of it." How often have you watched that proverb being repeated?

Once, during a counseling session with one of my more cynical employees, I asked him to give me a scenario of how not to make money in the business we were in. He grinned at me and asked, "You want me to tell you how *not* to make money here?" I nodded. "That's easy," he continued. "I do that every day."

Then I asked him, "In that case, what do you have planned for tomorrow?"

He stopped grinning as he realized that, like it or not, he had actually planned another day of low productivity.

ASK YOURSELF SOME SIMPLE QUESTIONS AND LISTEN TO YOUR ANSWERS

To help gain more from your time, you can answer a few simple, but tough, questions about yourself:

♦ What am I pretending not to know?

♦ What's not being done in my organization that should be?

♦ What's being done that should not be?

♦ What's being done that should be done more often?

These are questions we should ask periodically to challenge any standard operating procedure. We can ask ourselves, "If I had to do this in a whole new way, how could I do it better?"

Looking at your daily to do list in your daily planner, on-line calendar, or electronic organizer, ask about each item:

♦ What would happen if I don't do this at all?

♦ What things could be done just as well or even better by someone else?

♦ Knowing how many of these items are unproductive or inefficient, how many will I repeat anyway?

Ask your team members, "What things do I do that waste your time and/or block your productivity?"

Chef, the heat just went up in the kitchen. That last question is a very important one to ask. And believe me, they will answer it. Be prepared to do something about it.

THE VALUE OF YOUR TIME

I've heard it said that it's impossible to lead a successful life. The best we can do is lead one successful day after another. I personally think even that is too much to chew. In fact, people fail or succeed in 15-minute segments. That's right. We can all benefit from drastically reframing our sense of time.

Are you aware that, to a person earning $100,000 per year, one minute is worth a dollar? Multiply it out for yourself. A person earning $150,000 per year is earning $1.50 per minute. At $200,000 per year, each minute is worth two dollars.

This is all a means of drawing perspective on the question we should all be aware of throughout the day: "What was the value to me and my family of my last 15 minutes?" A very profound question like this should be tattooed between your index finger and your thumb, written on the back of the name plate on your desk, on the face of your watch, on a sticker in the cradle of your telephone, and in bold letters above your computer screen. At the end of the day, if you wrote yourself a mental check in the amount of what you thought that day was worth, would it total up to what a day should be worth if you were to double your income?

TAKE TIME MANAGEMENT SERIOUSLY

I frequently ask people if they plan their time, only to watch them produce an itty-bitty month-at-a-glance calendar with postage-stamp-sized squares for each day. Write down "pick up the laundry" in one of those squares and it looks like you've got a big day planned. A better-organized daily planner shows you the holes in your day where you can plan activities that are more productive.

Use an electronic calendar on your computer whenever possible. There's almost no end to the detail you can put in the Notes section. More important, you can e-mail the calendar to yourself and program it for automatic reminders that will show up wherever you receive your E-mail, which in this day and age of cell phones and electronic organizers can be anywhere in the world.

ORGANIZE YOUR SPACE

William Morris, the great 19th-century poet, artist, and craftsman, had some great advice for those of us in the 21st century: "Keep nothing that is not beautiful or useful." Take an early morning, an evening, or a weekend and organize your workspace, your attaché case, and your car (if you use it in your work); be merciless in throwing low-priority things away. Put things most frequently used in the most accessible places. Set up a file system that makes sense to you. Divide your job into parts and decide which of those parts needs the most organizing. With a computerized calendar, if you miss an assignment, pop it up and revise the due date so it will keep reminding you.

THE RIGHT WAY TO DO A TO DO LIST

Lay out a step-by-step plan (or master list) of organization, with a deadline for each part, and get started. The master to do list should contain all the tasks you want to complete, both high and low priority. Your plan should be written, measurable, expressed in results (not activities), realistic/attainable, and based on a date of completion. The value of a good plan is summed up in the carpenter's advice to "measure twice and cut once." The "to do" items should be labeled in three categories:

1. Do today, no excuses
2. Do today, if possible
3. Do today, if time is available after numbers 1 and 2 are completed

The tendency is to load up the to do list with nothing but high-priority items for the day, excluding low-priority items. Wrong. The little things can be ultimately important to our sanity, and accomplishing them is a good way to sustain a true sense of perspective. Remember the frogs? Swallowing the biggest one first is the way to start. But the job is not done until the little guys are gulped down too.

Almost nothing motivates us and elevates our mood as effectively as the sense of accomplishment gained from crossing items off a to do list. It's cheap therapy. Of course, the list clearly reveals what remains to be done. And a closer look can reveal if the list is going to outlive the day or vise versa, giving us a time reference.

MAKE SETTING PRIORITIES A PRIORITY

How is the priority system set up? First, we need to answer the question, "Am I efficient only at doing unimportant work?" It is always possible to be efficient without being effective. Some people call this job security. Don't overkill low-priority items with planning energy. The planning energy spent should match the priority of the task.

Always remember Dwight Eisenhower's words: "Urgent things are seldom important, and important things are seldom urgent." (A secret that your overnight mail service doesn't want you to know.) Urgent tasks require immediate attention, but they frequently have little or no impact on long-term goals, while important tasks are valuable to achieving long-term goals.

Peter Drucker gave us another jewel when he said, "It's more important to do the right thing, than to do things right." In other words, following the rules, the script, the SOP manual, whatever, is never as important as doing what is best for the greatest number of people in any given situation. In business, doing the right thing might mean taking a less profitable road for the moment, but it leads to higher profits later.

Accordingly, we should focus first on getting the right things done and worry about efficiency second. This isn't a license for shooting from the hip or being otherwise irresponsible. It is simply intended to liberate us from the bad habit of being pennywise and pound foolish.

TOMORROW BEGINS TODAY

I believe the difference between a winner and the also-ran can be as little as two well-planned hours per day. I recommend you take at least 10 minutes at the end of the day to plan tomorrow's activities. Those who already engage in this practice know how gratifying it feels to wake up in the morning with a head start on the day.

BE FLEXIBLE IN YOUR PLANNING

As a planning strategy, allow 10 percent more time than each task should realistically require. If you're just getting started with time planning, don't attempt to plan any more than 75 percent of your workday. Advanced time planners only plan 90 percent of their working hours. There will always be spillover and interruptions that need to be accommodated.

According to Phillip Musgrove, formerly of the Brookings Institute in Washington, D.C., everything takes longer than expected—2.71828 times longer, to be exact. Don't ask me how he measured that, but I prove it just about every time I book my speaking engagements too close together.

MAKE THE FIRST HOUR COUNT DOUBLE: DO THE WORST THINGS FIRST

Strive to make the first hour of your workday the most satisfying by remembering to swallow the biggest frogs first. Another way to think of it would be to have frog for breakfast every day. Hopefully, there won't be any left by dinnertime. Do the three things you least want to do first. If you leave unpleasant tasks for later, they tend to negatively flavor or just plain stink up everything you're involved in that day. Avoid the avoidance game.

INVENTORY YOUR EFFICIENCY

I agree with the successful people who say the first few hours of the workday are the most fertile and productive. So, when planning your time, schedule the most creative and demanding work during the time when you're at your personal best. For some people, their personal best time is in the middle of the night. Our internal clocks vary. Take a self-inventory and try to determine during what part of the day you're the most efficient.

Your self-inventory can be very simple. Just keep a log for one month, both at work and at home, documenting what part of the day is the most productive. When do you feel you're accomplishing the most? When are you tired? When are you alert? During what times of the day do you get along the best with other people, and when do others respond the most positively to you?

For most people, the first two to four hours of the workday are the most productive. The lull seems to come through the middle of the day, with productivity resurging into the evening. Your own personal record should inform you whether you are stronger early or late. You might discover a quick catnap in the place of eating lunch gives you a burst of energy through the afternoon, when you formerly felt bogged down for hours.

EXPECT THE UNEXPECTED

If a problem interrupts your best efforts, don't simply bear down on it harder. Sometimes it requires getting further away, not closer to it, in order to solve it. Back off and look at the situation from a variety of angles. Bend over and look at it backward and upside down between your legs. After gaining a broader perspective, break the problem down into its component parts and grade them in order of priority. Then move in and begin to work on the most important aspect of the problem.

LEARN TO SAY NO

Before you say yes to a commitment in the future, ask yourself, "Do I have time for this now?" If you don't have time for it right now, you probably won't have time for it later on. One of the reasons that 20 percent of the people always wind up doing 80 percent of the work is that the 20 percent either have an inflated concept of their abilities or, more likely, simply don't say no. (The 80 percent don't want you to find out about these time-efficiency techniques because the workload will automatically shift more evenly across the staff.)

According to Executive Productivity of Boca Raton, Florida, saying no is one of the five key steps to eliminating executive time wasters. Here's the whole list:

♦ Doing work beneath your abilities wastes time. On average, executives spend 53 percent of their time performing secretarial or clerical tasks. If others can do it, assign it to them.

♦ Tolerating too many interruptions wastes time. Schedule your availability and your unavailability. Set aside a quiet hour each day when all visitors and phone calls are absolutely prohibited. Don't be surprised if you get three hours work done in that one hour. Schedule another period when your door and your line are open.

♦ Handling trivial assignments while keeping the big job on hold wastes time. Attack the most important project early and work on it as long as you can. By 11:00 a.m. you'll feel as though you've accomplished a whole day's work. (My interpretation: by 11:00 a.m. your desk should be pretty much frog free.)

♦ Working without a plan wastes time. Take a few minutes at the start of each day to outline and/or review your objectives and priorities. By helping you organize your working day, those minutes can save you many hours.

♦ Saying yes too much can waste time. Make "No" the automatic response to demands on your time. "Yes" should be the exception.

Don't be discouraged if there are items left on your list at the end of the day. Many people are self-critical when they don't finish everything. Sometimes that is simply not a realistic or reasonable expectation. Why clobber yourself unreasonably? Take comfort in knowing that, with good time planning, you've made the most out of the time available to you. Getting even more efficient and effective tomorrow leaves you with a challenge you can look forward to.

CONDUCT A BRIEF, DAILY PERSONAL PRODUCTIVITY SURVEY

Take no more than five minutes at the end of the day to evaluate your productivity. Schedule the time for this evaluation. It's important to be aware of how you're doing. Not so you can beat yourself up for doing poorly, but so you can assess where you can do better and appreciate your own efficiency.

A SELF-MADE MULTIMILLIONAIRE'S DAILY EVALUATION

I have a friend who was illiterate at the age of 26. By the age of 49, he was extremely wealthy. He now reads five or six books per week. People like this fascinate me, and I asked him, "How do you get so much out of your time?"

He said that he evaluates his day on a daily basis and showed me a special daily planner he had printed. Each page represented one day, and there were four squares at the bottom of each page. To grade himself every day on a 100-point system, he writes a score in each box each day. His four categories, each one worth a maximum score of 25 points, are:

Simplicity (1–25)

On simplicity, he grades himself by asking, "Did I keep my day simple?" and, "Did I stay on top of my agenda or did it overwhelm me?" The beauty of watching masters at work is often found in how skillfully they keep disruptions and problems from knocking them off track.

Desperation (1–25)

When he named desperation as his second category, I asked him to explain. "Do I understand I don't get this day back?" he said. "That's an important question. Even if it's a day off, spent with my family at the beach." He was telling me to make the most of each day because I can never relive that particular 24 hours again.

Planning (1–25)

How good a job of planning was done? Most of us know the difference between truly thinking something out in advance and *winging it*. Everyone spends some amount of time flying by the seat of his or her pants. I've done it in supersonic fighters and I'm here to say that it's no smarter to fly by the seat of your pants at 60,000 feet than it is behind your desk or on a sales call.

Job Action (1–25)

Job action is defined as actually making a profit. Isn't it funny how profitability becomes the furthest thing from our minds while at work? Profits are made when plans go into action. Job action is probably the most vital category. I believe that hard work without talent is a shame, and talent without hard work or *action* is a tragedy.

CULTIVATE A SENSE OF PROFITABILITY

Almost every successful person I know has a keen sense of profitability. In a practical sense, they're placing a value on their 15-minute intervals the way we discussed earlier. This doesn't mean we should become obsessed with profitability. It means we need to be driven, in part, by awareness of how our efforts are turned into dollars and cents.

DEALING DECISIVELY WITH INTERRUPTIONS

I can't think of anyone who isn't frustrated by interruptions and the loss of time interruptions usually cause. As I've already discussed, all of us tend to make the same mistake over and over again, contributing to our own dilemma. The most common mistake is focusing too much attention on whatever lands on our desk and whoever drops in or calls on the telephone. All too often we stop in our tracks and spend valuable time attending to low-priority items. We allow others to plan our day for us whenever we allow them to interrupt and rearrange our priorities. There are several methods to help minimize interruptions in your workday:

1. Rearrange the furniture in your office so your desk does not face traffic as it flows by your door. Disrupt the line of sight between you and passersby.

2. Reduce the number of chairs in your office and keep them as far away from your desk as possible.

3. Place a clock where it is visible to you *and* anyone who is visiting your work space.

4. Don't automatically look up when someone walks in. This is a toughie. However, if you appear to be concentrating, people with unimportant business are less likely to interrupt.

5. Keep an interruption log for a week. Make columns that identify who caused the interruption, what time they came in and left, and the total time of their visit. Finally, note briefly what you think you could do to maintain better control over your time. (See Figure 5-3.)

6. When someone asks, "Do you have a minute?" learn to say no. Another toughie. You'll be surprised at how understanding people can be when

INTERRUPTION LOG				
Inter- ruption	Description	Time Begin/End	# of Minutes	Preventive Action To Be Taken
1				
2				
3				
4				
5				
6				

Figure 5-3. Interruption log.

you're up to your elbows in alligators. Saying no from time to time doesn't mean the end of communications with a person or persons. Instead, it is an effective way to establish appropriate boundaries that help everyone function more effectively.

7. If someone has a chronic habit of coming to you seeking advice or help, learn to respond by asking them what he or she thinks. You're being asked to do their thinking for them. So don't! If you refuse to do someone else's thinking, they will eventually stop asking. This doesn't mean you shouldn't offer a word of encouragement when they have a good idea. That encouraging word can also help them stand on their own capabilities while maintaining an appropriate boundary and allowing you to get back to your own tasks much faster.

8. If you have difficulty terminating a conversation in your work area, simply walk the person back to his or her work area and leave them there. Excuse yourself to go back to work. The message is subtle but clear.

9. Don't be part of the problem. The person being interrupted can become an interrupter. I sometimes catch myself slipping out of a work mode and into a social mode. Once again, excuse yourself and get back to work.

10. Keep in mind during the day the self-evaluation at the end of the day at 25 points each: simplicity, desperation, planning, and job action.

THANK YOU, ALEXANDER GRAHAM BELL

Thank you, Alexander Graham Bell, for that marvelous discovery, the telephone. Perhaps the greatest development in the history of communication is not the technology itself, but our ability to maintain control over it and not allow ourselves to be controlled by the telephone or the E-mail in-box. Here are some techniques based upon Stephanie Winston's book *The Organized Executive*:

1. Establish time limits when talking on the telephone. When someone asks if you have a few minutes and you determine you do, go ahead and say something like, "I have three minutes." Avoid using common blocks like five or 10 minutes. Using short and odd time segments will focus the caller's attention on being brief and to the point.

2. Start winding up a telephone conversation by saying something like, "Jerry, before we hang up … " What I just politely told Jerry was, "This conversation is almost over."

3. Don't hesitate to inform a talkative caller that you're in the middle of an urgent task and you'll have to call him or her back. Then, call back just before quitting time. People often use the telephone to take up time

and make five o'clock come more quickly; don't let someone recruit you in their scheme. Calling back at quitting time will usually result in a short conversation.

4. Ask the caller in advance how much time he or she needs to complete your conversation. Then suggest something a little shorter.

5. Steer the telephone conversation toward issues important to *you*, rather than following the caller's agenda. By asking a question the caller can't answer, it is possible he or she will appreciate that you're involved with something more important than what they had to talk about. Then, hopefully, they'll let you get back to your work.

6. Then, of course, there's the old standby of having your assistant call you on another extension if the caller or visitor is just too persistent to get the hint.

7. You can save yourself a lot of time by using a conference planner. Draw squares on a standard sheet of paper. Draw the squares in a variety of sizes because conversations vary in complexity and length. Write the name of the person you want to talk to at the top of each square and note the points you want to cover. (See Figure 5-4.) This will help keep you on track while you're on the telephone and will help you quickly recall your original agenda when someone, who isn't available at first, returns your call hours or days later. It's best if this form is on a piece of paper that's a different color than what's normally on your desk. When the person *finally* calls back, you can find your notes quicker.

8. Accept long distance calls whenever possible and talk on the other party's money.

BE A RIGHT-FINDER

Everyone experiences time emergencies we can learn from. For example, review an experience when you were called upon to complete a task in a shorter amount of time than you originally thought you had. Perhaps a deadline was moved up, but you got the job done in spite of the additional pressure. The question is, "How was I able to accomplish that in less time than I had budgeted?"

SPRINTING

Many people are engaging in what is called "sprinting." All this means is that they look at tasks that are scheduled to take a certain amount of time and decide they're going to accomplish them in half that time. What customarily takes a full day or a full hour will take only half a day or half an hour, and so on. Sprinting

CONFERENCE PLANNER		
Date _____		
NAME	NAME	NAME
NAME	NAME	NAME
NAME	NAME	NAME
		NAME
NAME	NAME	NAME
		NAME

Figure 5-4.

through a day or even an hour will demonstrate that tasks can be accomplished in shorter periods without the pressure of emergency.

A nonthreatening way to approach sprinting is to do it for a day and then return to your customary pace. My only warning here is to beware that once you've learned how much you can accomplish, you will probably be frustrated in accepting your former, slower pace.

TRY THIS *WHAT IF?* EXERCISE

How would you change the way you do your job if a medical emergency forced you to work only half days? Which tasks would you drop completely? Which tasks would you delegate or distribute to others? How would the role of family members, part-time help, and other staff members change? Which people you give time to now would you avoid under greater time constraint?

SPEED-READING IS ALIVE AND WELL: DO IT

There are many organizations anxious to take your money in exchange for teaching you to read faster. Your public library can tell you who offers speed-reading courses and for how much. If you don't think you can spare the time or make the effort to attend a formal course, then simply start moving your index finger or the point of a pencil under the text you're reading (including E-mails) as fast as your eyes can keep up with it, and that alone will at least *double* your reading speed.

Practice *jumping* your finger or your pencil down the page. You will soon begin to pick up entire phrases, major ideas, and concepts without having to read every word. By learning some basic techniques for "processing paper," you can spend less time reading each day, or read and understand *more* in the same amount of time.

1. Selective reading. I was relieved to learn that I didn't have to read everything that came across my desk. Neither do you. Prove this to yourself by throwing away anything you don't consider absolutely vital at first glance. See if your action is covered on the six o'clock news. See if the world truly ends.

2. Never pick up the same piece of paper twice. Never pick up a piece of paper unless you intend to do something with it. Tackle it or toss it, but do something with it. Don't put it back down to clutter your life again in the future. A wise time expert once said that a cluttered desk is a monument to delayed decisions.

3. Preview material for key words and phrases by reading the first and last sentences of each paragraph. If you're interested, go back and read more. If you're not interested, move on.

4. Immediately separate and organize all high-priority correspondence and respond quickly, even before you sort through low-priority materials.

5. E-mail features now make replying to messages fast and paperless. When you get a snail mail letter or written memo, write your reply on the original page and dispatch. If you feel a little guilty at treating your message and the other party with such informality, then get a rubber stamp or a sticker that reads, HANDWRITTEN FOR IMMEDIATE RESPONSE. PROMPTNESS BEFORE FORMALITY. The other party will be impressed

(especially if you bring it to their attention with your rubber stamp), and you'll save yourself and your assistant a great deal of time. File a copy of the letter with your response, thus cutting the amount of filed paper in half. When possible, e-mail your response.

HANDLING PAPERWORK

Time-planning consultant Alan Lakein has listed some helpful tips on handling paperwork. I've summarized and updated them a little to account for electronic mail and corresponding:

Sending, Screening, and Processing

1. Screen out items that go directly into the wastebasket and put them there.
2. Request an immediate reply. If it's a paper memo, leave a space for replies.
3. Write your requests in such a way that the recipient can reply with a simple yes or no.
4. File all previous correspondence and related materials together with new messages.
5. If you want to see advertising messages, collect a week's worth before reading them.
6. Highlight important ideas so you don't need to reread the whole thing when you refer back to the document or forward it to someone else to read.
7. Be brief with your responses. Two paragraphs max. Two sentences are better.
8. Have your assistant respond to as much of your correspondence as possible.
9. Include your assistant in processing paperwork and e-mail. Try to resolve each item as you go so it doesn't have to be dealt with again.
10. If an item goes through the system three times without action, put it in the dead file.

Improvements

1. Develop ways that your assistant can lighten your load.
2. Get off mailing lists. Block unwanted e-mail.

3. Eliminate unnecessary FYI copies and reports.

4. Train your staff to submit a recommendation with any problem report.

5. Require a one-paragraph summary on any report more than three pages.

RESPECT THE TIME OF OTHERS

Depending on your situation and personal style, many of these methods and techniques will not only make your efforts more time-effective, but also increase your respect for others' time. Practice what you preach. Lead by example.

◆ Don't conduct a $5000 meeting to address a $500 problem.

◆ Be prompt to your appointments and don't keep people waiting to see you. Promptness helps everyone's morale, including yours.

◆ Boil down your information to its most vital and salient points.

◆ Speak in headlines. If people want to know more, they'll ask.

◆ Sum it up first, not last. Begin at the end.

THE LEADER AS A TIME PLANNER

Allow yourself to enjoy the benefits of good time planning. It's important to frame all of this time-efficiency information properly, lest you think I'm suggesting you take on more work, more responsibility, and literally burn yourself out. The fact is, these time-management techniques, when employed properly, will reduce your stress level, lower the amount of pressure you're experiencing, and generally improve the quality of both your professional and personal life.

Perhaps most important of all, you will relate better and more meaningfully to other people, rather than allowing ineffective time use habits to smother you. Ask yourself, "Would I be more drawn to someone who confidently has it all together or to someone who is constantly under pressure and on the verge of losing control?" Note the word *confidently*. The proper use of these techniques will help transform personal and professional panic into self-assurance.

Strive to be more like the person to whom you are attracted and respect, whether that person exists in fact or only in your imagination. Others will respond in kind. What better definition for a great leader could there be than someone who truly behaves in a fashion consistent with his or her personal beliefs and values, constantly seeking newness in effective living?

It's important to understand that some people are driven by a need to achieve as a compensation for their own lack of self-esteem and self-confidence. Others are truly attempting to live life for all God meant it to be. The difference between these two motivations is most easily seen in how each person treats others along the way. One person appears to be running helter-skelter into everything they say and do, while the other person welcomes others into their world with open arms. There are healthy and unhealthy reasons for achieving. You can tell how healthy your motivations are by how much satisfaction you receive from your successes, in addition to how confidently you can accept your failures as valuable learning experiences.

All of us must look inside of ourselves and conduct a self-inventory to answer these questions. Just remember, few people apply the term over-worked to something they love doing. Such terms are reserved for tasks we feel we're being forced to do against our will. I'm encountering more and more people these days who have learned the difference. Such insight is helping to change lives.

TIME FOR YOURSELF

Leisure time is very important to me for many reasons, and effective time man-agement improves both the quantity and quality of leisure time. One of the most beneficial features of leisure time is the opportunity to recharge your batteries. There is a point of diminishing returns in an overworked individual, and a case of burnout can render people useless to themselves and others. Working oneself to death out of a personal compulsive need is not beneficial to anyone.

To avoid the erosion of morale and a general decrease in effectiveness, I've learned to schedule leisure time for both my staff and myself. Setting a good example when it comes to rest is just as vital as being a good model for proper work habits. Mental and physical renewal are vital components of a quality work ethic. Here's my two-step:

1. Plan some *quiet time alone* each day. Even the most die-hard, compulsive workers will accomplish more if they take time away on a daily basis. If you can't decide when you most need a break, or simply forget to take one, schedule a reminder to yourself to break two hours after you begin working, at midday (whether you eat lunch or simply walk in a park or a mall), and again two hours before you're scheduled to go home.

2. Break tough jobs down into more easily accomplished tasks. The result is an immediate feeling of accomplishment that reduces the ominous burden ahead. It's important not to become overwhelmed with the task. Breaks between finished segments help to keep a realistic perspective of *doability.* Don't forget to acknowledge your accomplishment by rewarding yourself when a tough job is completed. The "Salami Theory" states that slicing a task into small parts will not speed it up, but it will make the task easier to complete. And it's still salami.

Remember the great story, "Cheaper by the Dozen"? The father in the story said something like, "If you are awake for 16 hours per day, that's 960 minutes. Devoting a minimum of 9.6 minutes, or one percent of that time, to making someone else happy will brighten all of your hours." That's a mathematical approach to kindness, but a good idea. It can also be a morale builder for both you and the recipient.

END YOUR DAY RIGHT

There is even a right way and a wrong way to end your workday. The right way is to end on a high note or a point of accomplishment. Doing so promotes satisfaction, improves the quality of your relaxation time, and helps you return to work the following day more refreshed and eager.

If you must end your day with an unresolved problem, then write down a clear summary of the problem as it stands when you leave it. Before you leave, clear your desk or work area of clutter and distraction so you can attack the problem when you first walk in the following day. This means leaving that note, the summation of the problem, in the center of your desk. Now you have a good framework for pondering your situation in the hours away from the work place. The answer might come when you least expect it.

These preparations will also serve you well before breaking for lunch, so you'll get back up to speed more quickly and with less effort after your break. Reorienting yourself after breaking requires energy that can be saved with a little forethought before your break.

Employing these time-management techniques should help you avoid working on weekends, holidays, and vacations. I'm not suggesting you take on more work than you should in light of your personal goals and professional responsibilities. I am trying to help you accomplish more in less time so you can live a more balanced personal and professional life.

EFFECTIVE TIME MANAGEMENT = VACATION

All too often personal relationships with friends and family suffer because we are simply overloaded at work. This is too high a price to pay for success, if you ask me. What is it all for anyway? As I mentioned earlier, if work is simply a way to avoid personal responsibilities, then you would be better served to deal with the personal issues that are driving you to compulsive and self-destructive work habits.

Work effectively and then take your vacations, all of them. I used to pride myself on skimpy vacations until a mentor taught me that I was simply demonstrating my own lack of effectiveness in getting my work finished. Never having time to take vacations is not a badge of honor as much as it is a mark of ineffective time management.

KEEP YOUR LEISURE TIME LEISURELY

Take your time and relax. As I mentioned, you'll be a better worker, and more valuable to yourself and everyone else, when you've been recharged. Relaxing means spending some time alone and engaging in activities that refresh you and recharge your batteries.

This also means avoiding the urge to turn leisure time into a minimilitary drill. Ordering yourself and your family into a tight schedule is not relaxing. Rigid, compulsive structure might seem comfortable to you at first blush, but it's not going to leave you refreshed. Relaxation takes different forms for different people. However, it must take you out of your working pattern to be truly therapeutic.

There is a method for getting more out of the time you spend sleeping. The technique relaxes you before climbing into bed. It's called a "harmony bath," and you don't have to get into a tub to do it. Simply turn off the 10 o'clock or 11 o'clock news, with their "if it bleeds, it leads" format. Instead, spend the last 60 to 90 minutes of the day listening to relaxing music or reading or both. Make sure that whatever you're reading is also relaxing, such as poetry, the classics, or something inspirational. You'll find that sleep comes quicker and will be deeper and more refreshing

CLOSING THOUGHTS

Finally, some mythology of time management:

> *We trained hard. But it seemed that every time we were beginning to form into teams, we would be reorganized. I was to learn later in life that we tend to meet any new situation by reorganizing. And what a wonderful method it can be for creating the illusion of progress while producing confusion, inefficiency, and demoralization.*

Petronius Arbiter wrote these words in the year 66 A.D. Unfortunately, in many organizations, it is still true … so much for learning from history. Human nature hasn't changed much in leadership. The great playwright Somerset Maugham advised us to "Live life, don't portray it!" To me, that means aspiring to the highest and best use of our time. The difference between the self-made president and the self-made pauper can probably be found in how each person uses his or her equally allocated time.

CHAPTER SIX

THE FOURTH STEP: KEEPING MORALE HIGH WHEN THE HEAT'S ON

"Don't let the chickens roost over the well."
Anonymous

MORALE AND PERFORMANCE: CHICKEN OR EGG?

There is no such thing as a low-morale/high-performance organization or a low-performance/high-morale organization. If you think you have one, you don't have the level of productivity you could have. So, quick, where is the morale level of your team? Are you sure? The chicken-and-egg debate goes around and around over whether friction heating is caused by poor morale or poor morale is caused by friction and pressures from within the organization. Either way, the story always ends up with the leader on the hot seat.

Morale is generally defined as a state of mind involving one's sense of confidence, courage, hope, or zeal. High producers prefer not to leave a high morale organization even though they're offered more money somewhere else. Their concern is that if the new organization has lower morale, their production could drop because of it. Low or poor morale is negative, and people generally want to get away from it. Staff turnover is the tip of the low-morale iceberg.

Some people make the argument that turnover is good for an organization. Their logic is that new blood keeps creativity and innovation high because people naturally stagnate over time. Some managers even feel the experience of seeing others around you losing their jobs will keep you on your toes. Others believe staying with the same people for a long time promotes a sort of incestuous promotion cycle that weakens the bloodlines of the organization. No matter the reason, I have some fundamental problems with this kind of thinking.

When we have problems with our kids, we don't send them away and go get some more. The reality is, we do our best to get the best out of the folks we have. We don't just give up on them. As I've already mentioned, there are situations when it is in the best interests of the individual and the organization to part ways. However, when I hear someone tell me an organization must hire new people in order to gain new ideas, I'm troubled even more. The myth that new ideas can't come from people inside the organization indicates that the role of morale is being misunderstood. Besides, why would any truly creative person want to join an organization that is void of new ideas anyway?

A leader must plant his or her feet and commit to raising and maintaining the morale of the organization. A commitment to improving morale is a commitment to your people. The morale of your staff members is directly proportional to the quality of their experience in being a part of your team. In fact, the level of morale is a good barometer of how each of your people is reacting to your leadership. Keep in mind that you'll have no one working for you with a higher level of morale than yours. Show me the morale of the team and I'll show you the morale of the coach.

THE TEN WARNING SIGNS OF LOW MORALE

Low morale often creeps in without anyone realizing it, including the manager. One of the responsibilities of the good leader is to check his or her organization's morale pulse daily. Here are some symptoms of trouble:

1. Uncooperative attitudes
2. Lack of enthusiasm
3. Absence of commitment
4. Fault finding
5. Increasing complaints
6. Growing tardiness and absenteeism
7. Deterioration in the appearance of the work area
8. Breakdown in discipline
9. Long faces
10. Low morale as a rallying point

Uncooperative Attitudes. Generally, an uncooperative attitude is detectable the moment you approach a team member. You can quickly sense that something is wrong, even if you can't put your finger on it immediately. One of the most obvious indicators of a generally uncooperative attitude is an attitude of reluctance, or even one of being imposed upon, projected by a team member. Does doing little or nothing appear to be more important than dealing with you? The second you come into contact with a person who has a cooperative attitude, you'll recognize the difference. It's unmistakable. I believe people are fundamentally cooperative by nature. It's only when the environment is somehow contaminated that they become unfriendly.

Lack of Enthusiasm. A lack of enthusiasm can sometimes be perceived as a pervasive sense of boredom. People don't enjoy being bored. They must have a reason to avoid doing more interesting things. Either that or they're being restricted from doing more interesting things. It's true that an activity one person might enjoy could bore someone else. However, in an organization with high morale, we can assume the leader has done an effective job of matching people up with tasks and responsibilities that are in tune with their individual strengths.

Absence of Commitment. When there is an absence of commitment or a general sense of melancholy about what the organization is supposed to be doing, chances are good the same opinions are reflected in the organization's leadership. If the leader is not committed, there could be a host of problems, like poor communication, incorrect assignment matching, and so forth. As you already know, it's highly unlikely that team members are going to have or maintain any sort of commitment if the leader isn't committed.

Fault Finding. People who are not happy will tend to find fault in anything, everything, and everybody. When morale is high, even mistakes are not dwelled upon. When morale is low, even the greatest victories might be picked apart and talked down in an orgy of negative thinking. A person who is consciously committed to finding the good in people and their efforts will not be trapped in the quagmire of fault finding, which is nothing more than a cycle of negativity feeding on itself. In an imperfect world, there will always be faults to find in even the best people. Therefore, if someone chooses to be a fault finder, they'll have enough material to last an unhappy lifetime.

Increasing Complaints. When complaining seems to be a favorite activity, you can bet that folks aren't having a good time. I challenge you to show me a happy complainer. In an organization where there hasn't historically been much complaining, a noticeable increase is an indication that morale is slipping. Complaining usually takes place quietly, out of the leader's earshot. By the time the less than alert leader becomes aware of it, it's probably spreading rapidly and has had time to become fairly serious.

Growing Tardiness and Absenteeism. Blatant tardiness and absenteeism are generally grounds for termination and, at the least, an overt discipline problem requiring immediate attention. However, if absenteeism and tardiness appear to the leader's vigilant eye to be on the increase, they can be considered a subtle indication that morale is slipping. People who love what they do can't get enough of it and can't seem to stay away. The difference between people who love their work and people who are discontented is clearly evident in punctuality and attendance.

Deterioration in the Appearance of the Work Area.   Some very creative and productive people don't keep their work space very neat. How is a leader supposed to know when a change in the appearance of the work area indicates an erosion of morale? That depends on how well a leader knows his or her people as individuals. The key word is *change* in the appearance of the work area. People who are customarily neat and tidy are sending a clear message of dissatisfaction if they become sloppy and unkempt. This applies not only to the work area, but to the individual's appearance as well. On the other hand, if someone who is less tidy than the average bear, and possibly less fashionable, suddenly spends most of their time cleaning and straightening up, it could be a sign that he or she is bored or uncomfortable about something. Maybe they're out interviewing for other jobs.

Breakdown in Discipline.   The key word once again is *change* when discipline breaks down. There is a normal range of fluctuation in all things, and an effective leader will have a sense of how an organization operates on its best and worst days. Discipline varies greatly from one organization to another, depending upon the type of business being conducted, where the business is located, and many other considerations. However, if overall discipline appears to be breaking down over an extended period of time, start checking out possible causes.

Long Faces.   Long faces can mean many things. An individual's temporary low energy and sour expression can be caused by physical discomfort due to illness, emotional discomfort due to tension in the family, or any number of other nonwork reasons. The leader's concern should be primarily limited to how an individual's attitude affects his or her performance and the performance of others. A good relationship with each individual team member goes a long way toward diagnosing when a change in attitude requires attention and how much. Personal problems brought to work can become a problem for more than just the individual. The leader has to be an effective counselor who shows genuine concern for each person's situation, while keeping the overall best interests of the internal or external customer in sight. The subtle art of leading is, in part, the ability to read faces, voices, posture, and other indicators of unhappiness. A long face on everyone in the office, every day, is something else again.

When Low Morale Becomes a Rallying Point.   When the people within an organization begin to talk about how lousy it is to work there and reach a general consensus on the subject, the leader and the organization have a real problem. Discontent will affect different members of your team at different times and with different intensity, due to the different personalities involved. As with the increase in complaints, any collective discontent that virtually all of your people agree upon and openly discuss represents an advanced stage of discontent and is worth the leader's attention. When your people make no attempt to conceal their negative feelings, not only is something seriously wrong, but whatever it is poses a real threat to your organization's long-term morale and performance. No manager worth his or her salt would miss an indicator as obvious as consensus discontent in the ranks.

Interpreting the Signs

As a leader, you'll probably never encounter just one sign or no signs of low morale. When morale is strained or threatened, there will probably be a combination of indicators. Even when morale is high, someone might project signs of low morale, which don't pose an immediate threat to general well-being. An effective leader is good at reading and properly interpreting signs. Much of your sign-reading confidence will come from experience. However, knowing what you now know will give you a tremendous head start.

I once heard a group of salespeople refer to management as the "morale suppression team" who took their orders from the "sales prevention department." That is unfortunate. Yet when you stop and think about it, some organizations appear to be committed to undermining their own company's morale. They seem to think that an outbreak of higher morale somewhere in the company is a sign of frivolity and that the business isn't being taken seriously enough. I don't believe smothering healthy attitudes is a conscious goal for anyone, but some styles of management seem to nip enthusiasm in the bud whenever and wherever it's found.

Case in Point: A Certain Airline's Version of Customer Service

My speaking schedule takes me on the road for 90 to 100 appearances per year. As you can imagine, I spend a lot of time on various airlines. One day, I was in my seat, waiting for a departure, when a woman came into the First Class section and took the seat beside me. We didn't talk as we waited for the plane to be pushed back from the gate. When we were 10 minutes late and nobody had said anything, the woman and I glanced at each other. After another 10 minutes passed without an announcement and we still hadn't moved, several of the flight attendants gathered in the forward galley, only a few feet from where the woman and I were seated.

Although they drew the curtain, their conversation was easily overheard. In fact, we couldn't have failed to hear it if we'd tried. The flight attendants were emphatically renouncing their loyalty to the airline. They were trying to top each other's accounts of what a lousy company it was to work for. We were late taking off, and I was hearing the airline described in a way that left me thinking, "Now might be a good time to develop a fear of flying. For a former test pilot, that's shaky. Hearing the flight attendants talk, you would have thought this was the outfit that started the "kick the tires and light the fires" style of preflight inspection.

After listening to a large dose of this negative conversation, the woman beside me turned and sheepishly said, "They really shouldn't be talking like that." I told her I agreed, the discussion was inappropriate within earshot of the customers, but I also agreed with the flight attendants' assessment of the airline. I recited my own litany of horror stories about lost or delayed baggage, poor punctuality, and other complaints about this carrier. I was surprised at how intently she listened to my complaining.

"You sound like a person who is concerned about customer service," she observed.

"I conduct seminars on leadership, personal high performance, and customer service," I replied. Then I asked her what she did.

To my surprise, she said she was in charge of customer service. Much to my *embarrassment*, she said she was in charge of customer service for that airline!

I apologized for laying into the airline so severely. She said she appreciated hearing what people thought about their service. She went on to tell me that much of her job was to reply to the complaint letters people sent in. Apparently, she wrote a personal reply to each one. The way this outfit was going, I wouldn't have wanted her job for all the tea in China. Then came the shocker. I asked her what she did with the complaint letters after she had replied to them. She told me she kept them on file in her office.

"You don't give a copy to anyone else?" I asked.

"No," she replied. "I've been instructed that upper management doesn't want to see them." I couldn't believe my ears. It quickly all became clear. This was an organization that intentionally buried its head in the sand and then left its employees twisting in the wind to catch all of the flack for a poorly run company.

A company that desperately needed to close ranks and communicate effectively up and down the line appeared to be doing everything possible to alienate its own employees as well as their customers. I had to assume upper management simply didn't know how to address morale and productivity and therefore avoided the issue. Remember, employees treat the customers as they themselves are treated by management.

The way to absolutely avoid such a miserably counterproductive scenario in your organization is to recognize signs of low morale, such as those I just outlined for you, and to understand the causes of low morale that I'm about to discuss. Most of all, investment in high morale must be a priority for leaders, not an afterthought. The attitudes, good or bad, that leaders have toward company morale and customer relations will permeate the entire organization.

FILTER BUILDERS: WHAT MY BOSS DOESN'T KNOW CAN'T HURT ME

Everyone has a comfort zone. There's a point at which individuals become nervous and uncertain about the security of their positions. This is only natural. Losing a job or a reduction in job status impacts a lot more than someone's pride and ego. Throughout a man or a woman's professional career, he or she has built a lifestyle that closely reflects their professional success. The house they live in, the car they drive, the neighborhood where their kids go to school, the golf or tennis crowd they hang out with, even the church they attend. As a leader, you need to understand how much a person's life and lifestyle are tied to his or her position in your organization.

A person tends to become a filter builder over a long period of time with a company, although it can also happen quickly under the right circumstances. The filter builders know they can avoid rocking the organizational boat by making sure that the top decision makers don't get upset hearing bad news or by hearing about problems, which they tend to find disturbing. If you're a top decision maker, you need to be careful this doesn't happen to you. It's equally important to make sure that the information your next-in-line folks get is not being filtered.

The game is easy to understand in terms of the motivations I just described and in terms of how it's played. Everyone has a bigger fish just one step up the food chain. In management situations, everyone has a smaller fish one step in the other direction. If true, accurate, and factual information is being filtered or, worse yet, misrepresented, as it makes its way through the ranks, the top leaders are likely to be left in the dark about what's truly going on with their internal and external customers. How dangerous is this problem? There are some companies we used to hear a lot about that are now gone. They were filtered to death.

To be an effective leader you need real information, whether the news is good or bad. You have the power to fix problems and to help your people grow and develop. You can't do either of those things if you're operating with limited and/or inaccurate information. Filter builders are everywhere, protecting their backsides. Don't think your organization is immune. You must identify them and deal with them. Otherwise you're putting yourself, your organization, your customers, and all of your stakeholders at risk.

BECOME FAMILIAR WITH THE CAUSES OF LOW MORALE

Detecting the warning signs of low morale is only the beginning. To fully address the morale issue, an effective leader must understand what causes morale to start taking a dive. Only after the causes are determined can the process of morale building begin. Without knowing the causes, a leader might try in vain to correct the situation and never get to the real issue. Here are some of the most common causes of low morale:

1. When people don't understand their jobs
2. Unrealistic or constantly changing goals
3. Poor communication, which can take the form of:
    ♦ Constant criticism or Big Brotherism
    ♦ Inaccessible or absentee management
    ♦ Erratic and inconsistent discipline
    ♦ Being thought of as a number
    ♦ A manager's lack of growth as a leader
4. Overinflated organizational structure and overstaffing
5. Misemployment
6. Poor psychological work environment
7. When management isn't people oriented
8. When feedback is lacking
9. When training isn't adequate

This list is by no means complete. There are many variations on these and other causes of poor morale, depending on your unique situation and the combination of people involved. However, I've found this list covers most categories. In looking at each, it should be clear how attitudes within the organization could suffer, and it should be equally clear why and how attitudes about your organization from the outside can deteriorate.

When People Don't Understand Their Jobs

It's critically important for leaders to help their people fully understand what's expected of them. There are few things more frustrating than to be left in the dark about what exactly you're expected to accomplish. Even worse is the tendency on the part of some companies to keep their people in the dark as to their job expectations and then come down hard when a person fails to perform at a level that has never been defined.

If you don't think training is important, think again. Initial training and continuing education are your best hedge against misunderstandings and the resulting dissatisfaction when job expectations are not clear. I'm referring not only to organized training activities, but also to the ongoing personal counseling relationship between a leader and his or her individual team members. Make sure that each of your people fully understands what you expect and how their individual goals fit into the larger picture of the organization's objectives.

Unrealistic or Constantly Changing Goals

As I described in Chapter 4, goals must be realistic. If they aren't, you'll pay the price later in damaged morale. It's not fair to expect people to achieve unrealistic goals, and people who are treated unfairly don't stay happy for long. If you wonder how your people feel under such circumstances, simply consider how you feel when someone demands the unreasonable from you. By the same token, if goals are constantly changed, your people can't be expected to take them very seriously. What would be the point of working hard on a goal if it's likely to be changed or abandoned? The result of wandering goals and expectations is usually frustration and, of course, decreased morale.

Poor Communication

Poor communication seems to be at the core of almost any problem, in the workplace, the home, the school, or anywhere else. Poor communication in the context I'm using means more than just having problems sending and receiving accurate messages. I'm also talking about damaging messages. For example, it's not hard to mistake that criticism is an expression of disappointment and negativism. In that respect, criticism is clear communication.

Constant Criticism or Big Brotherism.   Criticism is poison. The more clearly and effectively it's communicated, the more painful and damaging it will be. Nobody enjoys being criticized. We are so exposed to it as children, at home, and/or at school, it seems completely natural to bring it to work with us. The net result of constant criticism is the feeling that you can't do anything right, which is simply not true. Take Ken Blanchard's advice and make it a priority to catch people doing things right. You'll be surprised at how much good is being done once you take off your criticism-colored glasses. This is a major reason I dwell so much on the powerful idea of talking to people's strengths, as I discussed in Chapter 3.

Inaccessible or Absentee Management.   As I also covered in earlier chapters, an effective leader is available to his or her people. The point is not to do their work for them or to hold their hands, but to be as heavily invested in the organization's efforts as anybody else. You simply can't join in your team members' investment if you're isolated or absent altogether. Every organization is different. How close you are to your team members' efforts and how much space you allow them is a function of the unique relationship between you and your people. If your people don't feel you care, why should they? You can't pay people enough to care.

Erratic and Inconsistent Discipline.   If the rules are always changing or the enforcement of company policy is inconsistent, the result will be frustration and an overall sense of unfairness. Morale will be damaged if your people can't count on consistency from their leadership. It's difficult to be consistent with discipline because we naturally feel differently toward different people. However, if the leader keeps the best interests of the entire staff in mind, consistency in discipline will improve. Don't give a favorite person extra slack at the expense of the other hard workers in your group. The others will be troubled by your inconsistency, and their morale will suffer as a result.

The manager sets the mood for an office, whether it's good or bad, within the first 15 minutes of his or her arrival. People have their radar antennae up constantly, and you can't hide your mood from them. Be honest with your people if something is troubling you. Don't leave them in the dark while making them suffer from your ill temper. As the manager's mood swings, so will the mood of the office. When a manager is in a bad mood, he or she and the team both suffer from it. The team continues to suffer from the uncertainty of the manager's moods for three additional days after the manager's bad day. I'm not recommending that you be completely cut off from your feelings, but it's important to be aware of how the leader's emotional mood swings affect the organization and to act responsibly. Your people tend to go up or down as you do. You have that power as a leader.

Being Thought of as a Number.   When people believe that they're thought of as a number, the resulting depersonalization is depressing. Naturally, morale will suffer if people don't feel appreciated as distinct and unique individuals. Walt Disney understood this and said, "The larger a company grows, the more personal it must become." Don't be fooled that personal relationships within an organization are merely a function of numbers. I've seen large companies that are extremely good at building healthy relationships among their people and small companies that are cold and impersonal

A Manager's Lack of Growth as a Leader.   One of the first things I talked about in this book was the concept that people within organizations get better as soon as the leader does. The point is, if the leader lacks personal and professional maturity, it's unreasonable to expect any better from the organization. When a leader promotes or merely allows pettiness, cliques, resistance to change, instructions to be ignored, and so on, he or she is setting the stage for terrible morale.

As I mentioned in Chapter 5, if the standard operating procedure in your organization is to wait until the manager asks for something the third time before it's acted upon, the manager suffers unnecessary hardship right along with the organization. Remember that an individual's peers are constantly briefing him or her right along with the manager. Low morale and immature work habits on the part of the leader will come around through the organization full cycle and turn up the heat another notch. Everything will be late, which increases pressure and friction.

Overinflated Organizational Structure and Overstaffing

An overinflated organizational structure, as well as overstaffing, causes inefficiency and confusion within an organization. When job boundaries begin to overlap and there are too many chiefs and not enough Indians, the atmosphere is bound to heat up with tension and suspicion. All of this instability will result in an erosion of morale. Top-heavy organizations experience up pressure from resentful people in the ranks who feel they are burdened with other people's work while the "fat cats" on top are not pulling their fair share of the load. In overstaffed situations, people often bump into each other and confusion reigns. Eventually, the self-starters will take over and the others will fall by the wayside. Before long a few people are doing most of the work and the resentment and hostility begins.

Misemployment

Earlier, I also discussed how important it is to recognize when an individual and the organization are not right for each other and to act accordingly. When a person winds up in a job they're not right for and vice versa, the leader must act to correct the situation if damage to overall morale is to be avoided. The airline I described at least had the sense to put the pilots in the cockpit and the flight attendants in the galley.

Poor Psychological Work Environment

A poor psychological work environment can be created by allowing any combination of these morale killers to exist or persist for long. If you step back and examine your working environment, you should be able to determine whether the atmosphere promotes good and positive feelings among the staff. The mood of a place will impact an individual's psychological well-being over time.

When Management Isn't People Oriented

One of the best ways to ensure a healthy and uplifting atmosphere is to place a high priority on Humanagement or people orientation. In an atmosphere where objects and accomplishments are held in higher esteem than people, it shouldn't surprise you that people will not feel affirmed. Morale hasn't got a chance where people are low on the priority list.

When Feedback Is Lacking

Performance appraisal, not criticism, is an effective method to communicate with and counsel your people. The result of quality, individual feedback is affirmation that the individuals in your organization are important and vital to the company's success.

When Training Isn't Adequate

Companies often publicly acknowledge a need for training and continuing education, only to withhold the strong emphasis such activities deserve in the organization. In my experience, the companies that place the appropriate emphasis on training and continuing education by elevating them to their proper role in the company's hierarchy realize a tremendous return on their training investment. The old-fashioned idea that training expenses represent money down the drain can actually cause companies to flush money down the drain and not even realize it.

Unfortunately, most companies still persist in relegating training and workplace education to the background. Training and continuing education can, at least, communicate the hopes, dreams, and ambitions of the company's culture to everyone in the organization. Training and education can be one of your most effective tools to generate synergy in your organization. Is your competition training their team members better and more consistently than you are?

PUTTING THE TEN FUNDAMENTALS OF A HIGH-MORALE ENVIRONMENT IN PLACE

Exactly which specific elements contribute to high morale in your organization depends upon your individual situation and the particular challenges facing the organization. No two organizations have exactly the same equation for high morale. However, there are some fundamental principles that apply to human nature, regardless of what your particular business is. These 10 elements of a high morale environment are like primary colors and can be mixed and blended in a variety of shades.

1. Keeping jobs interesting
2. Treating people fairly
3. Assigning responsibility
4. Welcoming new ideas
5. Fostering a sense of accomplishment

6. Recognizing effort

7. Offering fair and appropriate compensation

8. Supporting personal growth

9. Promoting a sense of belonging

10. Providing opportunity

Keeping Jobs Interesting

Some jobs are interesting all by themselves, while others are only important when considered within the larger picture of an organization's activities. An effective leader will be sensitive to the fact that some tasks are mundane and sometimes just plain boring. Why does the leader care? Because the morale of the workforce is at stake, and even the most boring jobs are vital to the overall success of the organization.

As a former supersonic fighter pilot and a current frequent flier, I appreciate that those people who put rivets in airplanes take their job seriously. Have you ever looked at how many rivets there are in a big jet? It must be boring as all get-out to put those things in every day at the factory. However, if the rivets aren't installed properly and something falls off the airplane in flight, quite a few people are going to have a bad day, including the company that built the airplane.

This example might sound silly unless you're reading this book on an airplane. If you're cruising several miles above the earth right now, you no doubt appreciate that even the most uninteresting jobs, like putting rivets in airplanes, are often vitally important. Flying the airplane will always be a more interesting job, but not everybody can fly the plane. So it's important to include the riveter, or anyone in a mundane job, in as much of the overall picture as possible. How?

♦ Consult with everyone on the team for suggestions regarding a more efficient approach or methods for quality control. In other words, involve them.

♦ Give constant feedback to people at all levels to keep them abreast of how their function contributes to the overall success of the organization.

♦ Rotate mundane tasks as often as possible and practical, without losing the benefit of special training and skills where necessary.

♦ Use the methods on the current high morale list, such as recognition and personal growth, to demonstrate how you genuinely value your people.

♦ If a boring or mundane task is not necessary or vital to the organization's success, get rid of it.

Welcoming New Ideas

The way some people are treated when they come to their managers with new ideas would make you think they're asking to burn the factory down. If a manager has not reached an adequate level of personal maturity and confidence, he or she might feel threatened when approached with new ideas—not necessarily by the person bringing the new idea, but by the change in the organization the new idea might bring about. Filter Builders are notorious for putting the kibosh on new ideas rather than for passing them up the ladder. When that happens often enough, people will keep their new ideas to themselves. And if people feel stifled, they're going to cut off their creativity and not be able to wholly experience their responsibilities. Don't simply keep your door open to new ideas, actively encourage and solicit them. Without new ideas, companies die.

Fostering a Sense of Accomplishment

A sense of accomplishment is basic to our human nature. From the time we're toddlers, we want to sense that what we do has some meaning and contributes in some way to the world around us. There is no argument whatsoever that people will work harder and more effectively if they feel that some good will come from their efforts, even if it's a small contribution. The need to feel a sense of contribution never goes away. If people throughout the organization feel they're accomplishing something and each individual has a role to play, your morale will be high.

Recognizing Effort

The topic of affimation is a close kin to recognizing strengths and providing positive feedback in recruiting and retention. It's difficult to maintain an individual sense of accomplishment without some sort of recognition, expecially over the long term. Management sometimes misreads the desire for recognition as a desire to blow one's own horn or have someone toot it for you. We must accept that people want their contribution to the success of the organization to be recognized and affirmed. Recognition is confirmation that what they do is important and helpful, not necessarily validation that they are good people.

Napoleon said that if he had enough medals to distribute to his troops, he could win any war. He didn't mean that he had an army of narcissists. He was acknowledging that the contributions of individuals to the greater purpose or goals of the organization must be recognized. When people expect their efforts will be noticed, they will pay better attention, and the quality of work will increase along with the morale. Remember, high morale goes hand–in–hand with high productivity.

One client of mine understands what makes salespeople tick. His clever technique might not produce results with, say, a computer programmer. But the programmer has his or her hot button too. All you have to do is find it and use it. Salespeople, however, tend to like recognition. My client had a life-size pasteboard cutout made from a photo of every salesperson in his office. Not some of them, not just the top producers—everyone. Each month the top producer's cutout is placed in the window, where it can be seen from the sidewalk. The recognition is obvious. But the other cutouts are not kept at the office. My client has his people take their cutouts home with them. That way the spouses start to ask why they're seeing the cutouts gathering dust in the basement, the garage, or in a closet instead of being taken to the office for their turn in the window.

New salespeople can begin receiving recognition early on, before they've had time to establish themselves. By having the new person give a report to his or her peers on what they've learned about their sales territory as well as the organization to date, you provide visibility and a chance to receive affirmation. You also encourage new people to jump in, meet their peers, and start learning from them as fast as possible. Ninety days in is a good target for making the initial presentation.

Treating People Fairly

The issue of fair treatment relates to the point I made earlier about consistency and discipline. I don't believe there is any evidence that people resent rules and regulations that are appropriate and enforced fairly. Rules and regulations become controversial and divisive when they're unnecessary, inappropriate, cumbersome, and/or expose a double standard.

Our sense of fairness comes from our childhood and is a constant issue as we grow up. If you've been the parent of more than one child, you probably have a keen sense of how children demand fair and equitable treatment. People can handle all types of regulations and controls as long as they prove to be necessary and, more important, are justly applied across the board. Favoritism in any arena will generate resentment and damage morale.

Assigning Responsibility

Just as an individual is motivated by a feeling of accomplishment and recognition, he or she will respond with enthusiasm to the assignment of responsibility. It's important to specify that the responsibility needs to be assigned on the basis of the individual's ability and competence. Loading somebody down with responsibility that is too heavy or out of proportion with the rest of the team will not build morale. In the correct context, responsibility is the raw material of accomplishment and recognition. If responsibility is the alpha, recognition is the omega.

Offering Fair and Appropriate Compensation

Compensation is a litmus test of how honestly management backs up its expressions of recognition and fair treatment. Even though studies prove that recognition and working environment are more important to workers than money, money is still near the top of the list. Appropriate levels of compensation vary with geographical region, type of job, health of industry, level of training, and other factors. However, the bottom line is that compensation, benefits, and incentive plans will either accurately reflect the relationship management has established with the individual team members or expose it all as false and misleading.

The practice from back in the 1990s, especially in high-tech firms, of hiring new workers for more money than company veterans doing the same work, took many of us by surprise. "They can't seriously be doing that" was one of the thoughts that came into my head when I first heard about it. But it was done quite often. Newfangled, high-tech executives and recruiters didn't see anything wrong with it. I mention it here for a reason. The collossal collapse of the dot-coms was due in large part to many a misguided management *faux pas*. If their concept of fair and equitable compensation was any indication, I can only shudder to think of some of the other management gems that ultimately sent billions of investor dollars right down the drain.

Supporting Personal Growth

Personal growth is not an option for successful people and successful companies. It is the opposite of shrinking as a person. When a muscle is not used, it doesn't continue to exist in its previous state. Atrophy takes place. In the same way, if people aren't growing and maturing, atrophy takes place. We begin to forget what we have learned and to slide back into older and less healthy habits. An investment in the personal growth of your people is an investment in the morale and productivity of your organization—and ultimately your success as a leader.

Promoting a Sense of Belonging

Many people spend a great deal of energy trying to isolate themselves from others. I'm no psychologist, but they are not the type of folks you want to build your staff with. People have a strong, innate sense of community, and attempts to run against that indicate problems. A sense of belonging is far more natural and faithful to our human nature. As individuals and as members of an organization dedicated to accomplishing something worthwhile, we want a sense of community. The sense of belonging produces not only improved morale, but also synergy.

There are different strokes for different folks. Computer programmers who are busy writing code, and engineers who are busy making calculations, are not the social butterflies you find among your sales staff. When you're building a sense of community in your organization, remember that there are different comfort levels and different appetites. You need to determine what is a healthy level of participation and involvement for everyone working in your organization. Then do your best to keep them all pulling their oars in the same direction. Helping them encourage each other is also a top priority for the leader.

Providing Opportunity

Opportunity simply means an ongoing sense of being alive with hope for the future. When people sense they have nowhere to go and nothing more to accomplish, they begin to atrophy. Although it's not generally known, some astronauts from the early and middle days of our space programs, especially those with major accomplishments, have experienced tremendous emotional letdowns because there is no sense of opportunity left for them. Younger astronauts have taken over, and those they replaced will never return to the level of adventure, accomplishment, and public recognition they once enjoyed. When opportunity is removed from the picture, morale will dwindle and could eventually disappear.

PUTTING IT ALL TOGETHER

A combination of these and other elements will produce high morale. It would be a mistake to weight each component of morale building equally or expect them to have the same meaning to each and every individual. However, the more of these elements you have and the larger the dosage, the higher your morale and your productivity will be.

THE FIVE LEVELS OF LEARNING

Abraham Maslow wrote that there are four levels of learning. I've listed them for you with the highest level on top and the lowest level on the bottom, in addition to one I added myself. You might prefer to call it a "ladder of learning." The reason I've chosen to hit this element of a high morale environment harder than the rest is because personal growth is a primary factor in whatever we think, say, and do. The levels of learning are:

Level 5—Conscious of Unconscious Competence (my addition)

Level 4—Unconscious Competence

Level 3—Conscious Competence

Level 2—Conscious Incompetence

Level 1—Unconscious Incompetence

Level 1.   At this level, the person is messing things up and is not even aware of it.

Level 2.   Conscious incompetence is the level good old Ticky reached the moment he picked up that hot horseshoe in Orie Hyfil's blacksmith shop. At that moment there was no question in his mind that he had messed up. He was definitely conscious of his error. Others announce when they've reached this level by saying, "Ah-ha. There must be a better way to do this."

Level 3.   Conscious competence is achieved when you're doing things correctly, but you need to focus a great deal of attention in order to remain competent. This is the most exciting level because a person who invests so much focus on a job has either just recently become competent at it or loves it so much that they want to think of nothing else. Doing something you formerly could not do is exciting.

Level 4.   The ability to do something correctly without even thinking about it is unconscious competence. This can become your personal auto pilot. However, there is potential danger here. When a job has ceased to become a challenge, complacency and boredom can set in and quality can begin to drop. You might be a person who has changed jobs in order to find something more challenging. You can challenge yourself right where you are by identifying aspects of your job you don't do well. If you go somewhere else to do the same thing, you will end up bored and changing jobs all over again. When you realize you're at the level of unconscious competence, it's time to make the conscious move to the fifth level I added. Boredom and a lack of challenge drives many people to the door. Most turnover in an organization happens at Level Four, when people are getting less and less stimulation from their work.

Level 5.   Becoming conscious of your unconscious competence reveals a great deal about you. For one thing, it brings you to another crossroads. You have some choices to make. You are committed to stimulating increased excitement about your own personal growth and development. One of the first steps is to identify those areas in which you need the most improvement. When you've identified such a skill and worked to become increasingly competent at it, you bring yourself up through Level Three again. When you once more experience conscious competence, you reexperience the excitement that comes with it. It's exhilarating to try new things that work, no matter how far up you are in the hierarchy.

PUTTING THE LEVELS OF LEARNING TO WORK

Knowing all of this about yourself is important, but understanding it as it relates to your team members is priceless. When you become unconsciously competent with your new skill, it's time to challenge yourself with another area that has been traditionally weaker in your personal inventory. If you need a list of areas in which you can improve and experience the excitement of making new things happen in new ways, go back through this book, begin with the characteristics of a great leader, and work that list and every one that follows, right up through the elements of high morale. There will always be something you can improve, and doing so will energize you and benefit the entire organization.

To reduce turnover, especially at Level Four, and stimulate unprecedented productivity in your people, get to work counseling them on their own growth on the ladder of learning. Learning, growing, and developing are the primary functions of training and continuing education. If your training and continuing education are boring your people to tears and never seem to make any difference in the organization, my bet is that your people aren't climbing the learning ladder. People get excited whenever they learn something new. You might want to make another sign for your wall that says:

What have I tried that's new today?

The more we learn, the more we realize how much we don't know. The result is a world of wonder. The flip side of the coin says, "A little knowledge is dangerous." So, keep learning! As models to organizations, it's important that leaders invest in their own personal growth. Don't expect anyone in your organization to make an investment you're not willing to make. There is a little truth to the saying that it's lonely at the top. It should be more than *not lonely* up there. It should be *exciting.*

KEEPING YOUR TOP ACHIEVERS HAPPY

I've found the following three characteristics in top achievers:

1. They are driven toward self-fulfillment.
2. They love solving problems.
3. They love discovering new and better ways to do the job.

Top achievers are not characteristically patient people when it comes to accomplishment and seeking out new challenges. You therefore need to follow some ground rules to provide them with the most fertile environment possible.

♦ Give them room to grow and develop their potential. When you recognize the difference in ability and ambition among people, don't ignore it. Support their quest for personal and professional growth by subsidizing training and continuing education through seminars, conventions, college, and technical classes, as long as the result helps the person grow and thereby helps the company achieve its goals.

♦ When a major change is about to be instituted, discuss it privately with each of your high performers first. Involve them in decisions whenever possible and at the highest levels practical. Their input and support can make or break your plans.

♦ High achievers, like thoroughbred race horses, enjoy running the race. They want to stretch and strain against their own limits, and they enjoy the challenge of the competition. Make sure you give them those opportunities, lest they get bored. Help them to discover *new* opportunities within the organization when they get too comfortable with the old ones. Encourage them to take on as much responsibility as possible without reaching their point of diminishing returns. Involvement in creative projects seems to have a stimulating and renewing effect on almost everyone.

♦ Don't depend on higher salaries and larger commissions alone to keep your high achievers happy. Money is important. But praise, recognition, and relationships are the very substance of motivation.

♦ Above all, keep the high achievers challenged. The effective leader understands that the driven person needs to keep stoking the furnaces. The fuel will be different with different people. Know your people and keep them in good supply of what drives them.

NINE EASY WAYS TO GET YOUR MORALE CAMPAIGN OFF THE GROUND

Recognizing that everyone is surrounded by individual issues that affect attitude and morale, the effective leader must be as well acquainted with each individual equation as possible. Factors can be negative or positive. The leader's challenge is to multiply the positive influences while minimizing the negative. Factors that influence morale, either positively or negatively, include:

1. Family
2. The training program
3. Economic conditions
4. Peer pressure
5. Relationships with clients and customers
6. Team pride
7. Friendly competition
8. Meetings
9. Counseling sessions

Family: Take Your Objectives into the Home

The family exerts enormous pressure, which can be positive or negative. The families your team members leave at home each morning and return to each evening will be either a major ally to what you're attempting to accomplish or a deterrent. If family members see their loved one coming home frustrated, exhausted, and/or irritable, they might well encourage him or her to leave your company and find somewhere that suits him or her better. One company became aware that new commission salespeople were likely to experience some resistance at home because the rewards are delayed in commission sales, especially at first.

Resistance to the delayed compensation from commission sales might not be the most important issue facing your organization. However, you can probably benefit greatly from what this particular company did to bring the family into the picture: it invited the families to attend an open house where they could become more familiar with how the company operates and the benefits they could expect from having a family member employed there.

This is important not only during training of new employees, but also periodically throughout a person's career. In addition, by sending an audiocassette tape home with the employee during training, including it in the homework for the following day (so the tape is sure to be played), the company sends its plans and benefits right into the home, where the family members are likely to hear them along with the employee. The result of including family members as team members will be increased support and encouragement for the employee's efforts at work.

Having the family respect you, the leader, and the company is a vital asset.

The Training Program: Reach Them on the Ground

The initial and ongoing training program you have at your company influences morale. Make the commitment that your people will never be out of a training program. All of us are constantly learning things, so you might as well invest in an effort to teach those things that will be most beneficial to the organization. The relevancy of your training and continuing education, as well as emphasis on tangible benefits, will help keep your training efforts on the positive side of morale building.

Economic Conditions: Help Them Cope Successfully

Although economic conditions in the country or the world are not under your control, you can help educate your people as to how changes in the economy can and will affect them on the job and at home. You can also smooth over rough economic times by teaching your team members how to sell in a tough market as well as how to budget and manage their own resources. Many people who feel they must earn more money can be helped by some education on how to do more with what they have. This information can help morale at home and, consequently, in the workplace.

Peer Pressure: Make Constructive Use of Peer Relationships

Don't be fooled into thinking that people leave peer pressure behind in the school-yard. Peer pressure is one of the most powerful ongoing influences on the morale of your organization. Peer pressure is constant and can have either a positive or negative effect. This pressure issue prompts me to say that an effective leader must have radar hearing constantly sweeping across the work area to pick up what's being said. The radar is to pick up positive as well as negative comments.

When a positive exchange is heard between two or more of your people, the manager should materialize at the scene as soon as possible to reinforce what's being said, thus building up both the giver and receiver by amplifying the compliment. If negative pressure is detected between team members, the manager needs to appear as soon as possible and say to the negative party, "It sounds like you're having trouble. Why don't you come into my office, where I can listen to your problem and you won't have to burden anyone else with it." About the third time the individual is invited into your office to explain how bad things really are, they might figure out that complaining to peers means a guaranteed trip to the manager's office. You might want to refer back to Chapter 5, where I set up some guidelines for conducting such discussions in your office.

Relationships with Clients and Customers

Clients and/or customers will influence morale in your organization. It's smart to establish creative and effective methods for dealing with customers and clients in order to exert some influence on the degree of influence *they* will have on your team members. I can think of one company that recognized the relationship between customers and employees and addressed the issue right in the reception room. (It's never called the "waiting room.") The company made this area as comfortable as a living room, complete with current magazines and newspapers, coffee, and personal conversation with the branch manager about the client's needs and why he or she had chosen that particular company to do business with. A great deal of helpful information was generated while the customer was made to feel personally cared for. The atmosphere spread throughout the office, and the result was a positive working relationship, which in turn built morale.

Team Pride: Take Advantage of It

Pride in the team is always important to morale. In the office I practically destroyed early in my management career, we ended up with all sorts of plaques and trophies for the excellence we ultimately achieved together. This is important to point out because I learned that when I briefed a new team member in my office, he or she was getting a second important briefing right after that. By seeing the trophies and awards in the office, the new person received a clear message that excellence was *expected* in that organization. The evidence of our success as a team provided a nonverbal but extremely effective briefing. The Brag Book I described in Chapter 3 is an excellent form of nonverbal briefing.

Friendly Competition: Use It to Build Esprit de Corps

Contests are a fun way to keep everyone focused on the goals of the organization. While they're most common in sales organizations, they can be effectively used in many other situations as well. If it's important to complete a design with minimal flaws in a short period of time, prizes for accomplishment might help keep everyone pulling in the same direction. If creativity and new ideas are called for (which they should be anywhere), contests can help bolster those efforts as well.

No matter what you do, make it fun and rewarding, with both immediate gratification—such as a prize—and long-term benefits. I learned the hard way that if you shout long and loud enough about something you feel needs attention, you'll probably be put in charge of the committee to deal with it. That's what happened with the way our company ran contests. I complained and promptly got the job of coming up with new ways to run contests.

COX'S CONTEST RULES

Here is my list of Cox's Contest Rules that we built many successful contests around:

1. Develop a theme that reflects the goals and objectives of the organization. Use a name that is a good metaphor for the nature of the desired accomplishment.

2. The contest should target the middle 60 percent of your staff. The top 20 percent are fired up without any assistance, and the lowest 20 percent require more motivational effort on your part than you'll ever get back in productivity.

3. The length of the contest should be consistent with the goals sought. It's important to keep the contest shorter rather than longer to avoid losing

the intended emphasis. Sales contests should typically run from 30 to 45 days. If you're going to run a longer contest you'd better have your doctorate in Contest Promotion. People don't stay interested forever.

4. Keep the rules simple. Each person should receive a printed copy of the rules as well as a list of the prizes. It might be good to send these to the employee's home in order to involve the family. Publishing the rules in newsletters, on Websites, and posting them around the office will also help.

5. Make sure the prizes are worth working for.

6. Make it fair to all by using appropriate handicaps based on past performance.

7. Set goals just out of your team's reach but not out of their grasp. In other words, they can't achieve the contest goal without extra effort.

8. Have numerous winners. First place through fifth, for example, recognizes the efforts of more than just one person. If there's only one prize and one person leaps ahead early on, the rest of the people will lose interest. If it's a team challenge, the whole team should share equally in the prize.

9. Offer a choice of prizes for each winner, to generate more incentive because of the increased personalization. The first place finisher wins this or this, the second place finisher wins this *or* this, and so on. Be careful when using money as a prize, so you don't inadvertently create a morale backlash after the contest is over. Trips are better prizes.

10. Give each person the opportunity to be recognized for his or her efforts, even without receiving one of the big prizes.

11. Promote the contest prizes with enthusiasm. If the leader has no interest in the contest, neither will the staff.

12. Keep promoting throughout the length of the contest, not just at the kickoff. The team has to think that this may be the most important thing currently in your life.

13. Keep an up-to-date contest progress display in the office as a reminder of how things are advancing. If your team is scattered geographically, use daily E-mails.

14. Send out flyers during and after the contest, announcing the leaders and the winners. This works well, especially when someone who might not be expected to perform competitively is leading or doing well.

15. Announce the winners when you originally promised to. Always make your announcements as close to the end of the contest as you can. If you don't, the impact is weakened.

16. Take pictures of the winners with their prizes or on their trips, to use in promoting the next contest.

17. Keep a file of past contests with the rules, participants, results, etc., including how well it succeeded in reaching its goals, to review when developing new contests. Relying on your memory for what worked well and what didn't is not enough. Complete your critique of a contest as soon as it ends and file it.

18. Major contests should not be held more than twice per year. You don't want to condition your people to feel that everything the organization does is intended to win a prize. A healthy working atmosphere is an ongoing prize for everyone in the organization.

Meetings: Use Them to Boost Morale

Even if your organization never has occasion to hold contests, you probably have regular meetings. Meetings are another major factor in the morale of your organization. The more frequently you hold them, the more you must concentrate on the effective elements of good meetings.

There are time-tested techniques for effective meeting planning. Begin a planning book in a three-ring binder or in a special computer file. The sections should include:

♦ *Themes for the future and support materials* can come from a variety of sources. You can clip ideas out of newspapers and magazines. This works very well if the media starts to talk about a "coming downturn." Your people will appreciate two or three meetings on a strategy that will help get the team through the slowdown, in case it actually happens.

♦ *Personal experiences* will help to illustrate and support the goals and objectives you're seeking in your organization.

♦ *Attention getters* should be listed in your meeting planning book and/or file. I once put a head of cabbage on the table in front of me to illustrate how I was going to help my salespeople to make more money. Of course, they initially equated cabbage with money. However, I regarded CABBAGE as an acronym for: **C**lose **A** **B**uyer, **B**e **A**ggressive, **G**entle, and **E**nthusiastic. It made them focus on my message and think. Another good attention getter for *salespeople* when teaching telephone techniques was to wrap a telephone on the desk with one-dollar bills or tens or hundreds to illustrate how important the telephone is in selling.

♦ *Places to meet* should be varied in atmosphere, to keep the meetings interesting. Try to match the environment with the issue to be discussed. I know of one sales manager who met with his people one out of every four times at his home, which was set beautifully near a golf course where the atmosphere was relaxing. This meeting also confirmed to team members that their leader lived by a philosophy that provided a great lifestyle.

◆ *A list of speakers* other than yourself should be kept in its own section or file in order to give you some variety and remind you who is available to make presentations to your people.

◆ *Past meeting notes* should be kept in their own section or file so you can be clear about what's been covered at each meeting and how successful it was. With good meeting notes to refer to, you can quickly tell if progress is being made or if you're covering the same information over and over again. If you are, adjustments need to be made.

With the help of your meeting planning book, lay out your meeting plan:

1. Pick a *theme*. It can be a play on words, a challenge, something funny, etc.

2. Select *points* to support the theme and form the outline for the discussion.

3. Add *support material* for each point: how a person can use this information, why these ideas work, etc. Use illustrations or personal experiences whenever possible.

4. Preselect three to four *key questions* to ask your people, the answers to which should reflect the theme you've chosen. Asking questions is a way to break the ice and get the meeting started. Questions also help tie information learned together at the end. Use them wisely.

5. Select *attention-getting devices*.

6. Prepare *visual aids* for the meeting.

For a 45-minute meeting, the manager should spend two to three hours preparing throughout the previous week, not the night before. Arrive an hour before the meeting is to begin. Arrange the chairs in the room to maximize everyone's attention and minimize distractions. Arrange everything else in the room with the same purpose in mind, including projectors, handouts, visual aids, name tags, etc. Have the coffee and refreshments ready to go well in advance so as not to delay the start of your session. Music is a great way to set a lively tone for a meeting while people are coming in and getting settled. Once your people are there and the meeting begins:

◆ It's not necessary to start a meeting with a joke. Too many people do and stumble right out of the gate. *Be yourself*, and leave the jokes to professional comedians. Use your attention getter instead. This is also the time to use your opening questions.

♦ Be sure to *talk with* your people, not *at* them. A good meeting has the tone of a discussion rather than a lecture.

♦ *Always expect the unexpected.* There is usually one sort of distraction or another at every meeting. The best way to keep your crowd's attention is to walk away from a distraction in the room and get quieter, rather than moving toward it and getting louder.

♦ *Stay relaxed* throughout the meeting. You'll appear more friendly and credible.

♦ Plan a *powerful close* that includes an inspirational challenge with a quick word of appreciation and thanks. I've been known to say, "We can do it. We have a strong team. I love working with all of you. You make my job easier. Now, let's go make something happen."

To ensure that you're conducting the best meetings possible, do a self-critique after each one. It's helpful to tape the session and listen to it later. After you listen, answer these questions:

1. Was I really prepared?
2. Did I start the meeting on time?
3. Did the people respond freely and easily to my questions?
4. Did I keep the meeting on track?
5. Did I refrain from lecturing or playing the expert?
6. Did I maintain a healthy control of the meeting?
7. Were distractions handled properly, without magnification?
8. Did I keep their interest throughout?
9. Did I make full use of visual aids and other tools?
10. Were the outlined points covered thoroughly?
11. Did I answer everyone's questions clearly?
12. Did the majority seem to enjoy the meeting?
13. Did I give them something to think about?
14. Did I close the meeting on time?
15. Did I learn something from the meeting? If so, what?

Counseling Sessions: Use Them to Teach and Motivate

The individual counseling session is one of the least understood yet most powerful tools a leader has to educate and motivate his or her people. A counseling session is a prime opportunity to initiate many positive changes. People want to change most often because:

1. They're uncomfortable with the current state of affairs. When the pain gets bad enough, they will commit to making something new happen.
2. They simply want a change because they're bored with the same old way of doing things.
3. They get excited at the discovery that things *can* change.

Many managers fumble the ball and miss a great opportunity at the last point. When you see a positive change and the resulting increase in morale and productivity, don't sigh and say, "Thank God for small favors" and then move on to something else. The moment something new and positive happens is the moment you should congratulate the team member and introduce that person to another possibility and then another and another and so forth. People get excited about their own growth and the leader should feed that excitement.

ONE-TO-ONE COUNSELING SESSIONS

Individual counseling sessions can be a powerful tool to educate and motivate people. Here's how to go about it:

Pinpoint the Skill to Be Worked On.   Perhaps you're aware that one of your people is having difficulty with time planning. Before that individual arrives for the counseling session, make a list of ways you think he or she could better utilize time.

Start the Session on a Positive Note.   Put your list aside until the person has arrived, you've closed the door, and thrown sincere bouquets at him or her about how much improvement there's been since the last counseling session. Praise that person's success. Talk about the improvement. Make no other comparison than to his or her individual growth since the previous session.

Establish Your Understanding of the Personal Situation.   Talk to that person about why they're working so hard. Talk about their goals. What are the time frames involved? If a son or daughter is going off to college in a few years, that's a measurable length of time in which to accomplish some things. Then break down the goals into easily understandable units. For example, how much money needs to be set aside to get the son or daughter through college? Break down the goals into smaller units to demonstrate how much you understand their unique situation.

Reveal the Area Targeted for Improvement.   Introduce areas that can be improved only after you've established how well you understand the situation and have helped that person to get excited about his or her ability to reach desired goals. Always remember to *attack the problem, not the person.* Your purpose is to open the door to discussing issues where this person needs improvement, not to shut them off with negative criticism. Tell the person you're counseling that you have some ideas to help them reach the goals you've been discussing sooner and/or with reduced effort. Do this by using the person's own strengths (see Chapter 3), which you have carefully analyzed. By introducing time-planning ideas as if they're your own, you're not telling the person that he or she is lousy at time planning. If you do that, you'll get a mental door slammed in your face every time.

Keep on Track.   Once you've opened the discussion, follow some rules to keep you on track:

1. Get to the point quickly.
2. Describe the problem you want to correct.
3. Listen to how the employee describes the problem.
4. Get agreement on what the problem really is.
5. Explain your ideas on solving the problem.
6. Have the employee sum up the problem and the solution.
7. Schedule a follow-up meeting on this issue.
8. Schedule your next follow-up session.

Item seven is not the next monthly counseling session, but a "How's it going?" kind of follow-up. A follow-up on the issue you've discussed is vital for several reasons. First, you need to see if there's any improvement, and the sooner you find out the better. Second, the employee needs your feedback if there is no improvement, and he or she desperately wants recognition if there is improvement. Schedule a follow-up session one week later at a specific time and keep your appointment. Imagine the letdown your employee will suffer if there is improvement to be celebrated and your secretary calls to reschedule. The leader has to make every effort to support the efforts of his or her people to improve, especially when requested to.

Come Full Circle/Set the Stage for Monitoring.   Finally, at the close of your counseling session, bring the discussion full circle by returning to the individual's stated goals. Reminding that person of how the new information discussed will promote the accomplishment of those goals will open the door to monitoring. Once the importance of, say, time management has been established, ask if that person wants a reminder if you notice old habits threatening the progress he or she has made. The employee will no doubt encourage you to monitor his or her growth in that area, thus opening the door to further coaching for improvement.

IF SOMEONE WANTS TO QUIT

If you've shown leadership in your hiring, it would be contradictory to neglect leadership in retention. I'm sure many people reading this might feel that some of my methods are melodramatic and lack professionalism. To some they might even smack of manipulation. I can almost hear voices saying, "It's not worth it. If they want to quit that badly, who needs them?" or, "That's ridiculous. These techniques would never work with my people." To these folks, I say a leader must believe in the value of working for his or her organization.

I have used the process I'm about to describe more times than I can recall, with tremendous success. So much so that I had a reputation of turning people around as they were headed out the door. Some people have to be drowned in affirmation to counteract their innate sense of failure, and once turned around, they are new people who are changed forever. Some of my brightest, long-term superstars went through this process with me and went on to tremendous success with our organization.

The 90-Day "I Want to Quit" Syndrome

Termination techniques are tools of leadership counseling and better serve for keeping employees than for getting rid of them. Once again, I'm referring to managing salespeople. However, with minor recalibration, these principles have broad application for virtually all staffers in a wide variety of organizations. A recent study confirmed a phenomonon I labeled several years before: the 90-day "I want to quit" syndrome. For whatever reason, some employees tend to lose sight of the future payoffs of a job and become overwhelmed with a sense of hopelessness approximately three months after joining the company.

The "Drown Them in Affirmation" Approach to Employee Retention

If you've been managing for very long, you've had team members enter your office before announcing that they've decided to resign. These are usually extremely good people you don't want to lose. When you hear the words, "Can I see you for a minute?" you start to sweat; *unless* you have a plan such as the one that follows.

USE THE ELEMENT OF SURPRISE

Once inside the office, the individual says something like, "I don't exactly know how to tell you this, but I've decided to leave."

At that point, you say, "Congratulations and welcome to the team!" By then the employee's mouth should be hanging open and you know you have his or her undivided attention. The person might think you didn't hear correctly and tell you again that he or she is leaving your organization. Tell them you not only heard correctly the first time, but you anticipated this conversation because *everybody* gets these feelings about 90 days into a new job.

Communicate that what they're experiencing is common for people in their circumstances. You can point to someone else in the organization—for this example, let's call her Kathy—who has experienced a similar dilemma, survived it, and is doing very well. Through means of identification, the individual in your office might no longer think that such feelings are unique to them and go back to work. But it's usually not that easy.

APPLY THE CONVEYOR BELT PRINCIPLE

The individual in your office might acknowledge that, even though others had similar feelings, they still want to leave. Then it's time for you to explain what I call the "conveyor belt principle." This principle states that all of the work someone has done to date is in process, and even though the fruits of labor are not presently evident, a little more patience will soon be rewarded. If this person understands the virtues of waiting for the benefits to cycle back to him or her, yet still insists on going, it's time for the heavy artillery.

PLAY YOUR TRUMP CARD

Say to this person, "Now I'll have to assign somebody else to carry on in the area or territory where you've been working so hard. They're going to enjoy the benefits you should be receiving for the hard work you've invested."

It's human nature to want rewards and recognition for work we have done. Nonetheless, your employee might be really set on leaving. What then?

IF ALL ELSE FAILS ...

If all else fails, it's time for "the grass is always greener on the other side of the fence, but it's just as hard to cut" segment. You say, "Why do you think you're going to be happier or work more successfully at a second or third choice employer rather than here at your first choice of companies." (Be sure to emphasize the word *first*.) Hopefully, your employee will realize that grass here is just as good as grass anywhere else. Of course, you might have an individual on your hands who has his or her mind set on leaving. To him or her the fact that it is new grass is reason enough. What do you do then?

TAKE IT TO THE TEAM

Use your top people to influence the one who wants to leave. Look at the employee standing in your office and say, "I've invested a great deal of coaching and counseling in you, and I want you to help me protect that investment by granting me one more hour; not 90 days, but one more hour. Have lunch with Kathy and me." Kathy is the person whom you identified earlier as the individual who once had the same desire to leave but thought better of it and went on to become very successful within the organization.

Your deal with Kathy is to buy lunch if she will share a personal 90-day, "I want to quit" syndrome experience with the person leaving. The lunch hour itself will be one of the most difficult hours you will ever endure, because you must keep your mouth shut, except to eat. You've set the scene. Now you must let Kathy sell the person on the folly of leaving after only three months. It should be clear that the person leaving hasn't considered all the angles yet, and peer pressure is hard to refute.

CALL FOR A MORATORIUM PERIOD

If, at the end of the lunch, the individual is still leaving, take him or her back to your office and say, "You've been working hard. Take two or three days off and get away with your spouse to the desert, the mountains, the river, the ocean, or wherever you want to go and think about what you want to do with your future. After that come back and tell me if you still think your wisest choice is to leave. If you still feel this way, we'll process the papers at that time." If the person has truly been working hard, the time off will sound like a little piece of paradise.

IF YOU VALUE A PERSON, ALWAYS LEAVE THE DOOR OPEN

If the person comes back after the time off and still wants to quit, do you process the papers? Not quite yet. First say, "The reason I hired you is because I sensed some real potential within you, and I believe it's still there. I hope the new manager you're going to work for sees that same potential. If he or she doesn't, you'll be losing valuable time in your career. So, give your new job your best shot. But don't forget to stop by from time to time and have a cup of coffee with me. I'll want to know how you're doing. Should it turn out to be less than you expected, don't hesitate to pick up your stuff and come on back home." Yes, use the word *home*. Say it softly. But it will ring in their ears.

If you've done your job right, you should have that person in tears. They might even soften enough to admit that your organization does feel a little like family. Your final hurrah should be a sorrowful account of how you'll have to go out and tell the rest of the "family" that this person is leaving. If the 90-day "I want to quit" person elects to stay with you, chances are good they'll never try to leave again. The process is simply too emotionally exhausting to experience twice.

THE FAREWELL INTERVIEW: MORE THAN JUST GOODBYE

In spite of the long and arduous process I just described for keeping good people on the job, it's important for the leader to diagnose, because the departing individual might be a symptom of widespread dissatisfaction among your staff. If the individual has weathered all of your attempts to keep them on the job, your focus should turn to the farewell interview as a study in how to make improvements where possible within your organization. Even if they elect to stay with you, there's a message in the fact that they wanted to leave in the first place.

EVEN TERMINATIONS SERVE TEAM GOALS

Although it might sound strange, the first order of business in the farewell interview is for the leader to explain the long-term goals for the organization. Then you ask the person who's leaving to help you achieve those goals by answering a few questions. It's often best to do this over lunch or somewhere outside of the office, where people feel less inhibited and more likely to talk freely. Ask them:

1. What are your long-term goals?
2. Why did you pick this time to leave?
3. What did you like most about this job?
4. What disappointed you the most?
5. How does your spouse and family feel about your work and this company?
6. Why did you pick our organization in the first place?
7. What are you being offered there that you can't get here?
8. How do you feel about the training you received?
9. How could we have helped you more?
10. Did we let you down in any way?

If you really want this person back, be sure to ask what can be done, if anything, to get him or her to return. Listen carefully to all of the information they give you: It's invaluable in developing a sense of what people are thinking and experiencing inside your organization. What if the person is gone and you would still like to get him or her back? Even though they might be working for someone else, all is not lost.

MAINTAIN POSTTERMINATION CONTACT

Send a handwritten note each month to that person's home. Be honest and say you hope things are going well and you're pulling for him or her to fully realize the potential you always felt they possessed. Invite them to stop by your office to say hello whenever possible and share some conversation over a cup of coffee. Keep these letters going for at least three months, because this is the time period over which that person and their spouse are going to be questioning the decision to make the move. Your letters convey to the former employee and his or her family that you still care and take a personal interest in their successful future. Chances are, your concern will exceed that of the manager for whom they're currently working.

IF THE PRODIGAL RETURNS, ENLIST HIM OR HER AS AN ALLY

If the former employee decides to return, kill the fatted calf and have a celebration. Never say "I told you so." Everyone in the organization knows the person left, so let everyone in the organization know that they have returned. Introduce the returning team member at meetings, post the announcement on bulletin boards, on the Website, in newsletters, everywhere you can. The message should be clear to others in your organization tempted by the "grass is greener" syndrome that you value your people ... *really* value your people. Where else will they get that? Now you have another Kathy who can assist you with personal testimony the next time someone else decides to leave.

TIPS FOR IMPROVING MORALE FOR EVERYONE

SEND A LETTER OF RECOGNITION TO THE EMPLOYEE'S HOME

Include the team member's family as much as possible in recognition for solving a particularly difficult problem. Since the family has heard a great deal about this problem too, it helps to acknowledge the employee's support base and the contributions family members make to success at work. You often see schools involve the family in recognizing quality efforts by students in the classroom. Taking similar action for quality work in business follows the same principle. People sometimes wish their spouses or children were more aware of what they do on the job. This technique helps not only to inform the family, but also to bring them into the picture, which increases their respect for you as a leader.

CALL YOUR EMPLOYEES AT HOME ON THANKSGIVING

Wishing your people well and acknowledging their family life keeps the leader and the team members more conscious of the important link between an individual's personal and professional lives. Any way a leader can show respect and genuine compassion toward the people in the organization will result in a more positive and productive atmosphere and higher morale.

TAKE ONE PERSON OUT TO BREAKFAST OR COFFEE EACH WEEK

The point of spending some time away from the office one-on-one is to communicate clearly that you have an authentic interest in your people as individuals and that you are not merely applying a new management technique. I constantly encounter situations where managers are instructed to take a more active role in their employees' affairs. The result is, managers simply make rounds and ask questions to which they really don't care to hear the answers. Or they emerge from their offices at the appointed time each day to mechanically slap everyone on the back and then disappear into their offices again. People know if your interest is real.

RECOGNIZE EMPLOYMENT ANNIVERSARIES

Many companies are good at awarding some sort of trophy, pen, watch, trip, or other token of appreciation when a person reaches a milestone in his or her tenure with the company. You can easily program electronic personnel files to remind you when a person has reached an anniversary. In fact, it can become so easy that many recognitions of this type become mechanized and lack personal meaning. Even the big boss from your corporate headquarters taking a person out to lunch to award the trophy can be a stuffy experience if you don't give the recognition proper attention and priority.

I applaud and encourage these methods of recognition, as far as they go. However, all of these efforts on the part of management will only seem as genuine and rewarding as the pervasive quality of the day-to-day relationship between a leader and his or her people. A fountain pen placed in the hands of someone who truly feels appreciated will mean more than a Hawaiian vacation presented to someone who is bitter over being a number for so many years.

ENCOURAGE PEOPLE TO PERSONALIZE THEIR OFFICES

Whether or not your people receive clients in their offices or are in highly visible positions will present some limitations on how outrageous decorating can become. However, within reason, it's always to your benefit as well as the individual's benefit for all of your team members to be as comfortable where they work as it is for them to be comfortable with what they're doing. An effective leader wants his or her people to be as personally invested in their work as possible and helps create a familiar and comfortable environment that promotes comfort and productivity.

Care must be taken to avoid one individual's tastes becoming offensive to others. As a leader, you're a sort of a village chief who needs to protect the best interests of the greatest number of people in the organization. Making people conform to cookie-cutter images and placing them in little identical cubicles might appear to increase productivity and order, but it will probably cost a great deal in morale and individual enthusiasm.

ENCOURAGE OUTSIDE ACTIVITIES SUCH AS FITNESS

The more ways you can help your people express themselves and more wholly experience the multiple dimensions of life, the stronger your morale is going to be in the workplace. Not only is physical fitness a worthwhile goal with positive benefits at work, but the sense of positive fellowship and community sets a tone that carries over into the work environment. Sports is not the only form of organized activity. Encourage people to form car clubs, hiking and camping trips, theater and movie clubs, and so on. The more you can encourage people to invest in activities that reflect their personal interests, the more completely they will open up to creative and innovative developments at work.

TAKE THE RAP ON OCCASION FOR GOOD PEOPLE

The two key words here are *occasion* and *good*. Even your best people are going to stumble once in a while. If you're willing to step in and bail them out instead of allowing them to suffer alone, people are going to understand how much you appreciate the good things they do. This should not be a regular practice, nor should you bail people out who don't deserve it. That would send a very different and less positive message. It might even be a slap in the face to your people who try harder. The well-placed and well-timed intercession on behalf of someone who is a solid contributor will make a stronger statement than almost any other gesture.

PROMOTE COMMUNITY PROJECTS

Businesses don't exist in a vacuum. Your team members and customers probably live in the same community. The community could be a neighborhood or the world. Regardless of the scope of your effort, it's important to promote community involvement among your people. You can offer company facilities for community meetings, blood drives, scout meetings, Bible studies, CPR training, and a wide variety of activities that reflect the needs and quality of life in your community.

Donations and sponsorship of worthwhile causes are also important. We are known by our actions as business people just as we are known by our actions as individuals. It's best to involve team members at all levels in determining how and to what extent the organization will become involved in supporting the community. You'll be proud when you see some of your people featured in the local news media.

ARE PHOTOS AND STAND-UPS FOR EVERYBODY?

As I mentioned earlier, some companies put a portrait or life-size stand-up of high achievers in the lobby or some other prominent place. Beware, most workplaces are not filled to the brim with narcissists that like to look at themselves. As a leader, you must be sensitive to whether public recognition might make your people nervous or self-conscious. Being aware of individual feelings within your organization can help minimize embarrassment or, possibly, help prevent team members from intentionally lagging behind in order to *avoid* being put on display.

RESERVED SEATS

By setting aside special seating in meeting rooms for high achievers and rotating the honorees each month, you can ensure that each achiever feels a sense of recognition in front of his or her peers. You'll also be promoting a sense that their ideas are receiving special attention in staff meetings. Take-home name cards on chairs give that impression of special treatment too.

VIDEO RECOGNITION

Use high technology to produce a *Day in the Life of (So-and-so)* for a super high achiever. Present the program as a gift. Put it on your Website. By making a small production out of an individual's activities, you're not only honoring them, but also reaffirming those aspects of their efforts that are most beneficial to the organization. This type of gift gives the individual the opportunity to share his or her accomplishments with friends and family. A video gift can also be used to reward an entire department. Don't forget, your company newsletters and newspapers are other valuable media resources for recognition as well.

TRINKETS, TICKETS, AND OTHER GIVEAWAYS

Concert, movie, or sporting event tickets make good prizes for individual or team efforts. T-shirts, coffee mugs, mouse pads, or other items with appropriate mottos, slogans, and/or personalized congratulations are appreciated in direct proportion to the amount of personal investment the leadership has in the individual or team effort. Sometimes, when recognition is in order, an advertisement in an appropriate trade or general publication extends your sincere congratulations.

LOOK BEHIND THE CURTAIN

Don't overlook the contributions of those people whose tasks might not be as spectacular or visible as others. A good policy to adopt is to recognize someone in a nonvisible support role every time you recognize someone in a more visible position. Recognize them together whenever possible, to promote the awareness among your people of how synergy works and how the efforts of everyone in the system contributes to the big picture.

KEEP AN ACCOMPLISHMENT YEARBOOK

Establish an annual publication that details who did what over the past 12 months and sets the tone for the upcoming year. Include pictures and case histories. This is a good opportunity to deliver much needed recognition in the context of the organization's overall goals. The impact of the annual publication can be increased by associating awards with it and even an annual awards dinner.

IN THE NAME OF ...

Another clever idea is to name a space or an object in the building with a small sign for someone who is a deserving recipient. Such acknowledgment can range from naming a cafeteria after someone who is an inspirational leader for everyone in the organization, to naming the photocopier after the secretary who has a special knack for keeping it running. This is another way that the workplace can be personalized while, at the same time, providing recognition.

There can be as many ideas for a list such as this as there are creative people and concepts. Your own situation might well give rise to other means of providing recognition. Don't forget: The most reliable source of information when it comes to what makes your people feel appreciated is your people.

CONCLUSION: DON'T FORGET NUMBER ONE

If the organization gets better after the leader gets better, then the leader needs to practice what he or she preaches! I've spent a great deal of time establishing the need for leaders to model the principles they set forth for others to follow. Morale and overall attitude are probably the most important examples a leader can set. I'll go so far as to say the leader's morale and attitude, positive or negative, is the most powerful force at work in any organization.

The leader not only sets the mood and the tone for the entire organization, he or she establishes the momentum. If leaders aren't as invested as they expect everyone else to be, all the speeches and trophies in the world won't improve morale. Even worse, if the leader's heart isn't in it, the speeches and trophies are resented for their hollow and manipulative nature. Your people will most likely respond positively to the same things you do. I had an employee once who told me her favorite feeling came after solving a tough problem. I felt the same way, but wasn't aware of it until *she taught me.*

The most powerful way I know for anyone to improve his or her own morale is to climb out of the rut they find themselves in when they insist on repeating yesterday. Top achievers not only love to solve problems and seek self-fulfillment, but also enjoy the search for new and better ways to get the job done. Improved morale at the top stimulates creativity and carries with it a productivity enhancing momentum.

Here are some practical methods for you to use to achieve higher levels of self-fulfillment and enhanced personal and professional growth for yourself:

1. Lay out a new list of goals. Be sure to break down each goal into daily tasks to assure accomplishment.

2. Go for a walk in the park, on the beach, or in the mountains. In short, get away to your own thoughts and hear what they have to say.

3. Read several books on a variety of topics to stretch your mind around someone else's thoughts and ideas.

4. Get away for the weekend, to a luxury hotel or spa, and pamper yourself and your significant other.

5. Exercise and get into better physical condition.

6. Buy something for yourself you've always wanted.

7. Invite interesting people who are not in your field over to your home for dinner.

8. Listen to good music and sing along at the top of your lungs.

9. Get your office and/or home totally organized and enjoy the moment.

10. Go see a funny movie.

11. List your assets and achievements.

12. Talk to somebody who always makes you feel good.

13. Take up a hobby.

14. Give help to someone who needs it. Invest one percent of your 16 waking hours of the day (approximately 10 minutes) in making someone else happy.

15. Take two five-minute mental vacations to renew your energy. Do this just before lunch and just before you leave for home.

If you can't manage to get yourself out of your bad mood by the time you reach the office, pull a 180-degree turn and get out of there. The last thing your people need is a leader with an infectious bad attitude. Remember, positive or negative morale begins with the leader. Everything in this chapter is first and foremost for you, the leader!

CHAPTER SEVEN

THE FIFTH STEP: CREATIVITY WHEN THE HEAT'S ON

The [person] who follows the crowd will usually get no further than the crowd. The [person] who walks alone is likely to find himself (or herself) in places no one has ever been before.

Creativity in living is not without its attendant difficulties, for peculiarity breeds contempt. And the unfortunate thing about being ahead of your time is, when people finally realize you were right, they'll say it was obvious all along.

You have two choices in life: You can dissolve into the mainstream or you can be distinct. To be distinct you must be different. To be different you must strive to be what no one else but you can be.

Alan Ashley-Pitt

WHEN THE HEAT'S ON, CREATIVITY IS YOUR FAN

When the heat is on, creativity is a necessity, not a luxury. If what you've been doing has not kept you ahead of the competition, you're probably in the hot seat. Treating creativity as an option is probably what helped to create the pressure you're under. As Ashley-Pitt pointed out, creativity is not always greeted with open arms in an organization, which tends to throw a wet blanket over creative thinking. Nevertheless, when old thinking gets you into trouble, you need new thinking to get you out.

Among other things, creativity lays the foundation for solving problems and managing change. It's important to understand what creativity is, how it helps you to be the most effective leader possible, and how you can stimulate it in your organization. I have never met anyone who wants his or her organization to dissolve into the mainstream. As I share ideas, methods, and techniques on creativity, bear in mind the goal is to be distinct in realizing your full potential and the potential of those you lead.

Creativity and the Coffee Bean

George A. McDermott, Jr., in the *Executive Idea Stimulator*, put it this way:

> *One day ... a long time ago ... in, say, a million B.C., somebody figured out that you could put things in water and boil them, throw out the water, and eat the things.*
>
> *(Somebody also figured out that that was called cooking, but that's minor-league creativity.) Cooking was very nice, but it was still a relatively new invention, and they hadn't worked all the bugs out yet. For instance: coffee beans, even after people cooked them, still tasted crummy. So, everyone gave up on coffee beans ... until some genius had a flash of inspiration. "Hey, maybe cooking doesn't always work the same way," he said. "Sure, the beans taste lousy, but we haven't tried drinking the water we cooked them in."*
>
> *If that doesn't sound like significant genius to you, ask yourself: Have you tried eating coffee grounds? Would the taste inspire you to drink the water?*

CHARACTERISTICS OF THE CREATIVE MIND

1.   Childlike sense of wonder

2.   Consistent openness to alternatives

3.   Unthreatened by new ideas

4. Eagerness for the future

5. Ability to test new ideas

6. Ongoing flexibility

Childlike Sense of Wonder.   Do not believe that you're not a creative person. Creativity is not a genetic trait. Anyone can develop creative abilities by understanding what creativity is. For example, a creative person is, first and foremost, curious and inquisitive. They are likely to read, travel, and explore a great deal. The creative person is likely to have some unique hobbies. Creative people truly enjoy the childlike experience of discovery.

Consistent Openness to Alternatives.   Creative people don't find satisfaction in limited alternatives. They want to discover as many alternatives as possible.

Unthreatened by New Ideas.   This can be a challenge for leaders who have creative people in their organizations. If you don't decide at some point which alternative to go with and refocus your people's attention on new tasks, they will keep coming up with new alternatives indefinitely. The good news is that a constant openness to new alternatives will often lead you and your organization out of the proverbial woods, especially during a forest fire.

Eagerness for the Future.   Some people stifle their own creative potential by caving in to fear of the unknown. You probably encounter several self-stifled people every day. You could probably even name names. For whatever reason, these people believe that what they're currently experiencing, as unpleasant as that might be, can't be as bad as an unfamiliar alternative.

In contrast, creative people feel that, however good the present is, there is always a better future waiting to be discovered. They are not threatened by the unfamiliar. Creative people seek the excitement of discovering the previously unknown. To creative people, the future is already familiar and comfortable. Creative people are drawn forward into uncharted territory by an eagerness for the future. To them, what lies ahead is more intriguing than the present.

Ability to Test New Ideas.   Henry Ford said, "Some of our best ideas have come from letting fools rush in where angels fear to tread." Don't encourage your people to be timid angels when it comes to creativity. There is plenty of time to be angelic when your organization gets involved with community service projects. The "fools" Mr. Ford talked about are really just normal people with permission to be a little unconventional when the urge strikes them. Eva LaGallienne said, "Innovators are inevitably controversial."

As an effective leader, you should see to it that creative people get quality feedback on their ideas, not criticism. Creative people are eager to test new ideas to see how they work. You could say the moment of truth or the peak of excitement for a creative person occurs when they actually try a new idea. A major joy in the creative process is seeing a new idea work. Of course, to truly creative people, as soon as a new idea works, it becomes an old idea. In an organizational context, it's always good to get feedback from others before a new idea is launched, providing the feedback does not block or stifle the creative impulse.

Ongoing Flexibility.   Creative people are not typically married to any one concept or idea. They rarely develop sacred cows. Where less creative people tend to cling desperately to the past or existing ideas, people who are more creative are willing to scrap something that doesn't work and move forward. Flexibility is driven in part by curiosity and eagerness for the future, and maintained by the sheer delight of moving on to new things when the opportunity arises.

FIVE FUNDAMENTALS OF CULTIVATING CREATIVITY

If Henry Ford and Eva LaGallienne are correct, creative and innovative people might be thought of as controversial fools. If you've experienced resistance or criticism during your creative moments, don't be surprised or discouraged. The more flack you receive, the more creative you must be. In spite of all the potential difficulties, you should be committed to creativity because you realize it's an essential component of personal and professional success. Here are some ways to go about becoming more creative:

1. Schedule more uninterrupted private time

2. Use the *kaleidoscope* approach

3. Be gullible

4. Anticipate mental conflict

5. Continue to look at far-fetched ideas

Buy Yourself Some Thinking Time.   When my boss told me he was looking for my replacement, I took some private, uninterrupted time to be by myself at the beach. At that point I was at a loss as to what to do. I didn't have any of the information then that I'm sharing with you now. Even though I initially stumbled across the correct action to stimulate my creativity, I can now recommend such isolation to anyone who is experiencing major problems. Most people in the heat of battle will feel they can't abandon the fight. Believe me, staying in the struggle with no good ideas or anything else to offer won't accomplish much.

You need to place more distance between you and the problem, not less. It's possible to lose perspective by staying too close to difficult issues. Going to seminars doesn't accomplish this. Going on crowded cruises won't do it either. In order for isolation to have a positive effect, your mind needs a chance to clear itself and get beyond the everyday clutter

Unrelated Pieces in Motion.   I often recommend to partners in a company that they get away to a mountain cabin together and write out a description of their company five years into the future. Isolation allows you to observe your situation through a longer lens. You can actually see the life return to someone's face after he or she has managed to put some distance between themselves and the problem. You can then return to the struggle refreshed and with something new and valuable to offer.

Remember looking through a kaleidoscope as a kid, watching the colors and shapes tumble and change? I look at creativity the same way, as pieces floating around in no particular order or formation. When I start to move the pieces around in my head, exciting thoughts begin to form. Tedi refers to my creative time as "being on the mountaintop" even though I'm usually in my own library. If you have the pieces in motion but haven't seen a good picture yet, keep turning the pieces. It will happen if you give it enough undistracted time.

Go Against the Grain of Skepticism.   Being gullible is like being the unconventional fool who rushes in where angels fear to tread. Don't be afraid of being fooled or being called foolish. Many people simply never allow themselves the luxury of being wrong. The fact is, we're wrong most of the time if we're committed to being creative. It's those rare moments when we're right that make the world go round.

No inventor has ever had more successes than successful failures. People who are afraid of being wrong don't trust new ideas. The creative person trusts every new idea until there is a solid reason to reject it. Just think of what a different world this would be if great inventors and pioneers throughout history didn't trust ideas others held no stock in. Don't give up your new ideas just because others might find them unorthodox.

Pressure Accompanies Progress.   Anticipate mental conflict during the creative process. Anticipate it so strongly that if you don't experience any internal or external conflict, you can assume you're not as invested in the creative process as you might think. Dr. Robert H. Schuller tells us that conflict is the "birthplace of creativity." A personal inventory of your life would probably reveal that when you experienced the greatest conflict you were also the most creative.

Unfortunately, many people stare helplessly at a conflict and say, "Woe is me." That's when you need to throw the conflict logs on the creativity fire, because there can be no progress without pressure. You can carry the argument a step further and say that moments of conflict are when you are most effective as a leader—if you have the appropriate commitment to creativity. I know many readers are scratching their heads right now and thinking that, given the amount of heat lately, they must be especially creative and not even realize it.

Be Careful Not to Throw Away Ideas Too Hastily.   Look at illogical and far-fetched thoughts with credibility. The reason most people so often dismiss a new thought is that it doesn't fit neatly into the existing scheme of things. Remember that all of those illogical thoughts rolling around in your kaleidoscope will eventually fall together in such a way as to create a great new idea. Just because an idea doesn't immediately present the entire answer doesn't mean it's not a part of a larger solution. Don't discard a thought that might serve as a springboard into a new idea.

KNOW WHAT MAKES AN IDEA SUCCESSFUL

The fellow I learned these principles from lost his job as a young newspaper reporter because he "lacked good ideas." His editor back in Kansas said that he was "void of creativity." Nobody knows the name of that editor, but almost everyone in the world associates the young reporter's name, Walt Disney, with creativity. In order for anything to become successful—a book, a company, a movie, yes, even leadership style—Walt Disney said that it must have (1) a *uniqueness* factor; (2) a *word-of-mouth* factor, and (3) a *flair* factor.

Uniqueness Factor.   The first criterion for your creative endeavor is to make sure it's unique. Why should anybody get excited about something that's ordinary? Walt believed that, unless something is truly unique, there is no reason to go out of your way for it. The question to keep asking throughout the creative process is: "How is this different from what I'm already doing?" or "How is this different from what the competition is doing?" Or you could ask: "How is this going to make things different in the future?"

Tapping into Natural Excitement to Generate Word-of-Mouth. The word-of-mouth phenomenon Walt lists results from the excitement people feel when they discover something unique. When people have a positive new experience, it's virtually impossible to keep them quiet about it. It could be a new book, a movie, a car, a piece of furniture, a pair of shoes, or anything else that makes a significant impression because of an unexpectedly pleasant experience. The big question we should ask ourselves in business is: "Am I a unique and positive experience to the people I work with or sell to?" If the answer is yes, you are successfully integrating creativity and uniqueness into your relationships. And the people you work with or sell to are probably talking you up to others.

Capitalizing on the Flair Factor.   The flair factor Walt Disney talked about means doing it *big,* doing it *right,* and giving it *class.* Something that is truly unique and generates the enthusiastic endorsements of others should be done with style. There are various reasons why people can be impressed with an idea. Some might be impressed with how well-planned it is. Others might be impressed with how effective it is. Others might be impressed with the image it conveys. Overall, people want to associate themselves with something classy.

FOUR-PART PROCESS FOR CREATIVITY ENHANCEMENT

I think of creativity as the "voice beyond silence." I've already talked about isolating yourself to experience a clear mind. In the silence of isolation will come the voice that is creativity. I built the library onto my home because I collect rare books, and that library has become a retreat for me. There are times when I can go into my library and induce creativity. There are other times when I stop eating in the middle of a meal and start taking notes because thoughts have begun to erupt.

Whether you're able to induce creativity or it simply happens when the time is right, the following four-step process will help you make the most out of your creative experience:

1.   Preparation
2.   Incubation
3.   Insight
4.   Verification

Do Some Homework.   If your intention is to create a new product or method for doing something, it's important to learn everything you can about that subject. In other words, do your research. Too many people think the birth of a new idea is enough. To make the new idea more meaningful, you must *prepare.* When Thomas Edison wanted to get creative in some aspect of his varied interests, he read about other people's experiments in the same arena. In doing so, he learned from the mistakes others made and didn't have to repeat as many failed experiences. He put pieces that other people came up with into his kaleidoscope along with his own before he started turning them. If you look only at your own knowledge, your picture will be that much less complete.

Give New Ideas Time to Incubate.   A new and creative idea begins to cook in the incubator. Once it's born, it needs time to get a grip on you, and vice versa. The incubator is a mysterious place. Nobody is sure why ideas grow in there, but they do. Have you ever pondered a new idea only to sit up bolt upright in bed at two in the morning with the completed picture clearly before you? The incubation period is a time when ideas take root or wither. Whether the idea takes root or withers is beyond our control. That's why, when an idea is incubating, we're not able to actively or consciously manipulate it. The kaleidoscope will often turn itself while we sleep. When the correct picture appears, we are awakened instantly.

Eureka! Await and Recognize the Moment of Insight.   Insight is the moment you receive a new idea. That moment when you sit bolt upright in bed is a moment of insight. We sometimes refer to insight as an innate quality some people possess. We're really saying that person has discernment. Insight is that glimpse of the suddenly clear and illuminated answer.

Coming Down to Earth to Objectively Confirm the Worth of the Idea.   Verification is not as much fun as being creative. Creativity flourishes in a mythical, mystical environment with no boundaries. The process of verification brings it all back to reality and begins to establish boundaries. It's difficult to exist in both worlds at the same time. Fantasy and reality don't mix well. Nevertheless, any idea born in the realm of creativity must be brought into the world of reality before it can be of any use to anyone. Therefore, verification, although not very entertaining, is a necessary evil if we intend to benefit from creativity.

THREE STEPS TO VERIFYING A NEW IDEA

1. Suitability: Will it solve the problem or simply be a *stopgap*?
2. Feasibility: Is it *affordable* and *practical*?
3. Acceptability: Who will *support it*?

Is It Suitable?   When evaluating the suitability of an idea, you must first determine if a permanent solution is required or if a temporary fix will suffice. This doesn't mean that every creative idea needs to be a solution to an existing problem in order to be valuable. But it is important to determine if the idea has long-term or short-term implications. When a problem exists, you must ask if the idea helps to bring about a solution. When the idea is not problem-related, it's still important to determine what tangible benefit the idea might produce. Is the idea *appropriate* for the organization?

Is It Feasible?   Feasibility is really an issue of ability. You and your team need to answer the question, "Can we do it?" When budgets meet effort, there can be a great deal of discussion. The leader shouldn't determine the suitability of an idea independent of his or her team members. I recommend including your people in decisions that affect them. An effective morale killer is the autocratic decision that an idea is doable. Few things are more annoying to people than to receive an assignment without any input. Managers might be more concerned with costs than the other team members. However, the practicality and amount of effort involved with carrying out a new idea directly affects the people in your organization. Like you, they are feasibility conscious.

Is It Acceptable?   *Acceptability* raises several questions, including:"Who has the final word on this? Will the people who have to carry out this idea accept it? Will this idea have a positive impact upon the people that matter most?" It's not hard to see how acceptability for some people might not matter if other, more important, people don't accept the idea. The people who say yes or no need to accept an idea if it's going to become reality. The people who have to carry it off must accept it if their efforts are going to be productive. The ultimate beneficiaries must accept the idea if everyone else's acceptance is to mean anything. The verification process can be summarized like this:

"Will it help?"

"Is it doable?"

"Will they buy it?"

DISMANTLE THE FOUR GREATEST BARRIERS TO CREATIVITY

Knowing what blocks the creative process is helpful to any leader committed to being as creative as possible and to developing and encouraging creative growth in every team member. If an individual or group of individuals seems to resist creativity or simply won't engage in creative activities, chances are that one or more of these four blocks to creativity is operating:

1. Habit
2. Fear
3. Prejudice
4. Inertia

We've Always Done It This Way.   Habits are hard to break, assuming we even *want* to. Some people will tell you they're just not creative. What they mean is that they're more comfortable with how things have always been than with how good things truly could be. Habits mean hanging on to the status quo. The result is to continually repeat yesterday, which we've already determined is the opposite of growth and creativity. The rallying cry of habit-bound people is: "We've *always* done it this way."

Why Can't We Leave Well Enough Alone?   Fear often explains why we stick with habits and other repetitive behavior longer than we should. You hear people constantly cautioning others that it's better to "leave well enough alone," or, "If it ain't broke, don't fix it." As I've already mentioned, many people opt to remain in an uncomfortable, yet *familiar* situation rather than take the risks involved with venturing into the unknown. Fear of what *might* happen keeps some people immobilized far more than fear of something known. Talk of "pushing the envelope" can send these people into cardiac arrest.

That Won't Work Here.   Fear and ignorance frequently team up to form prejudice. As I travel across America promoting creativity and new ideas, I encounter a great deal of prejudice. Prejudice exposes itself when you hear people say things like, "That wouldn't work here," and, "Our people wouldn't buy into that," and, "Our customers wouldn't like that." I hear some form of prejudice in almost every organization I speak to. After I've delivered my message and moved on, I get letters from virtually every organization saying, "Hey, it *does* work here!" Every letter like that makes me proud to be a "prejudice buster."

Don't Rock the Boat.   This is the rallying cry of the filter builders. Inertia stops creativity cold. If our fear is strong enough to immobilize us, we'll hesitate to make any move or to shift our weight in such a way that might rock the boat. Heaven forbid if we should tip too far and get wet. We would have to climb back in the boat. Even if an organization is following a specific road with its creativity, it's important not to exclude the possibility there might be other directions worth exploring. This is especially true of individual growth and creativity.

STORYBOARD YOUR CONCEPT

A tool that helps launch ideas into concrete actions is the storyboard. The concept of storyboarding is not new to people who create film and video productions. I learned it from someone I met two weeks after my boss announced the search for my replacement. At that moment I was receptive to almost any new idea that came in my direction. Mike Vance, creative consultant and author of *Think Out of the Box!* (coauthor: Diane Deacon), had worked for nine years with Walt Disney, who is credited with developing the storyboard concept. Mike was the first dean of the Disney University.

A storyboard is usually a large bulletin board with the title of the project across the top. Disney might have used one that said, "Mickey's Day at the Park." With the storyboard posted, his creative people could walk by and see the title. Immediately, images would come to mind about what Mickey could do in the park. The creative people would go away and sketch their ideas, bring them back and pin them to the storyboard. Walt would then call his creative people together and conduct what was called a "gag session." During the session they would put the ideas together and form a story, noting what the strong points were and where they needed to fill gaps.

A Case in Point: The Rain Parade

It was Walt Disney who realized that storyboarding could be useful for more than making cartoons. The storyboard method was used for everything from finance to development of new attractions for the theme parks. Several years after Disney died, Walt Disney World in Florida was ready to open. Mike Vance was walking through the nearly completed park with Walt's brother, Roy Disney, when Roy noted that, unlike in sunny southern California, it rained a lot in Florida.

Roy Disney was concerned that rain might drive guests from the park. My friend had an inspiration after one of the shortest incubation periods in history. While they were still walking down Walt Disney World's Main Street, he suggested having a "Rain Parade." Roy looked at him quizzically. Mike went on to suggest that when it rained, people could stand on the covered sidewalks and watch this special parade instead of going home. Roy said he liked the idea and told Mike to start a storyboard to develop it.

The result was yet another innovative Disney concept that turned a negative into a positive. Once the storyboard was in place, the ideas came flooding in, so to speak. One person in the organization suggested that the costumes for the

Rain Parade not be waterproofed, so the crowd could see the characters having fun getting wet. Such creativity! They were so successful at turning a negative situation into a positive one that visitors to the park who saw the Rain Parade went home and told others about it. The word-of-mouth popularity of the Rain Parade was testimony to the creativity of the organization, aided by the storyboard process. Where else would people tell their friends they hoped it would rain during their vacation?

The same type of creative genius was used on the West Coast when Disney imagineers developed a method for keeping people at Disneyland on cool summer evenings. Almost everyone in America has seen or heard of the Main Street Electrical Parade. The parade was promoted all day long, which made it impossible for parents to drag their kids through the exit turnstiles before they watched the parade. Once again, the storyboard technique brought many creative minds together in an environment where creativity is not only allowed, but also encouraged and rewarded.

How to Storyboard in a Business Setting

After my good friend Mike Vance shared the concept of storyboarding with me, I began applying the concept in my office and at home, and later, when I was promoted to the position of district manager, with my managers. Before they heard me saying "Let's Rain Parade it" every time a problem came up. "Let's take all of these negatives and turn them into positives," I would say. They thought I was off my rocker at first, but soon the departments were bringing in their storyboards, and new ideas were popping up everywhere. Managers don't want to show up at meetings with a blank storyboard if they've been given the task of gathering new ideas.

When the leader knows what methods and techniques to apply, negatives turn into positives, and conflict produces creativity. Any significant issue facing us became the title for a storyboard. We had our own gag sessions and began to string new and exciting ideas together into workable plans. Often our creativity was challenged because of the company's limited budget for creative projects. But that didn't stop us. We just employed a little more creativity.

One of the reasons storyboards work so effectively is because they keep the issues up in front of people in a way that always keeps the issues in the conscious mind. It keeps the project "in your face" and not hidden in a computer. Usually, in a business situation, the ideas that go up on a storyboard are written on index cards. However, ideas can come in the middle of the night, at a restaurant, at the ballpark, or anywhere and at any time. Don't be surprised to see storyboards with napkins, the back of envelopes, torn-off corners of team rosters, or almost anything else that can be written upon pinned up.

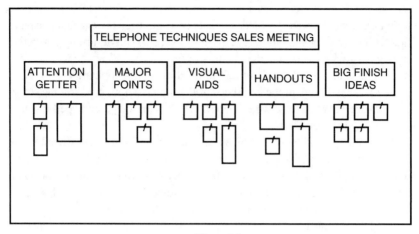

Figure 7-1.

In Figure 7-1 you see a storyboard for a sales meeting on telephone techniques. The project title is bannered across the top. Smaller strips of paper are used to classify the subsections that make up the project. For a recruiting storyboard, the columns might be titled: Career Night, Brochure, Advertisements, Competitors' Ideas, Hall of Fame, Brag Book, and other categories where we want to create new ideas. Many people ask me why I want to be constantly reminded of my competitors' ideas. The answer is that their ideas act as a stimulus for us to top them. In other words, a "burr under our saddle."

Don't expect people to line up outside of your office to contribute creative ideas. Unless your business is driven by creative activities, like Walt Disney's company, it's likely your people will have to be encouraged to participate in "idea storming." The team will be more apt to contribute ideas once they've seen you use it to creatively complete a project.

One company I worked with on storyboarding provided each of their salespeople with a little pocket-size flip chart of all the objections they were likely to encounter on the telephone as they were setting up appointments. All the salesperson had to do when they heard the objection was to spot it on the index, flip open the chart to the appropriate page, and be reminded of the best response. There was also a section for appointments and a record of how the call went. The entire flip chart concept was the result of a storyboard process. As you read the following chapters on solving problems and managing change, remember that storyboards are invaluable to these activities.

Keep in mind that storyboards on sensitive topics should be kept at home so the information developed won't be disruptive to your team. Another type that should be kept at home are storyboards for any meeting or celebration you are planning for your people. You don't want to spoil the surprise.

"IMAGINARS" FOR SYSTEMATIZING TEAM CREATIVITY

Walt Disney had his imagineers; I developed what I came to call "Imaginars" in place of seminars. These weekly meetings with my managers were, appropriately, held in our district's Imaginar Room. While most companies were having seminars, we were having Imaginars. A sign that hung in our Imaginar Room read:

NONE OF US IS AS SMART AS ALL OF US.

Our theme was a constant reminder that no one individual could offer as much as the corporate effort of the entire group. My people went in there with the express purpose of discussing solutions to problems and creating new ideas to put into action. Creativity was not only allowed, it was encouraged. Creativity was our first order of business. When we really wanted to dig deep into ourselves for ideas, we rented a room in a local resort and got away from the clutter of daily activities. We covered the walls with flip chart sheets filled with thoughts and ideas we later verified and put into practice. A typical scenario for such an Imaginar would be:

♦ Seating around tables set up in a U-shape

♦ A large flip chart on a tripod, with wide-tipped marking pens in varied colors

♦ Pads and pens for each attendee so an idea could be quickly jotted down in case someone else was presenting an idea

♦ Masking tape to hang up flip chart sheets that were filled with responses

I would begin with a topic such as "Unresolved Problems" and then ask them to give me any and all of these problems in no particular order. (Prioritizing came later.) Responses generally started slow but picked up speed. When there was no room left on that sheet, we tore it off and taped it to the wall. When the input slowed to a crawl, I asked them to get up, walk around the room and read each response on every sheet.

Then the two-part prioritizing process began. The first thing was to decide what problems should be considered as being in the Top Ten. Once that was decided, the second part of the process started by picking number one, number two, and so on.

The next step in the Imaginar was to storyboard the number one problem. The board was labeled and the subtopics were selected. Then ideas were asked for. Often, the problem couldn't be totally solved, so we took the board back, to continue working on it at our next weekly managers meeting.

We found that a genuinely creative environment allowed us to go beyond the ordinary, everyday questions that most business people ask themselves and to go deeper into the real meaning behind what employees and customers said they wanted and needed. As a result, we were able to gain a much better perspective and solve problems more effectively and permanently. Major issues that faced our company, such as a high rate of turnover in salespeople, dropped dramatically.

Another company I consulted wanted to start a franchise, but to avoid the type of failure some franchises have experienced. We held an Imaginar, got down to the core issues facing a franchise attempt, and really had a handle on the proposition before the company proceeded.

Another situation called for the development of a training program for sales-people who were moving into management positions and one for managers being promoted into a job where they would be managing managers. This Imaginar focused on what happens when a team member leaves the job he or she knows well and steps up a notch into an unfamiliar managerial position. We began by gathering a group of first-line managers and upper management. Some had been managers for two or three years, but others had made the transition to manager just a few months before. I asked them for feedback on what they remembered as difficulties during the transition. The list we compiled in the Imaginar that day became the structure for the company's new management training program. Storyboards were used to build the lesson plans.

The following list of their responses in the Imaginar is in no particular order:

Hiring
Firing
Time planning
Assuming a leadership role
Going from doer to delegator
Learning to think like a manager
Family and lifestyle adjustments
Being the example for the office
Learning to be impartial and just
Blending authority with empathy
Knowing when training is needed
Learning to deal with bureaucracy
Coping with the flow of information
Gaining the respect of team members
Understanding profit and loss and ROI
Understanding operations vs. administration
Coaching individual team members' strengths
Being looked at by team members as the company
Selling the company for recruiting and/or retention
Helping team members stand on their own two feet
Setting priorities for the office and the organization
Being held responsible for the department's success or failure
Shifting focus from individual production to office production

Helping people learn when and how to use their own creativity
Shifting focus from sales or production volume to the bottom line
Handling the difference between the perception and the reality
of management

All of these issues and more came from the managers themselves. That made them real problems as opposed to problems that executives might guess their managers are facing. The Imaginar and storyboarding techniques not only helped identify these challenges, but also produced solutions and recommendations from the managers themselves. People are always more receptive to ideas they had a hand in formulating. We took the Imaginar up to another level and excused the managers so that the managers of managers could run the same exercise. Some new issues emerged:

Being consistent
Keeping promises
Coping with conflict
Promoting managers
Counseling managers
Being unafraid to innovate
Teaching emotional control
Creating a management pool
Selling change in a positive way
Selling the company's big picture
Giving authority with responsibility
Developing one's own replacement
Helping managers grow and develop
Selling the company way to managers
Setting realistic goals and expectations
Making the office manager feel important
Balancing empathy with company policies
Recognizing the right people the right way
Understanding and working with superiors
Understanding and coping with competition
Developing independence among managers
Selling team members through their managers
Creating a leadership image and living up to it
Keeping an overly ambitious person on the team
Managing upward and downward communications

It takes people facing similar challenges to bore deep into identifying problems and their solutions. Imaginars can include a wide diversity of individuals from different departments and/or different levels of management.

The wide-open Imaginar is likely to produce wide-open ideas. When you need to focus more on a specific area or group of individuals, then participation becomes more restricted. As you can see from the lists, managers face a certain set of problems, and the managers of managers face a more highly developed set of challenges. In both cases, the same people that identify problems and potential problems also identify solutions—if you give them the creative license and atmosphere.

CONFIDENCE IS SEXY

It's not possible to turn every meeting into an Imaginar, but you can continually introduce new and innovative ideas to stimulate creativity and imagination. One of the techniques that I developed was to invite competitors to selected meetings, often year-end meetings, when I brought in well-known professional speakers. The very thought of inviting competitors makes some people feel faint. But it works. Showing how proud and positive you are about your team to their competition pumps up your team members' confidence and encourages them to focus on the organization's strengths, unique factors, and competitive advantages. Some of the best people from competing firms see what a dynamic organization you have and want to get on board. Like actor Jack Palance said in an aftershave commercial, "Confidence is sexy." Our confidence impressed customers, staff, and competitors.

SHARE THE WEALTH (OF KNOWLEDGE)

Having your managers make regular presentations to their peers helps stimulate an atmosphere in which we all learn from each other. Sharing experiences about how others run their offices can help managers feel less intimidated by many of the problems they face. Knowing that others are up against similar roadblocks somehow shrinks the barriers and makes them more manageable.

Encouraging managers and team members to come up with their own ideas for speakers and presenters can result in unusual and unexpected learning experiences. But nothing beats the full-blown Imaginar for unleashing creativity. You need to encourage and reward the innovative thinking that your people are capable of. The Imaginar provides a system and a structure to do just that.

BE UNIQUE

Your people and your organization are unique. Use the Imaginar process to explore that uniqueness. This information is valuable in a number of ways. Remember the gutsy move I described in Chapter 3? When interviewing potential new employees, I used to hand them a list of unique factors in our organization—a list my team members and I compiled in Imaginars. I confidently suggested to our potential new employees that they take the list with them as they interviewed with our competitors. Just giving them the list to begin with impressed the new recruits. They usually came back even more impressed and told us that our competitors had very little to offer them in comparison. It takes creativity to uncover your uniqueness and put it to good use. Figure 7-2 lists the five basic rules for conducting an imaginar.

FOSTERING A CREATIVITY-INDUCING ENVIRONMENT

Creativity flourishes in an environment of:

♦ Experimentation

♦ Playfulness

♦ Spontaneity

Creativity Calls for Experimentation

Experimentation is risky business. Creativity can create heat for the leader by stimulating up pressure *and* down pressure. A leader is likely to meet resistance from his or her team members as well as those higher in the organization. The thought of doing something new or different terrifies some people and makes

---

Basic Rules for the Imaginar

1.   *Set a time limit* so that you don't wind up wasting your group's efforts by not completing the process. Give the group enough time to spin new ideas, but then move along to organizing and verifying the ideas as well.

2.   Don't begin the verification process too soon. *The quantity of ideas is more important than the quality of ideas* during your idea gathering phase.

3.   *Avoid criticizing, complimenting, or questioning ideas* during the idea gathering phase. You don't want to chase good ideas back inside of people's minds for fear of embarrassment or feelings of inadequacy.

4.   *Encourage free-wheeling and piggybacking.* One person's idea can stimulate thoughts in someone else. Keeping the proceedings orderly and linear can stifle creativity.

5.   After the idea gathering phase is completed, *prioritize the top 10 ideas* prior to beginning the verification process.

Figure 7-2.

the rest nervous. Yet the leader courageously asks, "Why don't we try this?" The answer is almost automatic from his or her people: "Because we've never done it that way." To me that's just not a valid reason to block creativity. Yet, you'll hear it nearly every time a new idea is mentioned, if not in so many words.

The larger the company, the more likely the manager is going to be pressured from above not to venture out in new directions or to adopt new methods and techniques. During the years I spent working in a large organization, I was told many times not to alter course. So I learned to fudge a little. When the chiefs came around and asked what I was doing, I told them I was doing what we had always been doing. My answer pleased them and they moved on. Yet, in those early days, I used to wonder why, when the old ways resulted in poor productivity, upper management continued to discourage new thinking and approaches.

After telling upper management I was doing things the company way, I met with my team members and said, "This is what we're really going to do." Sometimes my team members looked at me with trepidation, but got excited when our new ideas started to show results. They were beginning to develop a spirit of adventure! Then, when upper management came to visit again and praise us for our improved productivity, I gently let them know what we were doing that had produced the positive results, and they gradually began to loosen up.

So don't be surprised when you race into a corporate meeting saying your organization needs to try new things and they look at you "like a new dog at the bowl." People don't want to hear that stuff, at least not at first. There is long-term value in being discreet and diplomatic. Softening the hearts of upper management and your own staff to creativity takes a gentle hand, not a sledgehammer.

Creativity Calls for Playfulness

An "environment of playfulness" simply means an environment that grants permission to have fun. In fact, it encourages people to have fun with what they do. Urge your people to play the "What if?" game and kick new ideas around. Some bosses will catch people brainstorming a new idea and demand they quit goofing off and get back to work. What poor, misguided souls. Their people were engaging in one of the most valuable exercises to improve production, and they were nipped in the bud. One of my mentors once told me, "Don't just do something. Sit there!"

Creativity Calls for Spontaneity

Take the "What if?" mind-set seriously. Keep the door to new ideas open constantly. Encourage innovation whenever possible. I know a retail merchant, Stew Leonard, who started what he calls the "One Idea Club." Each month, Stew selects about a half-dozen employees, making sure every job level and description is represented regularly, and drives them as far as two hours away to observe a store where customers are served well. The next day, the team that traveled together meets and each team member stands up and shares one new idea learned on the trip to use in their own store. This is another good example of sharing best practices among team members.

Stew Leonard has become a close friend over the years, and I admire his approach to all of the best practices in organizational life. Stew asked me to assist his daughter, Jill Leonard Tavello, in setting up Stew Leonard University, better known as "Stew U." Jill is the dean of this school that presents regular half-day seminars for business people representing hundreds of industries from around the world. They come to see why Stew Leonard's Dairy Store is a legend in customer service and was picked as number 22 on *Fortune* magazine's "100 Best Places to Work."

Stew is a strong believer in recognition and he spends time and money to make sure everyone in his organization is recognized on a regular basis. His three stores in Connecticut and New York have almost 3000 employees. Each issue of the company newsletter, called *Stew's News,* contains pictures of hundreds of his employees. Perhaps that's why *Inc Magazine* dubbed it "the ultimate company newsletter." Stew's way of doing business could fill a book all by itself. But more important to Stew and his staff, the way they do business *fills stores with customers.*

A FINAL CALL TO CREATIVITY

In my discussion of creativity and its value to any organization, I've covered characteristics of a creative person, environments where creativity flourishes, how to become more creative, what makes ideas successful, the creativity process, how to verify a new idea, what blocks creativity, and how to turn negatives into positives by invoking the Rain Parade theory and Imaginars. The thread running through all of these topics is *creativity.* Creativity is a stimulant to growth, increased production, and enthusiasm. Organizations need new ideas to grow. Organizations without growth begin to die. There couldn't be a better time than right now to tap the vast reservoir of potential in you and your team.

The best way to sum up this chapter is to quote from an Apple Computer ad campaign with the theme "Think Different." Perhaps we should all commit this piece to memory. Here's to the Crazy Ones:

> *Here's to the crazy ones.*
> *The misfits. The rebels. The troublemakers.*
> *The round pegs in the square holes.*
> *The ones who see things differently.*

They're not fond of rules.
And they have no respect for the status quo.
You can praise them, disagree with them, quote them,
Disbelieve them, glorify them, or vilify them.
About the only thing you can't do is ignore them

Because they change things.
They invent. They imagine. They heal.
They explore. They create. They inspire.
They push the human race forward.

Maybe they have to be crazy.
How else can you stare at an empty canvas and see a work of art?
Or sit in silence and hear a song that's never been written?
Or gaze at a red planet and see a laboratory on wheels?

And it's these people who are crazy enough to think
that they can change the world, and they actually do.

(Used with permission and blessings of Apple Computer Co.)

CHAPTER EIGHT

THE SIXTH STEP: PROBLEM SOLVING WHEN THE HEAT'S ON

"The world is a grindstone. Life is your nose."
Fred Allen, Humorist

A SHORT, TRUE-LIFE PROBLEM-SOLVING ADVENTURE TO SET THE TONE

My radar observer and I were tumbling out of 56,000 feet, wing over wing and out of control, when I remembered that three out of eight F-101 Voodoo crews before us had survived a pitch-up similar to this. But this wasn't a standard pitch-up. No one had pitched up at this high an altitude before. We had entered a nonstandard pitch-up called "inertia roll coupling," and our chances were getting slimmer by the second. I was aware that I had a problem requiring immediate attention and a creative, lifesaving solution. The heat was on! If ever I needed to be unorthodox and creative, this was the moment.

The manufacturer had supposedly built safety systems into the Voodoo to keep this from happening. As this 70-foot-long, 45,000-pound mass of metal tumbled toward the earth like an enormous rock, I had news for the manufacturer. A thought flashed through my mind. The Air Force had told me, "Don't worry. The safety systems will never let you enter a pitch-up." Right.

The negative "g" forces from the high-speed rolls (the airplane rolled at 400 degrees per second) were so strong that the blood vessels in my eyes started to rupture. I was on the verge of a red-out. I was the pilot-in-command and the fate of my aircraft and my radar observer was my responsibility. My radar observer was a tad concerned, as you might imagine. He might have thought I was incredibly brave to stay with the aircraft and attempt to save taxpayers several million dollars. Or he might have thought I was just plain stupid with an obsession to play the heroic jet jockey. He would have been wrong on both counts.

The truth was, the negative "g" forces had me about two inches out of my seat in spite of my 3-inch-wide lap belt and shoulder harness. The explosive charge (equivalent to a 35-mm cannon shell) that propels the seat clear of the aircraft during ejection would have been moving before it hit me. My spine would have been crushed by the impact. So I attempted to keep my radar observer calm while I figured out how to get us out of the mess.

As we tumbled toward earth I first attempted to fight the roll by forcing the controls in the opposite direction of the rolls to regain control. No good. In desperation, I figured that this fighter was designed to fly. Therefore, I needed to get air flowing over the control surfaces of the aircraft. I stopped fighting the controls and neutralized them.

I said the pilot's prayer very quickly as I reached for the T-handle to deploy my drag chute, normally used on landing. It worked. As we passed through 30,000 feet, about five miles below where the tumble had started, the added drag helped to get the air flowing over the aircraft and I was able to pull out and successfully return to base. As it turned out, the only damage to the aircraft was a bent drag chute door and a battered canopy. Both had to be replaced. The drag chute had caught with such force when I deployed it, the lines had actually bent the metal back. As for the canopy, my crash helmet had battered the inside of the Plexiglas so badly it was no longer usable. The unfortunate part was that my head had been *inside* the helmet as it repeatedly and violently banged off the canopy, resulting in more than a two-aspirin headache.

Here's the lesson for the leader in any field: *Don't fight your problems with brute force.* Sometimes you have to neutralize the controls and pop the drag chute.

LESSON 1: ALLOWING SOMETHING TO WORK AS DESIGNED USUALLY GETS BETTER RESULTS THAN PRESSURE

Thankfully, that near-death experience had helped me to become an effective problem solver under pressure. If I had continued to fight the controls, I would have still been fighting them as we made a "smokin' hole" in the desert. Only when I backed off and helped the aircraft do what it was designed to do did we succeed in solving the problem. The same thing applies to the people in your organization. They want to do a good job and propel the company toward its goals. When the heat's on and you're tempted to start forcing your imperial will upon them, it's time to back off and remember what things you and your people do best.

Maybe that's why I went to the beach when my boss told me he was looking for my replacement. Forcing the controls had not worked. Forcing them harder would have been counterproductive. Give the people in your organization room to solve problems. Use supervision, not surveillance. Surveillance builds an unhealthy feeling of "Big Brotherism."

Managers can be the number one source of problems in the organization. The problem-solving leader must remember that when the heat's on, for whatever reason, it's usually a result of unresolved or unanticipated problems. Make sure the people in your organization can come to you with problems before they get out of control. When they do come to you, listen. A great thought from *Cosmopolitan* magazine says that if you come to your boss early with a problem, you gain a partner. If you come late with a disaster, you get a judge.

I've talked about problem solving as a beneficiary of creativity. However, problem solving is such a major priority for the leader, it's important to devote an entire chapter just to that process. Someone once asked: "Why can't we be exposed to all of life's problems when we're 19 years old and know all the answers?" Unfortunately, problems are with us from the cradle to the grave. What marks a truly great leader is the acquired skill to solve problems effectively. Like so many other things in life, we get better at problem solving with practice. The healthiest organizations are those that are best at creatively solving and/or anticipating their problems.

LESSON 2: KEEPING A HUMOROUS PERSPECTIVE CAN LITERALLY BE A LIFESAVER

John Burgess, manager of the Briggs Cunningham Museum, tells the story about Rusty Roth and Chuck Yeager and how spontaneous humor brought Rusty back from the brink of disaster. It seems that Rusty was flying an XF-91, which was the first afterburner fighter, and Chuck Yeager was flying a chase plane. These two guys were fishing buddies who often scouted for early thawing mountain lakes during their flights.

Anticipating the great spring fishing, they bought thousands of worms in several big "flats," only to discover the thaw was still a few weeks off. Neither Rusty nor Chuck wanted to take care of the worms, and they shuttled the bait back and forth between their houses, usually in the middle of the night.

During this time, they continued to fly, Rusty in the XF-91 and Chuck flying "chase.". One day Rusty was putting the XF-91 through its maneuvers and wound up in a deadly vertical dive known as an "aerodynamic lock." He couldn't pull the fighter out of the dive. He literally had his feet on the console in the cockpit and was pulling on the stick with all his might. Chuck called him on the radio and gave him suggestions. Rusty answered, "I've already tried that. It doesn't work." It was no use. He was a goner for sure.

Knowing full well the "gravity" of the situation, Chuck said to his friend over the radio, "Rusty, what am I gonna do with all them damned old fishin' worms?"

Rusty pulled out of the dive—laughing!

Although I've had my share of narrow escapes in supersonic fighters, I'm sure glad that happened to Rusty and not to me. Humor causes us to look at things differently than we usually do. It also releases energies we don't know we have. Rusty's miraculous escape proves it. You'll be surprised at what it will do for you in the face of your problems.

PROBLEMS HAVE THEIR UP SIDE

Some benefits rise out of crisis. The Good Book says we should be thankful for problems because crisis builds character. I'll go one step further and say that crisis also helps to identify character. Churchill said, "You can tell the character of the person by the choices made under pressure." It's important for leaders to observe how each of their people responds to crisis. Who stays cool under pressure and who doesn't? Who is best at taking the heat and acting effectively to resolve the crisis? Are different people adept at handling different types of pressure situations? Know who's who in your organization as well as you're own problem-solving strengths and weaknesses.

A few months ago I had the opportunity to fly an F-16 Falcon through the sound barrier and up to a little over 1000 mph followed by some aerobatics. Yes, it's like riding a bicycle—it does come back to you. The pilot-in-command, was explaining from the front cockpit about the heads-up display that we could both see. It shows all the information that formerly was available only by looking down into the cockpit at the instrument panel. He went on to explain how it showed the status of each of the members of his flight, what tactical maneuvers they were doing, the condition of each fighter, and the fuel status in each airplane. And all that while he was seeing what was going on around him without being distracted. Wow!

Good leaders have to build their own heads-up display that allows them to know the exact status of each team member as well as what the current situation is, without being distracted. Meeting problems head-on develops your organization's ability to resolve problems over time. The more you do it, the better you become. This doesn't mean you should arbitrarily allow or encourage problems to develop. Every time a problem is confronted and licked, it should be a character-building education for you and your entire organization. Part of getting better at problem solving is getting faster at it. An organization that has been learning from its mistakes and problem-solving experiences will have a capacity for accelerated corrective action.

A problem that remains unresolved long enough eventually become a crisis. A smoldering issue won't get as much attention as a house on fire. If leaders and team members, for whatever reason, are unaware of the smoldering issues, there will eventually be a fire to put out. I realize it's a stretch to see a positive side to unresolved problems. However, one good thing about a crisis is that formerly unresolved problems will finally be handled.

People who solve problems develop increased self-confidence. A certain amount of empowerment comes with the experience of solving problems. The problem itself has an initial amount of power that's proportionate to the amount of disruption the problem is causing in the organization. To resolve the issue so there is no longer any disruption implies that those who attack the problem and defeat it have greater power than the problem. Holding dominion over problems is the substance of self-confidence.

The very existence of a problem or, worse yet, a crisis, indicates that existing methods and techniques are somehow lacking, and that new methods and techniques are called for. Depending upon the severity of the problem, minor adjustments might be enough to provide lasting solutions. If the crisis is sufficiently threatening, an entirely new agenda might be in order. Crisis calls for something that doesn't presently exist or, at the very least, calls for a different dosage of existing policy.

Addressing problems large or small should alert us to the possibility that other problems might be brewing. In fact, increased awareness of other problems is a major benefit of encountering problems and working through crisis. New competitive strategies can come out of adversity. I'll carry this thought further shortly. For now, I want to point out that once creative thoughts start percolating, the positive results usually go far beyond what's necessary to solve the initial problem. The quest for a simple solution can easily be the foundation for development of broader and more beneficial thinking.

SOME INSPIRATIONAL WORDS ON RISING TO THE OCCASION

Abraham Lincoln said, "The occasion is piled high with difficulty and we must rise high with the occasion." A smooth sea never develops a skillful sailor. Solving problems sharpens us. Problems often herald the arrival of good things. When you're up against a seemingly insurmountable problem, chances are you're on the brink of a great discovery. If you're not making mistakes—what author Richard Bach calls "unexpected learning experiences"—you're not making discoveries. Henry Ford said, "Failure is the opportunity to begin again more intelligently." And according to Wendell Phillips, "Defeat is nothing but the first step toward something higher." Look for problems. Become what Stew Leonard calls a "problem finder." Problems are darkness and solutions are light.

It's important not to get overwhelmed by the difficulties we face. We must become larger than the situations in which we're involved. We need to be constantly open to change. Flexibility is the other side of rigid indecision, and indecision never solved anything. We can't change the past, we can only change the future, which begins now. We shouldn't feel remorse about our problems; we must feel resolve. It is our duty to keep ourselves in condition to accomplish the biggest things possible in the moment. Roy Acuff got credit for saying, "There ain't nothing come up today that me and the Lord can't handle." Amen.

MENTAL PREPARATION FOR PROBLEM SOLVING

To mentally prepare for problem solving, you must first commit yourself fully to solving the problem. This means making a strong commitment to yourself and your organization that the problem you're presently facing will not come back for lack of a sound solution. Second, clear your desktop of all distractions. This is difficult. The top of your desk looks like the inside of your mind. But it's important to rid yourself of anything other than what's required to solve the problem at hand. At my seminars, I usually have one or two people faint on me when I compare the condition of a desk to the condition of the mind. Don't believe those little signs that say, "A neat and tidy desk is the sign of a sick mind." I tend to be as unorganized as the next person; so don't feel as if I'm being condescending with this. Experience has simply taught me how much disorganization can cost, and I've learned to be far better organized.

Lastly, work logically, step by step, from start to finish or from finish to start. Whether you work deductively or inductively, working systematically helps you avoid retracing your own steps. It helps establish goals that act as markers so you can pause in your process and pick up next time from a familiar and clearly defined point without losing ground. When goals are reached, appropriate rewards help to mark progress emotionally and launch the next stage of the process. Even if a goal represents a half-day or a full-day effort, a week-long effort or month's work, the reward is an important part of a problem-solving mind-set.

Here again are the three steps toward mental preparedness for problem solving:

1. Make a total commitment to solving the problem.

2. Clear your desk of all distractions.

3. Work on the problem systematically.

THE PROBLEM-SOLVING PROCESS

The Niagara River gorge is 800 feet wide with a 400-foot-wide river channel. Water rushes through the channel at 24 miles per hour. Engineers in the middle of the 19th century faced a major challenge when assigned the task of building a railroad suspension bridge across the chasm. No boat could withstand the current and drag a cable across the rushing waters. There was no helicopter in those days to "chopper" a cable across.

So, creativity came to the rescue. A contest was held in which the first young person who could fly a kite across and have someone grab the kite string on the opposite cliff would receive a prize of 10 dollars. Homan Walsh, nine years old, flying his kite from the American side, was the first to have a companion secure the kite string on the other side.

In 1915, Edwin Markham told the rest of the story like this:

> *The builder who first bridged Niagara's gorge,*
> *Before he swung his cable, shore to shore,*
> *Sent out across the gulf his venturing kite*
> *Bearing a slender cord for unseen hands*
> *To grasp upon the further cliff and draw*
> *A greater cord, and then a greater yet;*
> *Till at the last across the chasm swung*
> *The cable—then the mighty bridge in the air!*

By 1855 trains were crossing the 1160-foot-long bridge, 230 feet above the river, and it all started with a kite string.

Can the difficulties we face be that insurmountable? We have many more resources available to us now. Symbolically, we need to get more kite strings across our problems. Don't wait for the kite that will fly the bridge across. Nevertheless, now, as then, long journeys begin with small steps. More than anything else, we must not lose our perspective or, more important, our sense of humor, in the face of problems. At a glance, the six-step problem-solving process looks like this:

Step One: Identify and isolate the problem.

Step Two: Gather all relative information.

Step Three: List all possible solutions.

Step Four: Test possible solutions.

Step Five: Select the best solution.

Step Six: Put the solution into action.

Step One: Identify and Isolate the Problem.   What exactly is blocking our progress toward predetermined goals? Not everything is a problem. Learn to distinguish between a problem and an annoyance. Develop a perspective on the problem from all angles, otherwise you may just be working on a symptom of the larger problem. Leaders will view a problem in one way, while team members and customers probably see things differently. Who has the best angle? The view from the top is not always the most accurate.

Clarify the problem by writing it down in clear-cut terms. Illustrate the problem on paper or explain it to someone else who knows nothing of the problem to help ensure that you have a complete picture and are not assuming too much. Going through these exercises helps highlight the important information about the problem and dispense with the irrelevant.

Step Two: Gather All Relevant Information.   Anything that exists might somehow be helpful in finding a solution to the problem, including all relevant printed and audio/visual information. Talking to people who have addressed similar problems can shed a broader perspective on whatever you're facing. Consult your problem-solving journal, which I'll describe after Step Six.

Step Three: List All Possible Solutions.   Use storyboards and Imaginars and allow your mind to *freewheel*. Don't eliminate any potential solution out of hand. Remember, you're looking through a kaleidoscope and the picture will become clearer the longer you let the pieces tumble.

A great deal of mental energy will be expended in this step. Anticipate some frustration, disappointment, and depression. Keep reminding yourself and your organization that when the problem seems the most impossible, you're usually nearing a breakthrough discovery.

Step Four: Test Possible Solutions.   After you've listed the different solutions to the problem, ask these questions of each one:

+ How well will this particular solution work?
+ Is this solution affordable?
+ Can we implement this solution?
+ What new problems will this solution create, and can we handle them?

Step Five: Select the Best Solution.   A dry throat and sweaty palms might mark this step, depending on the size of the problem you're facing. This anxiety might be brought about by the fact that what you and/or your team think is the best solution you've been able to come up with seems bizarre to yourself and outsiders, in addition to being risky. The greater the innovation and creativity, the fewer will be the guarantees of success.

Don't let the risks at this stage frighten you into an endless cycle of procrastination. As Dr. Norman Vincent Peale said, you (and your organization) are only as big as the problem that stops you. Enthusiasm, mixed with a good measure of the unorthodox, is a reliable antidote for procrastination.

Step Six: Put the Solution into Action.   This means applying as much of the solution to the problem as possible. Don't allow your idea to fail because of too much timidity and caution. If the dosage is too diluted, the solution might appear ineffective when a more appropriate concentration of solution would have worked. I'm not suggesting that you throw out the baby with the bathwater. but it isn't much help when the cure is worse than the illness. The key word in Step Six is *action.*

A PROBLEM-SOLVING JOURNAL FOR FUTURE REFERENCE

After a problem has been solved, it's important to study the experience for the lessons it contains. Write a dated description of the problem and the solution in a journal, notebook, or a document file, answering these questions:

* How will I improve the solution if the problem emerges again?
* What can be done to prevent this problem from reemerging?
* Does the solution have broader application to other problems, even in other areas?

The initial solution to a problem might be the gateway to even better methods and techniques in the future. Peter Drucker summed up the true nature of solutions when he said that most solutions "fall between almost all right and probably wrong. As much as we would like the heavens to part and a clap of thunder to confirm that the solution we've selected is the right one, it's usually more a cautious optimism at best."

We are often tempted to view the first workable solution to a problem as the end of the story, when it might only be the first step in prevention of similar problems. New methods and techniques developed for the solution of one particular problem can frequently be successfully applied to other problems, just as the Disney Rain Parade in Florida led to the Electrical Parade in California and, later, in Florida.

Problem solving is a major portion of the leadership challenge, and all of the creative issues and characteristics of an effective leader come into play. An effective leader is an effective person. You don't find people who run a terrific organization and corrupt their family, or vice versa. Somewhere, somehow, given enough time, the private person's true colors emerge in the public person.

Someone who is good under pressure privately will be good under pressure publicly. Someone who appears to have a split personality, appearing strong under pressure at times and fragile at other times, is likely to be good at disguising fear. The effective leader doesn't cover up fear. He or she faces fear, acknowledges it, respects it, and then moves ahead anyway. Like other leadership skills, problem-solving skills and confidence can be developed over time. Crisis exposes character.

WHAT TO DO WHEN PEOPLE ARE THE PROBLEM

Anytime you have more than one person in an organization, there's a potential for conflict. How you manage disputes is extremely important to the health and welfare of your team. Don't expect to win any popularity contests as a fair and unbiased umpire. If you have successfully mediated a conflict, both sides will feel both vindication and disappointment. When nobody is completely elated at the outcome, you have likely maintained your objectivity. Even Solomon didn't make everybody happy. Don't expect to be more effective than Solomon, just be as effective as you can. John D. Rockefeller said, "I will pay more for the ability to deal with people than any other quality in a manager."

SEARCHING FOR THE UNDERTOW

Occasionally you get the feeling that something real-but-unseen is going on within the team. This undertow is starting to affect the team spirit in a negative way. The cause must be found quickly.

Take a pad of paper and draw a line down the center. This represents the fence in the Fence Technique from Chapter Three. You managed to get everyone on your side of the fence at one time, but perhaps one, two, or three might have drifted back to the other side for some unknown reason.

Start the exercise by putting your name on the left side of the fence. Then think of each of your team members and what you've noticed about them recently. If everything seems okay with that person, put his or her name on your side of the fence. Keep going through your team one at a time, searching for some change in habits, attitude, relationship, etc.

Let's say you finally come to Randy's name. All of a sudden, you remember that he's been coming in late and taking long lunch hours. Put him on the far side of the fence and keep going through your roster of names.

On down the list you come to Nancy. She's become very quiet when you're around. When you look at her, she diverts her eyes. Put her name on the far side.

Then a few names later you come to Al, who seems to have lost some of his enthusiasm, and his relationship with some of the other team members has been tense and even abrupt. Better put his name on the right side too.

You finish the exercise, then realize that the vast majority of your team members are on your side of the fence. That's not good enough. You want these three lost sheep back on the team.

Think in depth about each of them. Are there any other warning signs that you didn't notice in your first examination of them? How is the relationship between the three of them? Could they be planning to leave your company and start their own? Or is it just coincidence that the three of them are on the far side of the fence?

The next thing to do is have a casual, unscheduled meeting with each one of them, individually. It's the kind of meeting where you say, "Grab a cup of coffee and come on in for a few minutes" or, "I'm looking for someone to have lunch with. I'm buying. How about it?"

This relaxed setting is the time to probe, ever so gently, about how it's going. Talk family, goals, and future—anything that might give insight into the problem. Then ask, "Is there anything I can do to make this a better place to work? To build a stronger team?" Listen carefully to the answers.

Sometimes just letting them know you care will get them back. If the person does bring up a problem, go to work and do as much as you can to solve the problem or help the person solve it.

SIX-STEP APPROACH TO A TWO-PERSON CONFLICT

Here are some steps I've found helpful when dealing with people of all ages who are involved in various forms of interpersonal conflict:

Step One.   At the very first sign of a dispute, isolate the principal parties and meet with them, together, in person and face-to-face. Do not simply suggest they go work out their differences by themselves. This will result in the parties going back into the general population of the organization and recruiting sympathetic people to their particular side of the conflict. The divisiveness this creates will damage productivity and morale.

Step Two.   Don't allow yourself to be pulled aside to hear one party's version of the conflict. Insist that both parties be present before they plead their cases. Listen with empathy to both sides of the problem. Don't get caught up emotionally in one account versus another. Showing favoritism will discredit you as a fair and impartial leader, causing the other person to add some *fictional facts* to his or her side of the story in order to sway you back to their side. Let both parties know you want this problem solved quickly, efficiently, and fairly so it won't impair the productivity of the team.

Step Three.   After you've listened to both sides of the story, have the opposing parties repeat their opponent's version to the satisfaction of the opponent. This exercise tends to rid the process of any highly charged emotions. When people go through the motions of understanding the other person's point of view, it's virtually impossible to keep the hostility pumped up. Anger feeds on ignorance. Reciting the facts as the other party sees them has a tremendous calming effect and, more important, brings any misunderstandings to the surface. This doesn't mean the leader provides the interpretations. The parties involved in the dispute must accurately recite each other's perspective in order for this to be effective.

Step Four.   Without making a decision, schedule a follow-up meeting *later that same day,* if possible, so the dispute won't fester overnight. Inform the conflicting parties that you're not going to be rushed into a decision. Neither party can fault the leader for being methodical.

Step Five.   Independently gather any further facts, if necessary, and reconstruct the situation step by step. Make your decision and test its validity by leaving out personalities. The easiest way to eliminate the influence of personalities and test the validity of your decision is to reverse the roles in the new scenario. This is your uncompromising integrity at work.

Step Six.   At the follow-up meeting, both conflicting parties must be present. State your reasoning and then your decision. Reasoning always comes before the decision, so both people are following your logic toward the decision you've arrived at. If you start with the decision, the party who feels as if he or she has lost will tune out and won't hear why you decided the way you did. Furthermore, the party who feels as if they won won't really care how you came to your decision. If you don't do an effective job in selling the logic behind your decision, the party that feels a loss will appeal to a higher court—namely. the rest of your organization. Handle any questions or objections honestly and with diplomacy. Be straightforward.

The Third-Person Compliment

Sometimes people simply have personality clashes that don't result in any major conflicts, just constant irritation. This is why it's important for the leader to have individual knowledge of his or her people. Know each person's strengths so you can give each one a compliment on that strength and say, "I'm not the only person here who feels that way." The person receiving the compliment will want to know who else feels that way. That's your cue to identify the individual with whom that person has a personality conflict as the secret admirer. The fires of resentment will go out overnight because it's impossible to say bad things about someone who you think is saying good things about you. I can hear the accusations of management manipulation already, but I believe bringing people together for the best interests of the organization and their own personal growth is no vice. Dr. Norman Vincent Peale, who was undisputedly a man with uncompromising integrity, created the idea of the third-person compliment I've just described.

THE PERSONAL PROBLEM

Another reason an effective leader must know the people in his or her organization is so he or she can detect when personal problems are starting to affect someone's production. Edward Everett Hale once said, "Some people have three kinds of troubles: all they ever had, all they have now, and all they expect to have." Obviously, a good sense of what an individual's production has been over time is necessary to make such a determination.

If a leader senses that a personal problem has infiltrated the workplace and hasn't affected an individual's performance, approaching that person about the problem is risky. The first question you're likely to be asked is: "Have my problems affected my production or the quality of my work?" If your answer is no, you're likely to hear: "Then my problems are none of your business." Only when the individual's performance is suffering and, consequently, other people are being affected is it time to intervene.

HOW TO HANDLE A PRIMA DONNA

Prima donnas come in all shapes and sizes. They can be managers, salespersons, secretaries, assembly line workers, or anything in between. No matter who they are, they present a challenge. More than anything else, prima donnas like to complain about other people's work or personal habits. If anyone tries to coach them about their *own* shortcomings, the result is intense resistance. They don't want to hear about any problems they might have. Most of all, they never consider the possibility that they are a problem. Here's the five-step prima donna process:

Step One.   The most effective way to manage a prima donna is to engage them in a discussion about his or her strengths. They love to talk about how good they are. As they give you a glorious account of how they will increase sales, production, or whatever, take notes. Ask them to commit to a date when these great wonders will be accomplished. Have the goals and the dates for accomplishment written up for the person, and pledge your support to his or her progress. Promise to check in along the way to make sure that deadlines are being met, especially the deadline for completion. In a way, you are using the individual's own arrogance to ensure that they perform instead of merely talk.

Step Two.   If the prima donna is part of a project team, the negative influence is multiplied. It becomes important to make sure that he or she commits to deadlines and productivity benchmarks. This way, managing the prima donna can actually help the rest of the team plan and accomplish their tasks in the appointed amount of time. You can also prevent some major dissension and disruption that the prima donna could create.

Step Three.   Pick your battles. If something is not very important, don't go to the mat for it. A prima donna can make almost anything a battle if you allow it. Sometimes, discretion is the better part of valor. You need to have enough self-confidence to let the prima donna think he or she has won a victory or two along the way. As a leader, you need to concern yourself with winning the war more than getting entangled in minor skirmishes. Remember, though, minor skirmishes can lead to major battles if you don't keep your finger on the pulse of a situation.

Step Four.   Know your facts. Prima donnas are usually very well informed. If you get into a dispute with a prima donna, they'll jump all over any misinformation you might have and make you eat your words. As Kenny Rogers sang, "You gotta know when to hold 'em, know when to fold 'em." You don't need to inflate an already overinflated ego by letting him or her stomp you flat in an argument where he or she has better facts. Setting up a prima donna to win an argument with the boss doesn't do much for pumping up your image in the eyes of other team members. The team members know when the prima donna has won, even if you try to pull rank and declare yourself the winner.

Step Five.   Fire the prima donna. There comes a time when a leader has to make a judgment. If the prima donna is truly not manageable, despite your best efforts, and is a detriment to organizational productivity and success, you need to protect the hardworking, dedicated people in the company. Sometimes the best way to do that is through termination. As we said back in the Ozark hill country where I grew up, "You can't teach a pig to sing. It wastes your time and irritates the pig."

YOU'RE FIRED!

Just as it's important for an effective leader to hire people who are better than he or she is, it's necessary to terminate the employment of those who can't or won't fit into the organization. It might sound contradictory for me to say this after suggesting you hire unorthodox and unconventional people. Sometimes individuals wind up in your organization and it's simply not in their best interest, nor the best interests of the organization, for them to remain.

At times, the individual simply doesn't know what he or she wants to do, but their attitude and productivity continue to defy any effort you can make to bring them into line with the rest of the organization. At other times, people are simply disruptive and won't respond to your counsel. Whatever the specific reason, it is the leader's responsibility to determine when a person no longer belongs in the organization. Knowing that you've explored all avenues to give this person a fair shot at fitting into the team helps to reduce the guilt and anxiety that usually come with the termination of an employee.

It's also helpful to keep the goals and best interests of the organization and its people at the head of the issue, lest you begin to believe it's a personal issue between you and the disruptive employee. When you spend an inordinate amount of time trying to bring someone along, you're taking time away from your other team members and unnecessarily duplicating efforts.

When someone is simply not right for the organization, and vise versa, nobody benefits. The leader's effectiveness is diminished, the person's coworkers are negatively influenced, and the organization as a whole suffers. When fruit trees are pruned, they are sometimes cut back so severely that the tree appears damaged. However, in time, you'll observe a fuller and more productive tree than before. That's how it is with people and organizations. It may seem severe and harsh to let someone go, which is exactly why so many situations that call for termination are allowed to go unresolved for too long, but clean and precise farewells benefit both the organization and the individual over the long haul.

Termination Guidelines

Once you've decided to let someone go, follow a few simple guidelines that will help both you and the person you're terminating.

BE DISCREET

Out of respect for the individual, don't broadcast your intentions. Keep your agenda as private as possible. Ask for him or her to come see you at the end of a workday so they won't have to leave your office and face curious coworkers. Pick a time to terminate the employee when he or she can most quietly make an exit. Help the individual preserve their dignity in an emotionally vulnerable moment. A termination must be done in total privacy and in a climate of maturity.

GET TO THE POINT QUICKLY

Invite the person to take a seat as you close the door. Begin by saying, "As of this moment you're terminated. We had several problems we weren't able to work out." (This refers to the several counseling sessions you did with this person; the results of which didn't show enough progress to satisy you.) Keep in mind you are now talking to a *former* employee.

ASSUME PART OF THE RESPONSIBILITY

Your dialogue here should be sincere: "I'd like to assume part of the responsibility for not having brought out the best in you. That does not mean the next manager you work for can't really help you."

CLOSURE

Wish the person well and *stand up*! If you don't stand up at that moment, you're going to get one of the best sales presentations you've ever heard.

And if, as a result, you back off of your decision and give him or her one more chance, you've bought an even bigger problem. What generally happens is the person works very hard for a week while they're setting up interviews and clandestinely doing a number on your team's morale. Then, with a new job secured, the person walks into your office, doesn't close the door, and fires *you*.

NOTIFY THE TEAM

Let's use the name Bob. At the next team meeting address Bob's termination. The best way to do that is to say, "As you probably know, Bob was terminated this past week. We had several problems we couldn't work out. I'll take part of the responsibility for that. I'm sure that all of you, like me, wish Bob well in whatever he does." That's it. Then go right on with the meeting.

TURNING ADVERSARIES INTO SUPPORTERS

As I've said all along, leaders must know their people. If you pay attention, you'll be able to predict how certain people will react to certain kinds of news. If you don't know your team members that well, you need to study them more. Several people in every group tend to react more negatively than the others. These people can be extremely cynical and pessimistic. That attitude won't help you get things done. Plus, you don't need to set off a bomb that will blow your meeting to pieces. One of the stimulants sure to set these naysayers off is change—any kind of change.

The key to turning this situation in your favor is to isolate the potential adversary. As soon as you know that you need to make a controversial announcement, invite your strongest adversary into your office for a cup of coffee. Let that person know that you need some advice and feedback about an inevitable change that is coming up. Hit him or her with the change and let them hit the ceiling in the privacy of your office, not in front of the team. Ask for their advice on how to break this news to the rest of the team, then discuss the change and touch on all the reasons why the move needs to be made. Let them blow off steam in your office instead of in front of everybody else. Turn the conversation back around to how this can best be sold to the rest of the team.

Listen. Take their advice and use some of it. When you make the announcement, in a meeting or otherwise, you'll have supporters where there would have been detractors.

THE MASS WALKOUT

I received a panicky telephone call late one afternoon from a couple of clients who jointly owned a sales firm. One of their salespersons was opening an office just down the street, and my clients were watching in horror as the rest of their staff walked out the door to go work for him. The former salesperson was offering a higher commission. My clients were scared and didn't know how to deal with the situation.

After we discussed the situation briefly, I suggested that we look at it from all sides. We needed to help change their point of view. I suggested to my clients that they call the spouses of the employees that walked out and ask them what they thought of the change. We scripted some of the conversation they needed to have with the spouses. I told them to ask the spouses if they thought there might be a financial dip because of what's left on the table when someone leaves one firm and takes up with another one.

What about their leads? An established company generates more prospects than a start-up firm. Expenses would be another issue. Even if the commission percentage is better with the new firm, a start-up has less operating capital and the burden might fall more heavily on the salesperson's shoulders. Without attacking the former salesperson or his new company directly, my clients helped the spouses see that there were some serious concerns that hadn't been addressed. In doing so, my clients did them a favor because starry-eyed sales-people don't necessarily think this kind of a move through.

About ten o'clock that night my clients' telephone started ringing with calls from those who had walked out wanting to come back. Within three days everyone was back except for the poor guy who tried to instigate the insurrection in the first place. All it took was to help the salespersons and their spouses see the issue from another perspective. The same issue looks different if you look at it from the convex side of the partition rather than the concave side. Of course, my clients did a better job from that point on of leading their team members with the methods, techniques, and philosophies contained in this book.

KILL THE FATTED CALF

If you lose a seasoned producer who is well known throughout the company, in spite of your best efforts to keep him or her, don't get mad and tell that person that they"ll never be welcome in your office again. Keep the lines of communication open, as noted in Chapter 6 on how to handle the "90 day I want to quit syndrome." Invite the person back to see you and have a cup of coffee. Let them know that you want to stay in touch and hear about how they're doing. Send handwritten notes to his or her house about once a month, saying that they're missed around the office and that you hope things are going well.

Eventually, that person's spouse is going to point out that you care more about his or her future than the new boss does. Hopefully, your former employee will get the message without being reminded. The other message that will come through loud and clear is that the door is open for them to return. When that happens, you'll know what to do.

Everyone in your organization knows that he or she has left for "greener pastures." Often, the person discovers that the departure was a mistake and wants to come back. Welcome them back with open arms. Proclaim that the prodigal has returned! Kill the fatted calf! Announce it in meetings; put it in the company newsletter. Tell the world! This lets everyone in the company know they're better off staying with you.

At their first opportunity, team members will single out the returning team members and ask what it was like "out there" and why they came back. At that moment, the returning team member becomes a powerful retention tool, so make sure you do everything within your power to make the returnee fall in love with the company all over again, if they haven't already. If you suspect that someone in the organization is thinking about leaving, you can have your new advocate provide some counsel that might keep that person from jumping the fence.

THE FIVE WHYS

Serious problems can often be recognized and action taken, but the root cause, perhaps several layers down, is not eradicated. Working on a "symptom" guarantees there will be a recurrence of the problem. The effective leader starts on the surface, but goes deep, using the Five Whys.

Even though the questions are simple, the answers can make many people in the organization uncomfortable; maybe even feel a little pain. For example, someone points out that turnover is on the rise. You ask, "Why?" Right away you send the message that dropping bad news like a baby on your doorstep isn't the end of the discussion; it's the beginning. You might get a textbook answer like, "They seem to prefer working for some other company."

"Why?" you ask again.

"They expect to make more money," you're told.

"Why weren't they making enough money here?" you ask. "Do we need to adjust our compensation structure?"

"Well," the explanation goes on, "the other company has a better training program than we do."

"Why?" you insist. "Why do they have a better training program than we do?"

"Well," you hear again, "they spend more money on training and make it a bigger priority overall."

"Why do they spend more money and place more emphasis on training? How does their training translate into increased productivity and profits?"

When you ask "Why?" and sincerely pay attention to the answers, you'll find out valuable information about your competitors, the marketplace, and, most important, the barriers to productivity and growth within your own organization. The Five Whys process will give you valuable, usable information to fuel your strategic thinking.

The answer to the first "Why?" is never enough information. The answer to the second "Why?" is better, but still evasive and superficial. The answer to the third "Why?" puts a demand on truth and honest disclosure. The answer to the fourth "Why?" includes accurate and relevant information—even if some of it is unpleasant. The answer to the fifth "Why?" is the beginning of change; changes that need to be made in order to make your organization the most desirable place to work in the industry.

FACTORS THAT KEEP PROBLEMS TO A MINIMUM

If you've accepted that problems will always be present in any organization, large or small, you're ready to take on the following six methods for minimizing the disruption problems can cause.

1. *Keep the training going.* If you let the learning stop, your people will naturally begin reverting to old habits and routines that lower productivity. When you stop learning, you start losing. Continuous training requires planning and investment on your part. Support it and do whatever it takes to make your company what Peter Senge calls a "learning organization." Learning needs to be part of the daily routine, not something that happens every now and then. When team members are learning, they're thinking. Folks with their thinking caps on are in the best possible position to identify problems early on and take whatever steps are necessary to find solutions.

2. *Keep the team informed.* It's counterproductive to keep the team in the dark. Make an extra effort through your Website, company newsletters, meeting agendas, bulletin boards, and coaching sessions to let people know what is happening now as well as what's just around the bend or over the next hill. When people are informed, they feel involved and can put their brainpower to work for you in ways you might not have thought of.

3. *Keep listening and growing as the leader.* When your team members see that you're making an effort to get better at your job, they're more likely to do the same. The reverse is even truer: If team members don't see you trying to learn and grow, they'll definitely lose interest. Why should they care about growth if you don't? One way they'll discover that you're growing is by having conversations with you. As you talk about what you're learning, ask them what they're learning.Being an excellent listener is the best way to show your team members that a big part of *your* growth and development as a leader is to care about *their* growth and development. As you could chart each team member's growth in the last year, remember that they could do the same with the growth they've seen from you over the same period.

4. *Communicate clearly.* All of your best intentions to keep team members informed and to demonstrate that growing and learning are for everyone won't amount to a hill of beans if you don't get the message through. Use all the techniques and tools I've talked about throughout this book to shower them in information, then make sure they got the message by having them feed it back to you. If your team members can give a good accounting of what you're trying to communicate, you're doing a good job. But remember: When it comes to communicating, you can always improve.

5. *Provide regular counseling.* This is about more than casual conversation. By structuring sessions on a regular basis—not necessarily often, but regularly—each team member knows that they're going to have a chance to let his or her feelings and/or ideas be known. I can't emphasize enough how important it is for people to feel that they'll be heard when they speak. These sessions are also the best time to tap the team member's mind for problems, potential problems, possible solutions, and, generally speaking, what's going on in the trenches. This counseling is similar in nature to the counseling used in the morale campaign described in Chapter 6.

6. *Remember that team members are customers.* The people that work for you are always your first line of customers. If you don't think this is a big deal, think again. Your team members treat *their* first-line customers the way you treat your team members. Whatever's going on between the leader and the team member is passed on to your end customer. When I put it that way, many of the managers attending my seminars report to me that they couldn't sleep for several nights, just thinking about how differently they perceive their team members vs. their end customers.

HIGH TURNOVER/LOW PRODUCTIVITY: TURNING THE ORGANIZATION AROUND

After my boss told me he was looking for my replacement, I went to the beach and did some serious soul searching. I was out for two days; while everyone in my office knew that my boss was looking to replace me. The second evening, I called every member of my staff at home and asked them to attend a special meeting that Friday morning at eight o'clock sharp. "There is something I need to tell all of you," I said before I hung up. They expected me to announce my resignation or that I'd been fired. Furthermore, they expected me to somehow place the blame for my failure somewhere other than on my own shoulders, maybe even blame them. They were all there on time, just to see what was going to happen.

"Thank you for being here," I began. "When I was given this job, you were given the worst manager possible. At the same time, I was given the best office that I could possibly receive. I want you all to know that I am going to take my best shot at turning myself around. Not the company, not the office—me. My goal is to prove that I can be the kind of manager you want and deserve."

End of meeting. By looking the problem straight in the eye, I bought myself enough time to start improving. That's when I started working with their strengths instead of their weaknesses. The complaint calls about me that had kept the telephone at headquarters ringing off the hook stopped almost overnight.

Learning from Each Other

I succeeded in reinventing myself, and after two and a half years managing that record-breaking office, I was given an entire district of offices to manage. One of my first major challenges was to tackle the problems of high turnover and to increase productivity. Both were districtwide problems. I helped my managers to sharpen their skills by sharing information with each other. As I said before, "None of us is as smart as all of us."

Each manager was doing something right, but that didn't mean all of them were doing the same right thing, so it was time to share the wealth. In my first meeting, I asked them what they'd like to know about how the other managers were running their offices. I started listing their areas of real concern on my ever-present flip chart and taping the filled sheets to the wall.

The list included such things as handling office personnel records, handling personnel problems, personal growth books (sales and management), time planning systems, ideas for future sales meetings, presentation techniques, etc. At the close of that first meeting, I explained that our next meeting would be in one week. They would find out then how we would be using this list to everyone's benefit.

The next week, we met in the same room, which I'd renamed the Imaginar Room. Each manager was handed a binder that had the list of things they wanted to know about how the other managers managed. It was an outline format with about three inches of blank space after each item so they could take notes.

Then I announced that in one week we'd be meeting in Betsy's office so she could show us how she did all of these things. While she was catching her breath, the seven other managers' hands went into the air. Strange! They all had the same question: "Whose office will we be in the week after that?"

"I'll tell you next week and so on until we work our way through all eight offices." Keep in mind that this was a struggling district with bottom-dwelling production. Several district managers had preceded me into this position with little or no positive results. These managers suddenly knew that things were about to change. The best was yet to be—it was on its way!

My thinking was that each office needed to be shaped up, not only physically, but also organizationally. They each wanted his or her office to look and be at its very organized best. When their peers showed up at their office, they didn't want to be embarrassed.

Talk about a flurry of activity in those offices! Each manager was thinking his or her office could be next. They wanted to be proud of their office when their peers met there. A side benefit was that the 145 salespeople in those eight offices had never seen their managers moving at that speed. They too knew things were going to be different.

At the end of each of these meetings, the next office in the string of eight meetings was announced and they were all handed another outline like the one they'd been taking notes in at this particular office. After the series of meetings was completed, each manager had eight valuable note-filled outlines.

The ninth meeting was held back in the Imaginar Room, where we discussed what had been learned and what we were in the process of implementing. Production was on its way up along with morale. Thomas Edison once said to his workers, whom he called the Insomnia Squad: "There's always a better way to do it. Find it." We were seeing the results of that philosophy. No wonder this series of meetings became the talk of the company.

Each manager also had a weekly sales meeting for his or her individual team members. I announced that I would be attending these meetings but since they were all on the same day of the week, I couldn't attend them all at once. This meant that no manager had advance warning of my visit. "You'll know I'm there when you see me walk through the door," I told them.

After this had gone on several weeks, various managers called me to say they wished I'd come to *their* meeting the prior week because it was a terrific session. Before I took over as district manager, managers hated it when the brass came into their offices, much less attend their meetings. Now they were inviting me over. It was because they were now taking *pride* in their work as managers.

In our weekly Imaginars, I could have had my managers from the various offices turn in a written report each week and skipped my meetings. But I had every manager give a verbal report in front of his or her peers. There was a pride factor involved when they talked about their office's accomplishments.

They also felt a kinship around the entire challenge of managing an office and producing results. Although I never belittled any of them, I knew that they hated to put up bad figures in front of their fellow managers when they had an occasional down week. That their peers knew they had a down week made them work that much harder the next week in order to announce better numbers.

Surprise Instructor Series

Once we learned about all we could from what each manager was currently doing, it was time for the next step up. This was done with a weekly reading assignment for my team of managers. We went through business articles and business books one chapter at a time and discussed how the information related to what we were doing. I seldom acted as teacher. I gave out the assignments a week in advance but waited to announce who would be leading the discussion until the meeting. No one wanted to look unprepared in front of the others, so I usually had a room full of well-read managers. They quickly learned that this information could increase productivity.

It was also done in a spirit of fun, so no one felt that it was manipulative. There was no greater thrill than asking a manager what caused the increased productivity that past week and hear the answer, "Oh, it was something I learned a couple of weeks ago in our weekly lesson." Can you see how this fits into Level Three of the Five Levels of Learning discussed in Chapter 6? No wonder management turnover dropped to zero as production increased by over 800 percent in a five-and-a-half-year period. These managers were doing what they were learning!

The Unofficial District 13

After the intense weekly Imaginar, generally about two hours in length, my managers didn't want to break the mood or quit learning so they headed for a local *pub*. Officially, they were District 10 managers but they elected to call this informal meeting "District 13." As they gathered around the pool table, sipping a cool one or two, the discussion continued and camaraderie soared. They had become an elite team. Often managers from other districts asked them if they could come along to join in on these legendary discussions. They generally received a polite, "Sorry, but you just wouldn't understand."

Frequently I'd receive a call that started out, "Yesterday at our District 13 meeting ..." That meant they'd come up with an idea on their own and wanted to try it. I was impressed by how much creativity was unleashed once we started our learning process. I was invited weekly to the District 13 meetings, but I always declined. I felt that it was important to have time together that was truly their own and not presided over by me. When I left the company a little over five years later to pursue a career in professional speaking, District 13 gave Tedi and me a magnificent weekend at a beachside luxury hotel, all expenses paid, as a token of their appreciation. I guess they had developed some class along the way too. The District 13 invitations kept coming, and since I was no longer their district manager, I attended some of their meetings when my travel schedule permitted. All of those managers have done very well in the years since, either with that firm, other firms they joined, or companies that they started. I'll always believe that it was the commitment we made to learning and sharing with each other that led to their success.

NEVER STOP SELLING YOUR COMPANY TO YOUR COMPANY

One of the things you learn when you truly make learning a priority in your organization is how many good things are being done. I ask business people all of the time now, "When was the last time you heard something positive about your company ... from your company?" Invariably they say, "When they recruited me." Tremendous opportunities are being missed when you don't keep singing the praises of your organization, its people, and their accomplishments. As important as it is to portray your organization in the best light possible when recruiting talent, it never stops being important—not just to the outside world, but to your team members. They do not want to leave a company where exciting things are going on.

Report good news through all of the media resources I've talked about. Highlight improvements in sales, production, efficiency, or other benchmarking tools, even if the improvement is month to month. Report on the good works your team members are doing in the community and/or the causes your organization supports around the world. This is not something you, as the leader, can dump off on a public relations or corporate communications person. They might do the basic communications work, but the messages need to come from the top. Your team members must believe that the things they read about in company newsletters, on the Website, and anywhere else truly reflect your thoughts and beliefs.

CONCLUSION: RUMINATIONS ON THE ART OF PROBLEM SOLVING

In case you or anyone in your organization feels like nobody else has ever known the troubles you've known, I've listed some other folks with troubles to keep you company. Remember Elbert Hubbard's maxim, "When life gives you a lemon, open up a lemonade stand"? People who reflect the truth of reality back to us in wonderful sayings are people who obviously are not without problems themselves.

I have never heard of any better summation of life's paradoxical nature than the words Charles Dickens chose to begin *A Tale of Two Cities*:

> *It was the best of times, it was the worst of times.*
> *It was the age of wisdom, it was the age of foolishness.*
> *It was the season of light, it was the season of darkness.*
> *It was the spring of hope, it was the winter of despair.*
> *We had everything before us, we had nothing before us.*

Turmoil often gives us not only strength, but new direction as well. Problems are not to be feared or avoided, but rather, should be sought out and confronted with all the creativity we can muster. Problems and opportunities will always be with us. Take care of the problems before they take care of you. If you're planning to build your dreams of tomorrow, you must be honest with the reality of today. A man was watching a little boy with a new pair of skates. He fell several times. The man said, "Why don't you just give up?" The little boy, with his jaw set, quickly replied, "Mister, I didn't get these skates to learn to give up with. I got 'em to learn to skate." Falling down is reality. Don't ignore it. What is your "bounce back ability," or BBA? Luxury and comfort are rarely the crucibles for great victories.

Some great thoughts from some great people who were no strangers to adversity:

> *"Many men owe the grandeur of their lives to their tremendous difficulties."*
>
> Charles Spurgeon

"Adversity puts iron in your flesh."
Somerset Maugham

"Nature, when she adds difficulties, adds brains."
Emerson

"You shouldn't be robbed of your right to make mistakes."
Beryl Markham

"The Spartans did not inquire how many the enemy are but where they are."
Agis II

"Circumstances have rarely favored the famous."
Milton (blind, and wrote his first epic after he was 50 years old)

"The gods look at no grander sight than an honest man struggling with adversity."
Orison Swett Marden

"Often defeated in battle, always successful in war."
Macaulay's description of Alexander the Great

"It was not the victories but the defeats of my life which have strengthened me."
Sidney Poyntz

"Progress is what we have left over after we meet a seemingly impossible problem."
Norman Cousins

"Failure means mental surrender."
Orison Swett Marden

"Men are not the creatures of circumstances. Circumstances are the creatures of men."
Disraeli

"Both adversity and prosperity can make fools out of men. Prosperity makes more fools than adversity."
Elbert Hubbard

"Adversity unlocks virtue; defeat is the threshold of victory."
Orison Swett Marden

"Many of life's failures are men who did not realize how close they were to success when they gave up."
Thomas Edison

"We can only appreciate the miracle of a sunrise after we have waited through the darkness."
Anonymous

"The nose of the bulldog has been slanted back so he can breathe without letting go."
Winston Churchill

"When one door closes, another one opens. But we look so long and regretfully upon the closed door that we do not see the one that has opened for us."
Alexander Graham Bell

"A word of encouragement during a failure is worth more than a whole book of praise after a success."
Anonymous

"There comes a time in the affairs of men when you must take the bull by the tail and face the situation."
W. C. Fields

"When I was young I observed that nine out of every ten things I did were failures, so I did ten times more work."
George Bernard Shaw

"The absence of alternatives clears the mind marvelously."
Henry Kissinger

"Most people don't know how brave they really are."
R. E. Chambers

"I have learned to use the word impossible with the greatest caution."
Werner von Braun

"The only thing more desirable than talent is perseverance."
Anonymous

"It is not good enough that we do our best, sometimes we have to do what's required."
Winston Churchill

"Although the world is full of suffering, it is also full of the overcoming of it."
Helen Keller

"Success is partial to the persistent person."
Dr. Frank Crane

"I laugh when I can and live with the rest."
Willie Nelson

"You're never beaten unless you give up. You may have a fresh start at any moment you choose."
Mary Pickford

"It's always too soon to quit!"
Dr. David Tyler Soates

"Experience is not what happens to you; it is what you do with what happens to you."
Aldous Huxley

CHAPTER NINE

THE SEVENTH STEP: LEADING CHANGE WHEN THE HEAT'S ON (NOT JUST MANAGING IT)

"Courage is being scared to death but saddling up anyway."

John Wayne, Actor

CHANGE: THE ONLY CONSTANT

Jim Newton was the author of *Uncommon Friends*, a book about his close friendship, when he was in his very early 20s, with Thomas Edison, Henry Ford, Harvey Firestone, Nobel Prize winner Dr. Alexis Carrell, and Charles Lindbergh. These leaders of change not only had a tremendous impact on the 20th Century, but a continuing impact on all of us in the 21st Century and no doubt for centuries to come.

Jim was my most valued mentor and the one I spent more time with than any of my other mentors. I met him in 1981 and had many interesting conversations with him right up until his death—"graduation," as he called it—in 1999 at age 94. In one of our many conversations I asked him what driving forces these change leaders had in common. He said they had three. They were a sense of purpose, a spirit of adventure, and continued personal growth. As to the third force, he said, "They knew they didn't know it all." Jim then told me Mr. Edison's response to a reporter who asked him when he was going to retire.

"The day before the funeral," Edison answered.

Charles Lindbergh said that Jim was the closest personal friend he ever had. Lindbergh once said, "I take chances but leave nothing to chance," and I asked Jim what the quote meant. He explained that things Charles did were "chances" simply because no one had ever done them before. But leaving "nothing to chance" meant that everything had been well-thought-out, and the great aviator planned for any eventuality. This clearly illustrates the spirit of adventure shared by all of Jim's *Uncommon Friends*.

Change leaders are needed at every level of an organization, not just change *managers*. Too often we think of *change management* as giving into it slowly and watering it down as it goes. This is not to say that this means jumping in with both feet. It means that the change leader *takes chances but leaves nothing to chance*.

Has this change leader always had this cutting edge charisma? Most certainly not. He or she understands that growth in this area is a process. The more changes (both successful and with perhaps even a failure or two along the way) that are spearheaded by the leader, the more confidence and credibility the leader builds. The team then shows him or her more appreciation, respect, and trust.

My first formation flying instructor was a man of few but profound words. He explained in a preflight briefing that the pilot flying the number four aircraft should never takes his eyes off number three. Number three should never takes his eyes off number two, and number two should never take his eyes off the lead. "Questions?"

Since I was number two, my hand shot up. "Sir, what if the lead flies into a mountain?" I asked.

"Then I want four equal-spaced holes along the mountainside," he replied. No doubt his idea of a joke. Then he went on to say something I've remembered often: "I'm the lead and it's not in my flight plan to fly you into a mountain." That day I was "tucked in" next to his wingtip. I flew closer to his airplane than any other airplane I'd flown formation with up to that time. His confidence was contagious.

Later on when a pilot, perhaps with hundreds of hours in the kind of high performance fighter we were flying, was assigned to our squadron, he was unofficially checked out. When he was assigned lead, it was a fairly loose formation until we were confident of his confidence.

You're now in the rear cockpit of my fighter in a four-ship formation. At 45,000 feet, three multimillion-dollar supersonic fighters tucked in, number two off our right wing, numbers three and four off our left wing, with only five to six feet separation between each. No one airplane has more than 20 minutes of fuel left. Eight very important lives inside those four fighters. There is 40,000 feet of bad weather to lead my flight down through. We have just been advised to be aware of severe turbulence in the area. (It can sometimes make your palms sweat—not perspire, sweat!) There's the call from the control center. "Mighty Mouse One," the controller drones. "Flight of four, start your descent."

"Roger," I reply as I pull the throttles back slowly and push the nose smoothly down toward terra firma, with the rest of the flight doing the same. There's a voice echoing in my head. It's the voice of my formation flight instructor. What's he saying? What he always says: "It's not in your flight plan to screw up."

The turbulence is tooth-jarring. Everybody's hanging in tight! We're in the clear at 5000 feet, as forecast. There's the base. Four perfect 200 mph touchdowns. Four perfect drag chutes.

Debriefing time. "The flight?"

"Oh, it was a piece of cake. No sweat."

There is a lot of backslapping at the Officers' Club Fighter Bar, along with a few refreshments. Maybe, just maybe, one of the pilots in my flight will say what any lead prays for: "I'd fly into the jaws of hell with you." My number two pilot, standing next to me, throws his arm across my shoulder and says it! Suddenly, I'm having trouble breathing. What's that in my throat? Oh, it's my heart! This really has been a good day, even though my palms did sweat. Yes, sweat.

Confidence Inspires Change

Confidence doesn't come overnight. It's the by-product of a series of learning experiences. We take what we learn and embed it in our memory. We then take that experience, place it in our kaleidoscope, and look at it from different perspectives and in relationship to other change procedures we've used previously. Can a more efficient method be developed so the next change can be handled better? It's best to take notes on this process and its results. That way you can launch the next change quicker and more effectively.

As you become an increasingly seasoned change leader, you'll notice that your team's acceptance of the change factor goes up. Their confidence and trust in you and the process of change increases. They start to *tuck in* a little closer.

You're developing a cutting edge team that loves the new and exciting. The spirit of adventure is becoming a way of life. You're pushing the envelope. You're making the competition—who is still struggling to manage change—sweat. Yes, sweat!

Having worked with hundreds of different kinds of companies, I can safely say that too many of them are plunging into the future with their eyes fixed on the rearview mirror. The reasons for their reluctance to change are:

♦ Some people believe accepting someone else's ideas is like admitting personal inadequacy. This is similar to the old "It wasn't invented here" way of thinking, or "I didn't think of it so it can't be a good idea."

♦ Some people fear new projects will bring about new problems. At least with the status quo, we know what to expect from day to day.

♦ There is a mistaken belief throughout the business world that anything new must be harder than what we're already doing.

♦ Often, top management believes that, no matter how poorly the company is doing, avoiding new and potentially helpful ideas will at least protect their positions. This is why many up-and-coming executives are told not to rock the boat and become filter builders.

THE LEADER AS A MANAGER OF CHANGE

If something has been done in a certain way for two years, there's an 80 percent chance there is a better way of doing it. I'm not saying something should automatically or arbitrarily be changed. But expanding knowledge and resources will almost always create new and better opportunities. One way to test this is to look at an existing method or procedure that's been in place for two or more years and ask yourself how it would be done, given current resources, if today it had to be done differently.

You might find out the existing methods and procedures do not need to be continued at all. A necessary effort one day might soon become a nonproductive tradition or habit. What makes the difference? Change makes the difference. Knowledge seems to expand at a faster rate than understanding. New technologies arise before we know what to do with them. Efforts to solve a particular problem often produce a greater amount of valuable information than is required to resolve the original problem. As long as there are problems, people will seek solutions. As long as people seek solutions, knowledge will expand. The good news for those who desire progress is that there will always be problems to solve!

A couple of other indicators that change is called for in the organization include managers who refuse to delegate responsibilities, and a general attitude that nothing can be learned from competitors or other outside sources. The effective leader notices when the sound leadership principles are not being practiced throughout the organization. If someone refuses to delegate, chances are he or she believes nobody can do the job as well as they can. This dangerous thinking needs to be changed. Anytime people in an organization begin to believe there is no other way of thinking but their own, change is called for. This firm belief in the status quo will cause an organization to crash and burn in a hurry.

THE FOUNDATION FOR SUCCESSFUL CHANGE

Change can be frightening. Change means something new and different is going to happen. Laying the proper groundwork upon which new ideas can be sustained is tremendously important. There are two basic steps to laying the necessary foundation:

No Surprises

The people in your organization need to feel they will receive sufficient notice before any significant change is made. In other words, your organization should discuss and think through new ideas before implementing them. People don't develop a sense of confidence when they get blindsided with something they weren't expecting. Even if the new idea is a good one, to spring it on unsuspecting people will produce uncertainty, an atmosphere in which they tend to proceed cautiously and tentatively. What you want is a group of spontaneous people who have acquired a strong sense of confidence in your leadership through past changes.

Think It Through Thoroughly

The second step is much like the first. Time and energy must be focused in advance on the real challenges of a new idea or project. This will help create the atmosphere in which the new idea can grow and develop. People who always expect the worst will distance themselves from new ideas. People who haven't been prepared for the real ups and downs of implementing a new idea will do the same if they keep getting sold on the great possibilities of a new idea without the real nuts and bolts. I've heard it said we should plan for the best but prepare for the worst.

This sounds like reality therapy to me. Work to make sure your leadership is consistent and dependable. Put a *no surprises* rule into effect. Respect the feelings of the people in your organization. Avoid cooking up schemes in private and then springing them on unsuspecting people who will be expected to carry them out. When a new idea is to be launched, prepare your people for the real experience in their future. Don't set them up for disappointments by simply preaching the expected benefits of the new idea. Nothing is ever accomplished without some effort and investment by somebody. When the reality is presented up front, your people will be glad they bought in when the idea succeeds.

To help build a firm foundation for successful change keep these things in mind:

♦ Storyboards are excellent for helping to visualize both the benefits and the *potential problems* in launching a new idea. Look at the up side and the down side. This is a storyboard you'll want to work on at home. If it's in your office, you could start a wave of dissension.

♦ Remember how the majestic bridge over Niagara Gorge was built from a kite string as the first step. You know that the ultimate change is going to be a big one, but there's no reason to put all of that on the shoulders of your front-line people. The little boy who flew the kite wasn't expected to follow up and build the bridge. Instead of asking your people to build a bridge, ask them to get a *kite string* across as the first step.

♦ Use the Fence Technique to sell the change (see Chapter 3). The Fence Technique is an invaluable tool in achieving team commitment to the new change. Even a strong team still has to be sold on the change. So, as far as the new project or new change is concerned, picture all of your team members on the opposite side of the fence from you. Then, just like the process described in Chapter 3, target the most respected member of the team. Show that person how their individual strengths can be used in facilitating the change. Then the next most respected person, the next, and so on. Keep in mind that when you get about a third on your side, the most respected third, that's when the other two-thirds start to buy in more quickly.

SEEING CHANGE LEADERSHIP AS A SEQUENCE OF EVENTS

There are six fundamental phases required for successful change management. In a busy organization you are very possibly involved in several new projects at one time. These phases of change management will help you understand which phase you're in, on each project, as you work through the upcoming ten steps. The six phases are:

1. Education
2. Participation
3. Communication
4. Facilitation
5. Information
6. Rededication

Education Phase.   Inform employees ahead of time change is on the way. The heads up helps develop the sense of confidence in your organization I talked about.

Participation Phase.   Encourage input from all employees on planning and implementation. This bolsters confidence and enthusiasm toward the organization and the project.

Communication Phase.   This is the final presentation on how the change is about to be implemented. A storyboard showing all the final changes can be used in the presentation.

Facilitation Phase.   The change is under way. During this phase the leader's hands-on participation brings big benefits. Communicating and coaching can only go so far. The leader must get personally involved to demonstrate his or her personal investment in the project.

Information Phase.   Now the leader truly keeps his or her ear to the ground to determine what's working and what's not working. Informal, non-threatening encounters with your people will give you most of this critical feedback. This is when you might learn that proper delegation is not occurring or thinking is still too narrow.

Rededication Phase.   Enthusiasm and energy don't last forever. After the initial hoopla is over, it is important to evaluate and analyze the progress of the new project. Necessary tune-ups and adjustments are made to improve on the improvement.

THE LAUNCH

There are 11 basic steps necessary to successfully launch a new idea. Getting most of them right isn't good enough. It's important that all 11 steps receive your attention. These steps are like building blocks. The blocks on top are completely dependent on the blocks on the bottom.

1. *Let your enthusiasm for the new idea show.*   Your people get their cues from you. No individual in your organization will be any more excited about the idea you've endorsed than you. Your level of enthusiasm is contagious.

2. *Presell key people.*   When you're storyboarding a new project in your Imaginar, one of the important considerations is always, "Who needs to get behind this to make it fly?" You don't want somebody influential grimacing when you announce your new idea to the organization. Pick out these key people and meet them individually. Explain what the change is and ask for feedback. If they're going to be upset, it's better to have you as their sole audience versus the whole team. Also they'll appreciate your confidence in them.

3. *Explain all the reasons for changing.*   It's important to be extremely thorough when presenting a new idea. For the reasons I've already explained, you don't want to dwell on the positive benefits of the new idea and exclude the real facts about what it's going to require to get the job done. Many people might not fully understand the need for the change. Don't leave them in the dark. Make sure everyone understands the who, what, where, and why of the new project.

4. *Discuss the risks.*   Anticipate that your people are going to have reservations about venturing into the unknown. It's your job to present valid

reasons for assuming the risks involved. Good people will listen and respond. Don't expect anyone to follow blindly.

5. *Show anticipated results.*   Nobody likes to be sold a bill of goods that will never be delivered. There are good benefits to be realized for both the organization and the individuals involved or else you wouldn't be promoting this new concept. The key here is to be realistic. Demonstrate how the new idea will help the organization meet its goals, such as staying ahead of the competition, as well as promote personal growth for the people involved with achievable methods.

6. *Promote what the project is.*   Don't rely on what people might think the project is. Sometimes people get carried away with bands playing and flags waving. As realistic and accurate as you try to be, at least some of your people are probably going to selectively hear what they want to hear about the new project and potentially disregard the rest. Have them explain it back to you so you can determine how thoroughly they understand what you've tried to communicate. There is no more reliable way to measure someone's understanding of a new idea.

7. *Encourage disagreement.*   You can always expect some people to disagree with the new idea. However, it will strengthen the project if you *encourage* intelligent and healthy debate. This also gives the doubters their say and keeps them from feeling that nobody listens to them. And when you establish an atmosphere of openness, people won't feel that something is being thrust upon them.

8. *Establish short-range goals for each individual.*   Flying a kite is easier than building a bridge. If the task seems too large and unattainable, people lose interest quickly. When big jobs are individualized, the tasks seem more doable and each person involved has an increased sense of personal involvement.

9. *Keep influential people on board.*   By influential people, I don't just mean those in powerful, executive positions. I'm referring also to informal leaders in the rank and file, the people who sometimes walk up to you and say "We need to talk" and occasionally reveal a budding problem you haven't noticed. It's not enough to only get their initial endorsement of a new idea; it's important to keep them on board. And as the project progresses, these influential people you bring over to your side of the fence will continue to have an impact upon the ongoing morale of the group.

10. *Stay on top of problems.*   Be on the lookout for problems that pop up as the new project progresses. An unresolved problem that festers overnight or over a weekend can dampen the spirits of your team members. The effective leader needs to spot problems quickly and jump on them with lightning speed. This lets your people know you're with them and available to help wherever and whenever needed. The result is a strong sense of cohesiveness and confidence.

11. *Are you ready?* All the hard work you've invested to sell a new idea to the organization can be lost not only if you haven't adequately prepared everyone, but if you aren't prepared yourself. If *you* truly understand how a new idea typically develops, you'll be in a much stronger position to guide the change as it occurs.

Some Other Things to Consider

Benefits Bring Problems.   As a new idea evolves, positive benefits will begin to appear, accompanied by some real problems. Anticipate that the struggle to accommodate new methods and techniques won't be as much fun as discussion of the benefits was at the kickoff meeting. Since benefits are difficult to measure early, focus on the new problems and their effect on morale.

Anticipate Doubt.   At this stage of the game the threat to the organization's morale is the most critical challenge. People can begin to doubt and become discouraged as the process drags on. As the leader, you must be on top of these feelings and coach your people through them. Let them know that you're as invested in the change as you want them to be.

Don't Stop Selling.   Increased productivity and renewed morale will only be present after the leader has demonstrated patience and perseverance through the long process of continually selling the new project. With people in the organization taking their cues from you, it's important to go beyond verbalizing the work ethic and qualities of self-discipline required to get the job done. The leader has to model the qualities he or she expects. In other words, practice what you preach. If you start to sweat and look like you're going to jump off the top of the building, your people are going to lack confidence in you and the new project.

The Other Shoe Syndrome

If sweeping changes are needed, lay out a plan that covers the scope of all necessary changes. If you present the need for change after change in piecemeal fashion, tension will mount in your organization and morale will suffer. If too many changes are made too frequently, your people will develop the "waiting for the other shoe to drop syndrome" and won't become interested or enthusiastic about *any* change. As a leader, you need to avoid crying wolf too often lest you deafen your people to the sound of the real need for change.

CONCLUSION: EMBRACING CHANGE AS A WELCOME FORCE

If you work hard on selling change and not hard enough on implementing it, your people will become cynical, and rightly so. One of your main selling points on change is the fact that the last change was so successful. In other words, the well-planned implementation worked. Focusing on past successes in change implementation is similar to focusing on strengths instead of weaknesses, and has similar positive results.

It's important that your attitude about change goes beyond merely tolerating it. If you continue to perceive change as a threat or as an enemy, you'll be doomed to a lifetime struggle. The terms used to define change are positive and full of opportunity. "To make different or to alter," for instance, sounds to me like an opportunity to spice things up and keep them interesting. "To substitute one thing for another" makes me think change requires a flow of new energies, new people, and new ideas.

Change, in perspective and in context, is to be welcomed. For us to see change as a friendly force, we must remain adaptable. We need to go beyond what's timely, in our attitudes, policies, and procedures, and truly become timeless. Timelessness is the ultimate adaptability, and vice versa. By definition, adaptability is the ability to make something fit for a new or more suitable use. The ability to adjust to a new situation or environment means we're not bound by time and circumstances.

A leader in a world of constant change must be adaptable. If such flexibility doesn't come naturally, it can be learned. The future has no healthy place for those who insist on remaining rigid and inflexible. Not that adapting means forcing change. Rather, it implies vigilance and open, informed acceptance of new and possibly unfamiliar people and ideas. Adaptability is not an option in becoming and remaining an effective leader and remaining competitive or attaining competitiveness in the global marketplace. Change guarantees we will never lack the opportunity to be competitive.

We need change leaders whose team members will "tuck in" real close and fly into the jaws of hell with them.

CHAPTER TEN

MEETING TOMORROW'S LEADERSHIP CHALLENGES TODAY

"Some drink at the fountain of knowledge. Others just gargle."

Anonymous

"The trouble with ignorance is that it picks up confidence as it goes along."

Anonymous

AN ISLAND OF EXCELLENCE

After speaking to an audience, I often have a manager come up to me and say, "Danny, I really want to grow and develop as a leader, but the managers at all levels above me certainly don't. What can I do?"

I give them two bits of advice. One is that you can't change anyone or anything above you in the company. You can't manage the corporation from your level up, so don't even try.

The second nugget I pass along came from Joe Topper, who was in one of the audiences I'd just spoken to. He explained that he couldn't do much about changing anyone above him so he had decided to become an "island of excel-lence" within his sphere of influence. He would get so good at what he was doing that something great was bound to happen.

That's the spirit! That's what I'm talking about!

No one is as interested in your career as you are. No one is more interested in your future than you are. Take the responsibility of becoming an island of excel-lence within your present company no matter what anyone else is doing. This will pay off for you in three ways:

1. You will become more valuable, perhaps even indispensable, to your present company. A sustained high-performance record of accomplish-ment can buy a bright future for you and your family.

2. The better you get at producing results, the more valuable you become to the competition. You're number one. You need to look after yourself and your family. If your employer won't compensate you for what you're worth, a proven record of accomplishment through sound lead-ership is valuable on the job market.

3. Finally, there might come a time when you want to strike out on your own. Every time you learn and improve as a leader, you become more skilled as an entrepreneur. And the more skilled you are as an entrepre-neur, the better your chances of succeeding on your own.

LEADERSHIP IS MODELING

We are all working for the future. I'm excited by the changing world in which we live because the future is rich with possibilities we haven't even considered. Someone once said we don't grow old, we become old by not growing. The ulti-mate threat to our future is stagnation. Continued personal and professional growth is essential to a tomorrow that will be better than today. The managerial moment of truth comes when you realize that, as the leader, you are the trigger for change in and for the organization. The people in the organization will pay the price in time, energy, and money to grow and develop in their jobs as they see you do the same as their leader.

WALLS

In Chapter 1, I introduced you to the enclosed world of self-imposed barriers. I mention them again because there is no greater threat to future growth and devel-opment as individuals and leaders. The timelessness I mentioned in Chapter 9 can never be accomplished if we're restrained by self-imposed barriers of any kind.

The adaptability that will prepare you for tomorrow's leadership challenge is anchored in your personal uncompromising integrity and the other leadership qualities to which you aspire. The leadership qualities I outlined in Chapter 1 are timeless virtues, as good tomorrow as they are today. Such qualities might be even more critical to leading in the future than they have been in the past. Looking back over the past 10 or 20 years, it's easy to see that the leadership challenges of tomorrow never get any easier. In a world that changes as fast as ours, the future will always be more complex and varied than today.

A Special Birthday Lesson about Walls

A few years ago I took my wife Tedi to prison for her birthday. When I bring this up in my live seminars, I usually get a few raised eyebrows until I explain why. She told me it was a birthday she wasn't looking forward to and that she felt like getting out of town and doing something different. I couldn't think of anything more out of town or different than for her to spend six hours of her birthday locked up with the prisoners in San Quentin.

A friend of mine ran a course for the inmates called "People Builders," and I called him up to see if we could attend. He graciously said he would make all of the arrangements and closed our phone conversation by telling us not to wear Levi's when we visited the prison.

"What's the matter with Levi's?" I asked.

"The inmates wear Levi's," he explained. "In the event of a riot or breakout, the guards shoot at Levi's."

We left our Levi's at home.

When we arrived at the prison and the huge steel gate slammed shut behind us, I sensed my terrific idea might not have been so terrific after all. The sound of the second gate slamming shut must have been amplified. The enormous clang echoed between the high concrete walls, and I felt a chill creep up my spine as Tedi and I stood facing "the yard."

We were standing next to the "adjustment" center, where I understand that, before they're through with you, either your attitude or your body will be adjusted, so to speak. Above the adjustment center is death row.

The guard at this second gate was expecting us. "Your People Builders class meets over there," he said, pointing across an almost empty yard. "See that group over in that corner with the sport shirts?" he continued. "Go through the door right behind them."

Assuming he wasn't going to escort us over there, we started the walk alone. Halfway across this surreal setting I looked at Tedi and said, "Happy Birthday, Honey."

"I hope so," she replied.

As we got closer to the casually dressed group standing just outside the class-room door, one of them spotted us. His face lit up with a big smile and he walked out to meet us. He extended his hand and said, "Hi, I'm Julian and I'm a poet."

With that, he reached into his pocket and pulled out a copy of a poem he had written called "Give a Child a Smile." I read it quickly. It was charged with emotion. I commented on the deep feeling in the last line. He said, "Yeah, if I'd had more smiles when I was a kid, I wouldn't be where I am today."

I looked down. Julian was wearing Levi's.

More of the Levi's-clad group started to gather around us and introduce themselves. One of the guys explained that they didn't get to wear the sport shirts all the time. It was allowed only "when we go out to a night class." I didn't consider this "out," but I guess he did when he compared it to sitting in his cell.

Tedi and I entered the classroom just as it was time to start the six-hour session. The decor was contemporary prison. I'm talking stark. Among the rules of the People Builders program was that you sat in your steel folding chair for six hours without so much as a rest room break. Try running a corporate training session like that sometime!

Tedi and I were heading for the back corner when we were told to sit in the middle of the audience, which numbered about a hundred. They didn't allow visitors to sit together, so we were separated. There were no guards in the room and no weapons, except, I suppose, those the prisoners carry. I'd realized by now that this was to be no ordinary stroll in the park.

The two guys who sat on either side of Tedi whispered in her ears all evening about what was going on and what had happened in previous classes, and she whispered back to them. Only at the end of the class did she learn that one of them was a child molester and the other a rapist. There's a lesson in that about preconceived notions. I was glad I didn't have any prior notions about those two. I don't think I would have heard a word of the program.

I was seated between two interesting gentlemen. The man on my left was the heavyweight boxing champion of San Quentin, and he looked just like the heavyweight boxing champion of San Quentin should look. I have never seen such a face on a human being before or since. It looked like he wadded his face up at night, stuffed it in his mouth, and slept with it that way.

The fellow on the other side of me had mastered the clever trick of somehow sticking his thigh out of the arm hole in his sleeveless sweatshirt. I figured anything that large had to have been his thigh; I'd never seen an arm that big. The funny thing was, he had another one just like it hanging out on the other side. When I learned this man graduated to the "Big Q" after he killed a guard at another prison with his bare hands, I wasn't surprised. Scared, yes, but not surprised. He was obviously strong enough to strangle someone in each hand at the same time if he had a mind to. If either one of those guys had leaned over and said, "It's tonight. We're going out of here." I would have said, "I'm with you. I've got the car keys right here in my pocket."

Throughout the six-hour session the one point that was hammered and hammered again was: Don't worry about the past and don't worry about the future. That leaves us with the *now*. Our focus should always be on the fullest *present* we can live. The future is nothing more than an approaching series of nows.

Energy spent regretting the past or worrying about the future is energy drained away from the now. Along with this, they also hammered home the concept of accepting full responsibility for ourselves in the present.

There is no greater challenge to leaders, old and new. There is no greater promise we can make to ourselves and to our organizations than to live as effectively as possible in the present. There is no better way to prepare for change than to live effectively in the now. Living responsibly today lays a solid foundation for tomorrow. No one is remembered for how well they repeated *yesterdays,* but for how they built *todays.* This all became clear for me toward the end of the San Quentin seminar. It was like flying out of a dark cloud into crystal clear air.

When the group leader looked out over the assembled prisoners and said, "You guys have an advantage over people on the outside," I thought he was making a joke and hoped the bookend human wrecking machines on either side of me had a sense of humor.

It wasn't a joke. Even though we were sitting in the closest thing to hell on earth and staring out the window and across the yard at death row, the advantage the leader was talking about became clear. He said someone in prison can see his or her walls. There's no question where or how high and thick the boundaries are. People on the outside, like you and I, can't see our walls. We all have walls that are just as effective at holding us in as the walls of San Quentin, perhaps even more so. We just can't see them. But they're there just the same.

The leadership challenge is clear. As leaders, we are engaged in the effort to help our people climb over their walls. Personal and professional growth can't happen in that kind of personal captivity. Our first order of business must be to climb over our own self-imposed barriers, then help others to grow beyond theirs. We never get rid of our self-imposed barriers, but we can discover they're on wheels. We must simply keep pushing them further and further out.

Changing economic and social pressures help push the walls back in on us and the challenge becomes greater. Our effectiveness has to increase constantly in order to ensure progress into the future. The walls have a tendency to roll back to their original positions, and we must respond by pushing them back. The heat is *always* on.

FOUR ALL-IMPORTANT WORDS

Dream

Dream the great dreams. Unplug. Pull out the stops. Go for the top. Dream. Dreams give us places to go and things to do. They are the good things in our lives, yet to occur. What if you did go after the rest of your potential as a leader of people? Dream that dream so vividly that you won't even notice any pain in getting it—to borrow a phrase from George Foreman.

Study

Study everything you can get your hands on to help make your dream come true. Study books, journals, and other published information. Listen to tapes and watch educational videos. Spend time with people from whom you can learn, either at lunch or by enrolling in classes and/or seminars. Make it a lifetime principle to never delay the remedy of anything that's holding you back. Anything that adds to your effectiveness is cheap, no matter what the cost.

Plan

Plan your time and time your plan. Give your time some structure and turn up the heat on yourself when you need to move along. As I mentioned earlier, it's okay to have a tiger by the tail if you know what to do *next*. Without a plan, plunging headlong into the future is a risky and potentially unproductive proposition. The bad news for nonplanners is they're going to plunge headlong into the future whether they have a plan or not. People who know the importance of planning understand how vital it is to design the future. Sure, lots of things will spontaneously happen to us along the way, but a plan gives us a course to follow.

Action

A plan was not meant to remain a plan. Put it into action. A study was done a few years ago of people who attended a seminar or some other such learning experience. They found that if you haven't made some change as a result of the learning experience within 72 hours, all of the time, energy, and money involved in attending the seminar was wasted.

PROFILE OF TOMORROW'S LEADER

The leader blazes a trail for others to follow. In doing so, there will be markers along the way. Knowing that the organization's future rests on the success of the people on the team, the leader seeks qualities that will lift him or her above the timely and into the timeless, thus inviting everyone in the organization to do the same. Here are 10 qualities I believe will be in the profile of tomorrow's leader:

1. Tomorrow's leader will be a remarkable builder of team spirit.
2. Tomorrow's leader will be self-reliant and confident and will teach team members to do the same.
3. Tomorrow's leader be creative and not afraid to take risks.
4. Tomorrow's leader will understand the value of change.
5. Tomorrow's leader will be fair, not afraid to challenge or be challenged.

6. Tomorrow's leader will be open to new ideas and perspectives.

7. Tomorrow's leader will possess a far greater understanding of people.

8. Tomorrow's leader will be organized and adept at setting and working priorities.

9. Tomorrow's leader will be on a continuing high personal growth curve.

10. Tomorrow's leader will be in balance in his or her business and personal life.

You might want to scramble these qualities in order of priority, depending upon your situation. However, the manager who demonstrates these qualities, along with the others outlined in Chapter 2, is a leader for the future. Greatness is timeless. These timeless qualities describe great leaders.

THE ULTIMATE CHALLENGE

Never be less than your dreams. Someday you may look back and ask, "Did I really build my dream or is it too late?" Let me assure you that it's *never* too late. In business, we realize our dreams by building up internal and external customers. An organization is alive and vital when the leader helps people grow and climb over their walls.

The ultimate reward is not the promotions, perks, and larger paychecks. As nice as those things are, the ultimate reward is the ability to go home at the end of a day and say to yourself, "I saw someone grow again today and I helped." That's what it's all about as a leader. Seeing people grow is the only experience in business that brings your heart up into your throat. When your team members see their own growth along with your matching growth as a leader, their memory of you and the difference you made in their lives will be vivid and inspiring for years to come.

So, what do you need to get started on in the next 72 hours?

Decide.
Begin.
Don't stop.

For further information on Danny Cox's speaking
programs and recorded training courses:
Danny Cox
Acceleration Unlimited
17381 Bonner Drive
Tustin, CA 92780
(714) 838-3030 (800) 366-3101
www.dannycox.com

INDEX

About the Authors

After ten years flying fighters at almost twice the speed of sound, **Danny Cox** turned his need for speed into a leadership system for the business world that transformed a declining organization into a booming industry leader. This high-performance climb of his district of offices resulted in an 800 percent increase in productivity in a five-and-one-half-year period. He shares this high-performance system in convention keynotes, seminars, and sales meetings for organizations throughout America as well as in numerous foreign countries. His exceptional speaking skills have earned him a place in the National Speakers Association Hall of Fame. He is also an elected member of the elite Speakers Roundtable, a group of North America's top twenty speakers.

John Hoover, Ph.D., has successfully used Danny's leadership techniques as an executive with Walt Disney Productions and McGraw-Hill. He now helps corporate and public sector clients to learn and apply the concepts of *Fearless Leadership,* internal and external communications, and how to form and sustain internal and external strategic relationships. Dr. Hoover is an adjunct faculty member at Aquinas College in Nashville, Tennessee, where he teaches Business and Psychology. He also teaches Fast Trac™ New Venture and Business Planning classes for the Nashville Area Chamber of Commerce, and is a Tennessee Supreme Court Rule 31 Civil Mediator. He belongs to the American Society of Training & Development, and the Organization Development Network.